Walking Barefoot
The Tilonia Way

Selected Articles of Sanjit (Bunker) Roy and Others

Edited by
Heather MC Malcolm
with inputs from Aruna Roy

Published in 2024 by Bennion Kearny

ISBN: 978-1-915855-06-0

© Copyright 2024 Bennion Kearny

Copyrighted material used with permission. All Rights Reserved.

No part of this publication may be reproduced, stored in a retrieval system, or transmitted in any form or by any means, electronic, mechanical, photocopying, recording or otherwise, without the prior permission of the publisher.

This book is sold subject to the condition that it shall not, by way of trade or otherwise, be lent, re-sold, hired out or otherwise circulated without the publisher's prior consent in any form of binding or cover other than that in which it is published and without a similar condition including this condition being imposed on the subsequent purchaser.

Bennion Kearny, 6 Woodside, Churnet View Road, Oakamoor, ST10 3AE, UK

Cover image: © Raghu Rai

Acknowledgements

This anthology is a commemoration of 50 years of Barefoot College. Representing College alumni, Aruna Roy suggested the publication of a selection of Bunker's prolific contributions over the years to magazines, newspapers and journals – a selection which would, in effect, trace Bunker's and Barefoot College's contribution to the ongoing discourse about development. As ideas for the anthology took shape, it was thought appropriate to include some of the numerous articles written by others about Barefoot, too.

Many people have helped bring the book to publication, and I would like to thank them all. Special mention has to be given to Aruna herself, not only for having the idea in the first place but also, with Bunker, for giving friendship, ideas, unwavering support, commitment, advice and encouragement, as well as providing material for informative introductions. There are others at Barefoot, too: all those in Barefoot's IT sections for help throughout, and everyone who produced cups of *chai* and delicious meals on the occasion of working visits. I particularly wish to thank those working in the Tilonia Campus' Barefoot College library, not only for their endless good-humoured patience when asked to hunt down yet another article but also for providing socks in cold weather… surely beyond all reasonable expectations!

Valuable assistance also came from other libraries, both public and private, in the United States, Europe and the UK, some of whose staff went to considerable effort to help me track an article down. I do not know all your names, but I appreciate your help very much and am grateful to you all. Thanks are due to Tilonia volunteer Ann Remedios, who helped prepare articles and the glossary, and secured several copyright permissions, and there are special thank-yous, too, to designer Laila Tyabji for allowing me to include extracts from her own wonderfully vibrant reflections on Barefoot College's 2022 re-creation of the first Tilonia Bazaar, as well as to photographer Raghu Rai for permission to use his stunning photograph of Bunker for the front cover.

And, of course, I am grateful to all the publishers who agreed to let me use their articles. In alphabetical order, I want to thank:

Deccan Herald; First City; India Today; International Agricultural Development (Research Information Limited); *IRC International Water and Sanitation Centre; Kurukshetra; Mainstream; New Scientist; Racing Towards Diversity; Regeneration and Renewal* (Haymarket Media Group); *Renewable Energy World; Resurgence* (The Resurgence Trust); *Seminar Magazine; Sources,* UNESCO; *The Indian* Express (© The Indian Express (P) Limited); *The New Times; UBS Optimus World* (UBS Optimus Foundation); *The New Zealand Herald; The Telegraph Calcutta; The Unesco Courier; United Nations Chronicle 1; United Nations Development Forum; United Nations Economic and Social Commission for Asia and the Pacific* (ESCAP) *Agricultural Information Development Bulletin; World Economic Forum; Yojana.*

In addition, I am grateful to the author for permission to use 'Rural Doctor', and to the Baig family for allowing me to reproduce Ms Tara Ali Baig's evocative piece from 'Portraits of An Era'.

Without such goodwill, there would be no anthology. To the great majority who waived copyright fees, I extend particular thanks.

Any errors are mine alone.

Heather MC Malcolm

Selected Awards and Recognitions for Bunker Roy and Barefoot College

- Jamnalal Bajaj Award for Science and Technology, 1985
- Padma Shri, 1986
- Education for Productive Employment Award, ESCAP HRD, UNESCO for Asia and the Pacific, 1995
- Save the Drylands Award for controlling land degradation. UNDP, 1997-1998
- Indira Gandhi Paryavaran Puraskar Award, Government of India, Ministry of Environment & Forests, 1998
- 2000 a+u Architecture and Urbanism. Barefoot Architects, Tilonia, India
- Nuclear Free Solutions Award, Berlin, Germany, 2000
- Children's World Award, Stockholm, 2001
- AGFUND Prize for Voluntary Work, 2001
- A+U (Architecture and Urbanism) Award, 2002
- The Schwab Foundation for Outstanding Social Entrepreneurs, World Economic Forum, Geneva, Switzerland, September 2002
- The Stockholm Challenge Award for Information Technology (Category Environment), Stockholm, Sweden, October 2002
- The Tech Museum Award for Innovation Benefiting Humanity, California, November 2002
- St. Andrew's Prize for the Environment, Scotland, May 2003

- The Ashden Award for Sustainable Energy, London, July 2003
- Conrad N. Hilton Humanitarian Prize, 2004
- World Culture Open Awards, New York City, 2004
- The Petersberg Prize for Information and Communication Technologies for Development, 2004
- The Tyler Prize, California, USA, April 2004
- The Tech Museum Award for Empowering India's Rural Poor to Develop Their Own Communities, California, 2005
- The Skoll Foundation Award for Social Entrepreneurship, 2005
- US$ 1 million ALCAN Award for Sustainability, 2006
- 12. L-RAMP Lifetime Achievement Award, Madras, 2007
- ICONECS International Conference on e-content and Sustainability and Manthan Award, 2007
- *The Guardian* identifies Bunker Roy as one of the 50 environmentalists in the world who could save the planet, London, 5th January 2008
- Schwab Fellow of the World Economic Forum. Barefoot College. Focus: Education, Solar Electrification, Rural Development, Technology, Rainwater Harvesting, Women Empowerment, 2009
- The Sierra Club Green Energy Award, USA, June 2009
- Suez Environment – Water for All Foundation – Paris, July 2009
- Robert Hill Award for Promotion of Solar Energy: 24th European Photovoltaic Solar Energy Conference, September 2009

- Conde Nast Environmental Award, Washington, November 2009
- *TIME* magazine identifies Bunker Roy as one of the 100 most influential people in the world, April 2010
- Skoll Foundation Award for Social Entrepreneurship, 2010
- Green Fighters 100 Eco-Lifestyle Magazine, Japan, 2010
- Asian Excellence Awards, Social Entrepreneur of the Year, London, November 2011
- Giraffe Heroes International Award, USA, 2011
- The Blue Planet Prize, Tokyo, Japan, November 2011
- QIMPRO Platinum Standard. Statesman for Quality in Education, 2012
- CF Andrews Distinguished Alumnus Award, St Stephens's College, Delhi
- CNN IBN Real Heroes Lifetime Achievement Award, 2013
- Humanity4 Water Award, New York, September 2013
- Clinton Global Citizen Award, New York, September 2013
- IMC Juran Quality Medal, 2014
- TOI Social Impact Award, 2015
- Hon. Fellow of City & Guilds of London, 2016
- Social Entrepreneur of the Year, Business Standard, Mumbai, India, March 2017
- Hon. Degree Bachelor of Law, Princeton University, June 2017 (first Indian to receive this award in 40 years)
- ILEA Leadership Energy Award, Kuala Lumpur, Malaysia, November 2017

- Earth Care Awards, 2018
- TSS Social Enterprise Global Awards, Hyderabad, 2021
- Women Exemplar Program, Dhapu Kaki Health Category, C11 Foundation, March 2021
- India Sanitation Coalition Award (FICCI) for Community-led solid waste management system under best non-profit engagement model in sanitation (Rural) category, 2021

On the occasion of its 50th anniversary in 2022, Barefoot College received letters of congratulation from HH The Dalai Lama, HRH Prince Charles, the Schwab Foundation-World Economic Forum, and the Chief Minister of Rajasthan, among others.

About This Book

AS STATED IN THE ACKNOWLEDGEMENTS, this anthology grew out of a suggestion made by Aruna Roy, as a Barefoot College alumna and close associate, that it would be a happy contribution to Barefoot's celebrations of the 50 years of its existence – 1972 to 2022. Providing a record of the history of SWRC[i]/Barefoot College's public action from the perspective of its founder and others through the years, the articles would collectively establish the College's legacy. In addition, the collection would present invaluable research material and add substantially to the body of knowledge on an important development process that has made a huge difference to many lives, not only in India but beyond its shores. It would give insight into how – through years of innovation, experiment and testing – Barefoot College found solutions to a host of problems that affect the rural poor. These range from practical issues, such as how to provide electricity and pure drinking water to rural villagers in drought-prone areas, to strategies for developing self-belief in marginalised people so that they have the confidence to act on their own behalf and become leaders fighting against corruption, bullies and cheats.

So, it's about many things.

It's about the realities of life in rural India. It's about the challenges of establishing a sustainable model for decent living, one that others around the world have been able to adapt and adopt for their own, and the things that helped. It's about the people of rural India with their skills and knowledge and wisdom, their courage and grace and long-suffering strength.

But most of all, it is about the achievements of a group of people who, determined not to accept that this was how things had to be,

---

[i] Social Work and Research Centre, the earliest name for the organisation which came to be known as The Barefoot College. It is also sometimes known simply as 'Tilonia' after the village where it's based, so while sometimes there are references simply to 'SWRC' it can also be referred to as 'SWRC/Barefoot College' as here and 'SWRC/Tilonia'.

tried (and are still trying) their damnedest to make sure that the people of rural India and elsewhere had something better.

The extraordinary man whose inspiration began it all, Sanjit 'Bunker' Roy, is a man of contradictions: caring and compassionate to the poor, unrelenting and implacable to those at all levels of society who harass and exploit them. Quiet and dynamic. Reserved, yet as a man who loves his country, unafraid to speak out against the things that are wrong, and prepared to live with the personal costs. Willing to stand up and be counted. One who chose to live simply according to the principles set down by Mahatma Gandhi and whose vision of what the world could be like is as sophisticated as simplicity itself, yet who has been invited to take his place on the various stages of the world. Even in the highest of places, it seems, there are people who realise that a vision like his might be the only way for humanity to survive.

In the early years, when the idea of the College was still germinating in Bunker's mind, there were, in effect, two Indias: that of Delhi, Mumbai, Kolkata – the cities – and Bharat, the countryside, rooted in tradition, which provided for urban needs through farming and crafts. But Barefoot College's fifty years have seen many changes, predominant among them the rise of mass production that spread out from the cities, and the growth of technology, which brought computing, the Internet and mobile phones.

As a result, there is now a generation to which a world without instant communication is unknown, a generation with a different mindset from that which prevailed in the 1970s, 80s, 90s and even the early years of the 21st century. This is true even in Bharat. Young people from rural areas don't want to be like their parents. They don't want to be farmers any more. Literacy levels have risen. Certification and degrees are more common and have become desirable and meaningful to those young people as passports to jobs and another world. But in spite of all this, in Bharat, most of this generation still lives in rural reality.

As I wrote above, taken together, the articles provide what amounts to a history, offering 'snapshots' of Barefoot College and Bunker's thinking as the years came and went. Both Bunker and those who wrote about SWRC/Barefoot College from an outside perspective acted within the contexts in which they lived at the time. Language was different; attitudes were different. But the realities and challenges of village life, good and bad, remained.

Barefoot College has adapted to changing times and still has relevance and meaning in people's lives. How much so can be seen in the following paragraphs, quoted with the kind permission of their author, designer Laila Tyabji.[ii] They were written for the occasion of Barefoot College Tilonia's anniversary celebrations in New Delhi in 2022.

April, 2022

Last Saturday at Triveni Kala Sangam was total nostalgia.

It's 50 years since Bunker Roy, a dashing Stephanian alumnus and national squash champion, disappointed his family's expectations and went off to rural Rajasthan to set up what became Tilonia, the Barefoot College. Many other rural development initiatives followed over the years … but Tilonia was the first rural campus, and possibly still the only one covering such a gamut of different initiatives – education, health, water, environment, rural livelihoods, women's empowerment, waste management, solar energy…

The strategy was both blindingly obvious and utterly brilliant – combining traditional local knowledge systems with newer urban solutions in ways that could be understood and implemented by local communities, including neo-illiterate rural youth as well as hitherto homebound women. An example of this was their Solar Mamas – village women who learnt how to manufacture and service solar lanterns through colour coding rather than written manuals

---

[ii] Laila, a long-standing friend to Barefoot College, is an Indian freelance graphic and interior designer who has also worked with costumes and theatre sets, garments and textiles. She co-founded and is currently Chairperson of the NGO *Dastkar*, which aims to give traditional craftspeople the design, development, market information, and entrepreneurship training they need to thrive in the mainstream market. In 2012, the Government of India honoured her with the prestigious Padma Shri, the fourth-highest Indian civilian award.

and so were able to not only electrify their own villages but teach women all over Africa and Eastern Europe the same skills, unimpaired by any language barriers. Seeing them working on electrical switchboards and setting up hand pumps in their colourful Rajasthani costumes was a delightful sight! Another example was Tilonia's messaging — often ground-breaking and revolutionary for the times and in that traditional society, but conveyed through puppetry and folk songs that struck a chord. On Saturday, too, the 50-year Tilonia journey was told through an illustrated scroll that slowly unrolled to the sound of songs and stories, in the manner of the painted phads used by itinerant Rajasthani bards of old. So ingenious and evocative.

Incidentally, it was at Tilonia in 1982 that I first learnt to use a hand pump myself. I was doing a weeklong design workshop with the patchwork appliqué women, one of our very early Dastkar projects. In my earlier six months in Kutch, there had always been someone to dash and fetch me a bucket of water, but in Tilonia, self-help was the mantra — I loved it.

I loved Saturday at the Triveni, too. Spread out under the trees was a recreation of the very first Tilonia Bazaar in 1975, the forerunner of so many craft bazaars of the future, including Dastkar. I remember going there with my mother, just a couple of years before her death, and our joy at first seeing those bell-tota mobiles that became such a trademark of Tilonia. My mother bought a block-printed ghagra with a lovely tasselled sash. It was all there again now — the embroidered leather and wood chairs, the patchwork and appliqué bedspreads with elephants and camels, the block-printed kurtas and tops, the hand puppets, interspersed with photographs, posters and music of the intervening years. And Delhi-ites in 2022 seemed to be enjoying it all as much as we had in 1975. In the the Auditorium inside, the much-loved master puppet and Master of Ceremonies Jokhim Bhai (Chacha), presided over the proceedings with his usual animation and humour.

Hearing those stories and songs, and meeting Bunker and Aruna again, was a happy reminder of those long-gone days. How young (and slim!) we were then, our hair black, filled with optimism and energy… Is it only in retrospect that those seemed simpler, more innocent, less cynical times, when one truly believed that ideas and idealism could effect social change, when the rural urban divide seemed an exciting challenge to be bridged rather than an insuperable and growing schism? When the warmth and satisfaction of real partnerships forged with communities working and growing together seemed as exciting a life path for the urban young as personal ambition and corporate growth plans?

It was good to relive those times; we must try to evoke that passion and spirit again.

Laila Tyabji

Some practical notes

The greatest challenge in bringing this anthology together was the mass of material. There were well over 120 articles written by Bunker alone, plus several others he co-authored, and at least 60 by journalists who had come to Tilonia from all over the world to discover for themselves what all the fuss was about.

The original articles came in diverse forms. Spanning the late 1960s to the early 2000s, they took many physical shapes – journals, books, newspapers, magazines – and were in varying states of preservation. All, however, were printed media which had to be brought into a digital form amenable to editing.

The pieces fell broadly into two categories. One dealt with Bunker's radical thinking about, and often disruptive comments on, the political and social system in which SWRC/Barefoot College and Tilonia's villagers were placed. The other category dealt with what SWRC/Tilonia is and does (its vision/ ideology/ philosophy/ methodology in practice). Those in the first group broadly make up Chapters 1-5, and those in the second group Chapters 6-12. Chapter 13 takes the Barefoot story beyond the articles through URLs to interviews and films, while Chapter 14 offers an overview of Barefoot College's achievements and how they might be built upon.

Though most of the articles were written by Bunker Roy, as noted above there are also many from journalists who visited Tilonia over the years. Apart from misprints being corrected,[iii] their articles have been left much as published, to honour the integrity of the original work.

[iii] Except in the case of articles from two publishers, who asked that no changes of any sort, major or minor, be made.

An Indian readership will naturally be familiar with Hindi terms, but since this book might have a wider audience, there is a glossary at the back. There is also a list of acronyms.

I hope you enjoy the anthology.

Heather MC Malcolm, Edinburgh, 2024.

Table of Contents

1: A Young Man Finds His Voice 1
NZ as Seen Through Eyes of Indian 2

2: A Village is a Different World 5
Village Realities 7
   Rural Credit 13
Don't Turn Your Back on Tradition 22
Despotism 24
Futile Untouchability Law 32
   Rural setting 32
   Letters of complaint 33
   More humiliation 34
   Real answer 35
Due Process of Law 36
   Sale deed 36
   Tenancy revision 38
   Semi-literate lawyers 39
   Effective possession 40
Beware of Educated Man 41

3: The 7th Planning Commission: Pathway to Consultancy 48
NGOs – Changing Role 52
Voluntarism and the 7th Plan 61
   Upgrading skills 62
   Monitoring machinery 63
   Appropriate technology 64

New awareness 65
For Prime Minister, a Word of Advice 66
Participation in Development 71
Let Voluntary Agencies Plan Their Own Schemes 79
Raw Deal for Rural Poor 84
Action is Called Right Now to Avoid a Rude Shock! 89
    This TV Onslaught! 90
    Poor Delivery System! 91
    And the Crucial Issue! 92
The Rural Self-Employed 94
Voluntary Agencies: Twenty Years From Now 99

4: And So It Goes On 108
The Wages of Sin 110
Required: A Code of Conduct 113
    National Debate 113
    Will Do Much Good 114
    Not Voluntary 115
    Undignified 116
Bane of Foreign Funds for Volunteers 117

5: The Elephant in the Room 123
Among the Eyeless in Oslo 124
Villages as a Positive Force for Good Governance:
The Right to Information 127

6: Bunker Roy and the 50-Year Pilgrimage 131
Portraits of an Era (excerpt from chapter 8) 133
Rebuilding Grassroots Potential 139

Table of Contents

1: A Young Man Finds His Voice 1
NZ as Seen Through Eyes of Indian 2

2: A Village is a Different World 5
Village Realities 7
    Rural Credit 13
Don't Turn Your Back on Tradition 22
Despotism 24
Futile Untouchability Law 32
    Rural setting 32
    Letters of complaint 33
    More humiliation 34
    Real answer 35
Due Process of Law 36
    Sale deed 36
    Tenancy revision 38
    Semi-literate lawyers 39
    Effective possession 40
Beware of Educated Man 41

3: The 7th Planning Commission: Pathway to Consultancy 48
NGOs – Changing Role 52
Voluntarism and the 7th Plan 61
    Upgrading skills 62
    Monitoring machinery 63
    Appropriate technology 64

 New awareness 65
For Prime Minister, a Word of Advice 66
Participation in Development 71
Let Voluntary Agencies Plan Their Own Schemes 79
Raw Deal for Rural Poor 84
Action is Called Right Now to Avoid a Rude Shock! 89
 This TV Onslaught! 90
 Poor Delivery System! 91
 And the Crucial Issue! 92
The Rural Self-Employed 94
Voluntary Agencies: Twenty Years From Now 99

4: And So It Goes On 108
The Wages of Sin 110
Required: A Code of Conduct 113
 National Debate 113
 Will Do Much Good 114
 Not Voluntary 115
 Undignified 116
Bane of Foreign Funds for Volunteers 117

5: The Elephant in the Room 123
Among the Eyeless in Oslo 124
Villages as a Positive Force for Good Governance:
The Right to Information 127

6: Bunker Roy and the 50-Year Pilgrimage 131
Portraits of an Era (excerpt from chapter 8) 133
Rebuilding Grassroots Potential 139

Affirmation 142
The UN and Poverty II: Why the Millennium
Goals Won't Work 154

7: The Experience of Tilonia 158
Six Good Reasons to Go the Tilonia Way 160
    The Different Options 161
    The Six Good Reasons 162
    Involving the Have-Nots 164
    Community Accountability 165
    The Mythical System 166
    As it Goes at Tilonia 167
Why Not Now Demystify This Technology! 169
    As It Goes in Rajasthan! 170
    And Its Pitfalls! 171
    The HPM is Born! 171
    And The Job He Did! 172
    And The Demystification! 175
    And the Problems! 176
    And Why This Prejudice? 178
Barefoot Pioneers 179
The Barefoot Approach: Diversity and Inclusion -
The Path to Innovation 184
    Innovation 184
    Promoting a Different Vision of Enterprise 184
    Dealing with Success 185
    Learning from Failure 186
    You Do Your Best Work When You Are Insecure 186

8: A Place in the Sun ... 190

Preventing the Deserts from Growing:
The Barefoot Approach ... 193

    The Urgency is Missing ... 194

    Focal Points Must Be Made More Accountable ... 194

    Environmental Conservation Measures ... 195

Where Water is More Precious Than Milk ... 199

Not a Drop to Drink ... 201

Water on the School Roof ... 203

An Uphill Struggle ... 207

India's Self-help Solar Villages ... 208

    Solar Pumps Bring Life to Dying Villages ... 210

Lighting Up Ladakh ... 212

Barefoot in Afghanistan: Solar Electrification of Villages in Afghanistan ... 215

    Solar Light ... 220

    Cost-effective ... 220

    Conclusion ... 221

Rwanda's Semi-literate Grandmothers Aspire for Solar Engineering ... 222

9: The Greatest Wealth of All ... 229

Rural Doctor ... 232

Barefoot in Tilonia ... 237

Adding Insult to Injury ... 240

10: When Learning is Fun ... 244

India: The Children's Republic ... 247

    Food First ... 248

Lessons Instead of Bedtime Stories: Night Schools in India ... 250

Tried, Tested and Proven 251

Five Years of Basic Education 251

Unique Children's Parliament 251

Sincere Thanks 252

School for Life 252

Needs-based Education with a New Perspective 252

In Tilonia, Everyone's Equal 253

The Children's Parliament: Not Just Role-Playing 254

Making Life Better on Your Own Initiative 254

11: The Art of Communication: Tradition, Puppets, Street Theatre and the Digital Camera 260

Gadgets are Not Enough 263

Reaching the Poor Through Puppetry: A Powerful Medium for Fostering Rural Development 265

12: Tilonia Bazaar: Where Tradition Meets Contemporary India 273

A Rich Craft Heritage – Tradition Meets Modernity: Some Photographs 275

13: Barefoot's Online Footprint 289

Lights, Camera, Action: Barefoot Films and Online Links 292

The Tilonia Experiment 292

Schooling and Education 293

Water 295

The Environment 296

Solar Energy 297

Women's Empowerment 299

Health 300

    Social Media Platforms 301

14: Foundations for the Future 302
    Ordinary People Doing Extraordinary Things 303
        Water 303
        Health 304
        Barefoot Teachers, Barefoot Schools 304
        Breadwinning! 305
        Greening the Desert 307
        The Battle for Justice 307
    Recent Work 308
        Managing Waste, Creating Employment 308
        Fighting Covid 309
        Power to the Women – Opening up the World 310
        A Level Playing Field 310
    Gandhian Principles in Every Project 311
    And the Future? 312
    Lessons for Us All? 314
    Some Thoughts 316

Appendix I: Glossary and Notes 325

Appendix II: Abbreviations and Acronyms 335

1: A Young Man Finds His Voice

Heather MC Malcolm

IT MIGHT SEEM STRANGE TO BEGIN an anthology of articles focused on Tilonia's Barefoot College with a piece about New Zealand! But as an introduction to Barefoot College's founder, Bunker Roy, it's oddly appropriate, coming as it does from a time in his life when all paths were open, a time before he chose to dedicate his life to the marginalised people of rural India.

He wrote it when he was in New Zealand, competing as India's national squash champion in the international championships. It was for the third time, but it was to be the last: already the idea of how else he might work for India had begun to germinate.

In 1965, the state of Bihar suffered drought conditions that brought widespread famine. With a small group of friends, Bunker volunteered to help. That experience changed his view of life so utterly that he abandoned his glittering prospects and came to represent India very differently: as Founder of Barefoot College and its Director for the next 50 years or so.

In 'NZ as Seen Through Eyes of Indian', we see that even as a young man (he was 26), Bunker was unafraid to voice his opinion publicly, and share ideas. It was to be the start of a long career of committing thoughts to paper, pointing out what he saw as wrong and urging action. The young man who was to write, work, and write again in support of India's villagers was on his way.

NZ as Seen Through Eyes of Indian

Bunker Roy

Originally published in *The New Zealand Herald*,
1 September 1971

Bunker was the No. 2 player in the Indian squash rackets side which competed in the recent international team and individual series in New Zealand

IN MY JOB as an Indian social worker, I have seen things that people in New Zealand could not imagine. I have seen a man and a dog fighting over a piece of meat in a street, men eating leaves off trees to stave off hunger. So it is not unlikely that my impressions will be strange or different.

The population of New Zealand is less than the number of people living in New Delhi. It is not surprising, therefore, to find a personal note creeping into practically everything – the radio, television and the press. These services seem to speak to the people of New Zealand as if they are one large family.

An Indian family of five has to survive on $20 a month and this prevents them from buying nutritious food. On this salary, they must feed, clothe, and educate their children. Education is a must: unless one has a degree the chance of a job is very remote. The alternative is to start begging or go in for politics. In other words, become a Communist.

There is as little chance in New Zealand of a person becoming a Communist as there is in India of not becoming one. The other day, I read of someone wanting to leave New Zealand because he thought the labour unions here were loose-principled and unscrupulous. If he experienced the highly specialised and organised form of blackmail of labour unions in India, he would thank his lucky stars that he was living in New Zealand.

It amazes me that a student of 15 can leave school and get a responsible job without having to go to university. It indicates how much common sense is valued over intellect, how much a practical bent of mind is preferred to a theoretical background and how little emphasis is laid on degrees.

In India, intelligence is judged by the number of degrees you hold. We are by far the greatest theoreticians in the world. Gandhi noticed this and said that India needed to combine Intellect with Labour: too much of either was bad.

There is no danger of New Zealanders ever becoming like this: their background and upbringing have been so different. But they run the risk of being isolated from the intellectual and cultural world. There is so much emphasis on outdoor life and sporting activities that they have virtually taken the place of culture. In the long run, this is bound to have serious repercussions on mental make-up.

Already, there are symptoms that only an alien can notice: the conspicuous lack of interest in reading thought-provoking books or the development of the mind; the absence of frequent classical concerts, plays and art exhibitions.

The popularity of television and the lack of patronage of the arts and New Zealand culture is likely to have two effects. It is likely to produce very boring people. The people of the present generation thankfully did not have television to distract them, with the result that those over 30 are extremely social and delightful to talk to. The subsequent generation, exposed to distractions like television, is not inclined to follow intellectual pursuits and is in grave danger of becoming boring.

The second effect is already becoming noticeable: an amazing inferiority complex among the younger generation. Every so often, I have met boys and girls who are already working who have told me they never went to university because they did not have enough brains. This is not for them to judge. In fact, I found them pleasant, intelligent and just the right sort of material for a sound university education.

After seeing the quality of the students getting degrees in India, I am convinced that the boys and girls who opt out of higher studies here are being foolish and letting a marvellous opportunity slip away.

A side effect of neglecting education is the absence of intellectual curiosity. For instance, ask any Kiwi what Maori names stand for, and he will not know. In all fairness, this ignorance is not confined to the younger generation. Like everything else, Maori names have been taken for granted.

The history and culture of the Maori is the history of New Zealand. I was fascinated by the Maori rhythm and dance movements which I saw in Wellington. It is a heritage any country should be proud of. Perhaps one way of bringing about a certain amount of understanding of the Maori language is to have English translations alongside the Maori names for towns, roads and rivers.

What more is there to say? Bernard Shaw once remarked that the Swiss could be the most boring people in the world because they were awed by their own scenery. One could not say the same of the people of New Zealand in spite of the fact that they have such an incredibly beautiful country.

Reprinted courtesy of The New Zealand Herald

2: A Village is a Different World

Heather MC Malcolm

IF BUNKER EVER WANTED A MOTTO, it might well be 'people first' because, for him, the importance of their lived reality comes far, far ahead of the material things, statistics, surveys and reports so beloved by highly educated people.

In Chapter 2, he introduces many of what were to become recurrent themes in his work and life, including the statement that the rural poor needed a practical approach to tackling their problems, not a theoretical one, one which demands real understanding – an understanding that can only be gained by living in villages. In the two articles featured here, written in 1980 and 1984, he made very clear his view that intellectualism had nothing to contribute to rural development. Quite the opposite; controversial as ever, he turned conventional thinking on its head by showing how, to a villager, 'educated' did not mean knowledgeable, competent or even trustworthy. For that villager, studies set up by social scientists intending to help him could have terrible consequences when the local powerful discovered he had spoken up about the truth of their activities. His job and his ability to secure credit might be lost. His house might be burned down, and worse. But what did the social scientists care? By then, they had their data and had moved on to report-writing, seminar-attending and furthering their careers on the back of it. These 'blinkered intellectuals' did not belong to the village and did not understand how broken its systems were.

Bunker uses the term 'educated men' with heavy irony. As with many things, he has a different take on what education actually is. The world, in general, thinks of it as what is learned in school and college and, in general, as a Good Thing. Not so Bunker. For him, all that should be called 'literacy'. Real education, the stuff that matters, comes from local knowledge and experience. And the experience that the villagers he wrote about had of educated men was that the expert who came flourishing a paper qualification was at best unhelpful and, at worst, actually dangerous – the more so as such people often wielded great power over life in rural villages (and still do). Lacking an understanding of rural realities, arrogant, refusing to learn and blind to their ignorance, they produced misguided plans that led only to exploitation of the poor, and thoughtlessly encouraged the adoption of new and damaging technologies. Their ignorance exacerbated the misery of the rural poor since it blinded the 'experts' to the level and nature of corruption that made life a living hell for those who had to live with it.

And the problem lay not only with urban-based experts coming from outside. To the rural poor, government functionaries living in villages were often considered 'educated', and were seen as using the knowledge and skills gained through this education to exploit them – the poor – while feathering their own nests. Such educated men, he wrote, were responsible for keeping the poor ignorant of schemes to help them, diverting funds to themselves and never being questioned about it. They engaged in 'intrigue, manipulation and harassment' and 'because of them the poor [were] never free from fear'.

And the last thing such educated men would want, said Bunker, was a 'Developed Man' who would ask questions and upset the apple cart. 'We do not want humans,' he wrote ironically. 'We want robots who respond predictably within reason – as defined by the educated man.'

Catch-22.

Village Realities

Bunker Roy

Originally published in *Seminar*, Issue 236, April 1979

WE ARE USING STATISTICS in rural development like a drunk man uses the lamp post: more for support than illumination. As of now, the number of loans we have dished out, the number of villages we have electrified, of farmers we have helped with seeds, fertilisers, insecticides and pump sets reads like a Ripley's 'Believe it or Not'. But has anyone stopped to think what is happening in the rural areas? Is this type of development doing any good? Is it, for instance, changing people for the better?

CRUCIAL QUESTIONS. Important issues, all of them. To my mind, we are being swayed by unscrupulous, selfish, ignorant people who have pretensions of being spokesmen for the rural poor. This includes a galaxy of bureaucrats, self-styled experts and members of the rural oligarchy, the dominant minority who are the least interested in the poor and their development. They are only interested in themselves and since there is no dearth of gullible people, influential or otherwise, and with all the financial resources at our disposal, in effect we are being taken for a massive ride. Willingly. With great style, we are showing what fools we can be. Who cares for reports, who cares for surveys, who cares for bankable schemes? In the ultimate analysis, they mean nothing to the 300 million people who live below the poverty line (if there is such a thing), who earn less than Rs.1000 a year, who still face fundamental problems like where their next meal is going to come from and who will beat them up next while the magistrate and the police watch the fun on the side.

We take great pains in balancing budgets and coming up with watertight schemes which look terribly impressive – reams and reams of data and statistics going on for thousands and thousands of pages – all for what? So that the small and marginal farmer can become a landless labourer? So that 99% of the budget of a primary school is spent on the salary of an indifferent, couldn't-care-less teacher and only what is left is supposed to be spent on books, teaching aids, training, renovation of school and educational tours?

We arrange for so-called experts in rural development who are costing us the earth to draw up, for *lakhs* and *lakhs*, some ludicrous plan ostensibly designed to help rural artisans; we think plastics as a small-scale industry is the last word in progress and development; we are all for power looms in villages because they are likely to generate employment and make cloth cheaper.

AND THE REPERCUSSIONS of all this? It is too bad that Gandhiji's 'last man' has to migrate to the cities, to live in unspeakable poverty and persecution because as a potter, as a leather tanner, as a weaver, his livelihood has been taken away from him; this is progress by Indian standards. It is too bad that the knowledge, the skill and the experience of centuries has to die in the slums of Delhi and all this master craftsman can look forward to is to become a daily wage labourer on some construction site; it is not possible to fight against this inevitable process. Why? Because we do not have the courage to stand up and say this is wrong, it is cruel, we must stop it. We are willing to swim with the tide. We are willing to be guided by bullies. We are not willing to take a stand and expose ourselves to explanations. So whoever shouts the loudest, whoever shrieks the most must be right; why question it at all? Whoever expresses the most concern must be feared because he must be the most committed.

RURAL PUBLIC OPINION – the moneylender, the landlord, the rich farmer – says that rural development is electricity, it is pump sets, it is tractors, it is good seeds and fertilisers and mechanised farming. And the bureaucrat, the responsible person who doles out the funds, nods with as much wisdom as he is capable of and says, yes. Rural development, it is subsidies, it is free service because the rural population is on the verge of starvation; the bureaucrat agrees. Not a beep in protest out of any of them. Not a word in favour of the rural poor – the impoverished rural carpenter, potter, leather tanner, weaver, blacksmith and Scheduled Caste. And if there is a word in favour which includes making the right noises when it comes to action, fighting these people and mobilising the depressed sections of rural society to get their rights back, no one is willing to fling the first stone.

WHAT HAS HAPPENED to all of us? Where are all our motivated and committed Marxists who talk nineteen to the dozen away from the action, the risks and the dangers? Gutless, all of them, with nothing to show, with no scars to reveal, yet in writing papers and in post-mortem exercises they have no peers. When, if ever, will they go into the countryside to practise what they preach? When are they going to gather up some courage, some convictions and some conscience and set out to do what they profess to believe in, and see what it takes? What does it matter if they are proved wrong? The intelligentsia are not likely to lose their virginity if they come running back to safer ground with their tails between their legs – so long as they know what it is like to live and work and suffer in the rural areas with the poor. Then, at least, they would stop pontificating as if they knew the answers to all the questions.

TRAGICALLY ENOUGH, the cause of the rural poor is being defeated by those very people who call themselves social scientists. They study the rural poor from a distance as if they were specimens in the zoo instead of treating them like human beings, instead of throwing in their lot with them and taking all the knocks, the beatings and the uncertainties. No, for that our social scientists have no time. The ultimate result our intellectuals wish for must be in the form of a book or report. What happens after the data has been collected, what happens after the lives have been studied, what follows after hours of pointless advice have been given, is really not the responsibility of the intellectual at all, whatever may be his political leanings. He may find that as a result of this interference, the agricultural labourer loses his job or has to go without daily wages for a week as punishment for revealing all; the rural artisan may have lost his village market; the Scheduled Caste man loses his access to the only credit he has ever received from the moneylender; the *Dalit's* house is casually burned down.

What does the social scientist care? He is impotent in these matters. In India, he is basically a coward. He will talk about Marxism; he will start frothing from the mouth about mobilising the rural poor and starting an agitation to get their rights back. But he will do it from afar. He will see that he himself is not involved. Since he does not have the courage of his convictions, the peasant, the agricultural labourer and the Scheduled Castes are really pawns and puppets whose minds and lives he thinks he can fiddle around with – but only from a distance. Witness the bits of sensational information that come out of studies and reports, which are taken as indications of in-depth research. We go into ecstasies over such observations. But that is about all we are capable of.

WHAT IS TERRIBLY FRIGHTENING is the fact that rural development strategies are in the hands of these few dangerously incompetent and impractical people, intellectuals all, every last one of them belonging to established urban-based institutions with degrees a mile long to their names but no practical experience in the rural areas to call their own. That is, if you do not count their brief encounters with their *dhobi* or sweeper as rural experience.

It is obvious that we have a forum in the urban areas championing the cause of the rural poor, but it is equally evident that no such attempt has been made to establish a voice in the rural areas where the action is. Where have all the voices gone? What has happened to all of us that we should speak so emotionally about the injustices and the unbelievable horrors the Scheduled Castes have to live through every day, yet no one, literally no one, has the guts to do anything practical about it? We are all so fond of sitting in air-conditioned offices expressing what should be done, what can be done, what may be done, but never what we are going to do ourselves.

This is the natural outcome of blinkered intellectuals who have absolutely no idea of the real-life problems people face. What is preventing them from living and working in the rural areas? What stops them from taking a house/hut in a village and seeing for themselves what it is like to live under such oppressive conditions? They would see how a magistrate in the lower courts can be bought or influenced by vested interests so that justice is denied. They would see how the police are used to browbeat the rural poor till their backs are broken and remain broken; how the *patwari* fiddles with the land records; how the co-operative society run by the higher castes swindles the Government out of funds or disperses funds to fictitious Scheduled Castes and that there is no agency that can probe into these affairs. They would see how government health officials use medicines to carry on private practice.

THERE IS NO END to all the hanky-panky that goes on. But we intellectuals must live through this experience, must feel what it is like to be powerless, impotent and completely helpless with everything going on right under our noses. Just reading about it is not the same as being involved in it. In the ultimate analysis, the development of the rural areas is not going to take place without this sort of personal involvement and exchange of experience. The *patwari*, the primary school teacher, the *gram sevak* and the *thanadar* know that the District Collector (DC) comes to their village once in a blue moon. If and when he does come, it is only for half a day, during which time it is their responsibility to see that only small problems are discussed, the visit is kept free of controversies, and sensitive issues are avoided. Once the DC leaves, the field is open to them to do what they like, because the person most feared, who is capable of terrorising to the extreme, is not the DC but someone like the forest guard, for instance. He is a law in the area. He is invincible. No one, not even the minister, let alone the commissioner, wields more power and can scare the hell out of the rural poor as effectively as this forest guard can.

WE CAN SIT IN SEMINARS and make fundamental changes, we can say all the right and nice things that should be done and include them in the recommendations, but at the village level, the situation never changes. For all the mighty laws we make, for all the circulars and directives we pass from the clouds to the village level, the attitude never changes; let us face this for a fact. Let bureaucrats claim otherwise, but they themselves do not know how flippantly these orders are treated, how much they are a source of amusement and derision. Perhaps because they suspect their own lack of credibility, they do not come as often to the rural areas. They would rather do the planning, the fiddling with numbers and the minor adjustments that promise the world but which have no hope of being implemented in the proper manner. But we have institutionalised this process of deception so completely that it is not possible to discontinue it.

The planner may be a man from Harvard or Yale or Cambridge, but the implementer is supposed to be a BDO (block development officer) or an agricultural extension man risen from the ranks; can there be a situation more tragic for the rural poor than this? The formulator of the integrated plan sits in the Indian Institute of Management; the implementer is supposed to be of equal mental calibre, is supposed to make practical sense out of much nonsense and then gets clobbered for it if it does not produce the desired results. What is written by an agricultural economist hailing from some high-powered university abroad (role experience = nil) is expected to be translated into practice by an agricultural extension man in the village who got the job in any case with a bit of *sifarish*, certainly not for his brains.

But, of course, our ingenious policymakers have thought out a way out of this one, send them for training, they say. Where to? To the IITs, of course, based in metropolitan areas because their staff do not have the time to go to the rural areas. In any case, there are no rural-area facilities for training. In other words, if the *gram sevak*, the agricultural extension officer, the BDO and the like have not yet been bowled over by the complications in the plan, the idea is to do so in the training programme. They are taught irrelevant things, they are lectured on insignificant topics of little or no importance and then sent back to tackle the practical problems on their own. To suggest that the trainers should go through an unlearning process themselves is, of course, being impertinent.

WHAT CHANCE IS THERE for any programme planned and implemented in this manner where there is such a vast difference between concept and practice? And rural development: at what expense? We talk of agricultural development in the same breath as rural development – but for whom? The rural poor? They think of fundamental problems, basic survival problems like food to eat, a house/hovel to live in, clothes to wear for wife and children and a life of peace. We cannot ensure even this. After three decades of planning, after building such a colossal infrastructure, such an amazing delivery system, we are not in a position to guarantee these basics.

Instead, according to official statistics, more than 100 million families survive on less than Rs.500 a year; a third of the 575,000 villages have inadequate water to drink; more than half the rural households live in temporary houses made of grass and mud; one out of every four persons sick is suffering unnecessarily; nearly five million die every year due to exposure, poor nutrition, non-immunisation and lack of proper medical attention; currently, one out of every four Indians is an agricultural labourer: more than 20 million people are unemployed in the country, there are 161 million illiterates in India today. Such fundamental problems and we still persist in talking of seeds (high-yielding varieties), fertilisers, pump sets, tractors and the like – for whom, may I ask? Who is likely to benefit, if not the richer farmer? Even where there is electricity in a village, who actually benefits? In fact, who else but the higher and richer castes can afford it? Is this the sort of rural development we have in mind?

Keep the rural areas away from these misguided people. Save us from these impractical experts who have no idea of the misery and suffering that the rural people have to undergo. Rural development in their hands is about the worst disaster that could happen to the rural poor. If nothing else, the poor are going to be destroyed with the kindness our urban-based wizards are about to shower down in the rural areas as patronage.

Rural Credit

IT IS TIME TO FORGET the credit world of make-believe. It is time to show up the high and mighty credit policymakers with *lakhs* at their fingertips for what they are and call their bluff. Some plain speaking to these fellows, these jet setters of high finance, might yet save the situation from sure disaster, that is if they care at all. These types are so concerned about the spit and polish, the well-formulated schemes, the planned documents, and seek forums to make outrageous promises so desperately, that they need to be told a thing or two. If we cannot make them do without three square meals and more besides, for a start, at least, we can bring them down from the clouds and corner them, to tell the truth for a change. But by the looks of it, this is going to be tough.

Is it too much asking them to come down to where the action is? Not at the State Capital. Not at the district headquarters. Not even at the sub-divisional or Block level which, to all our urban-based rural development experts, is really going to the back of beyond, to the verge of civilisation. One would think it was another way of asking them to live in the Stone Age. It's like using a four-letter word in genteel company; the reaction is the same.

BUT, AT THE VILLAGE LEVEL where the action is – listen, all you stuffy bank managers out there reading this piece – you will be surprised to know that people actually live there; they live and work and laugh and cry and survive like all other human beings. In spite of tatty clothes and torn shoes and an altogether bedraggled appearance, like all other human beings but to a lesser degree than the urban sharks entirely owing to circumstances, they like making a fast buck now and again, they like indulging in a bit of one-upmanship, and they also cheat and go back on their word. Which does not make them any different from some of the respectable types we meet in the urban areas. We call the rural poor who do not respond to the schemes churned out by the banking system illiterate, ignorant, crafty, dishonest, everything uncharitable under the sun. Scratch them with manicured nails and smell beyond the Old Spice lotion they dab on generously and pick them out one by one from the posh colonies in any city and then let us see if there is any difference, if there is anything to choose between them.

Like all human beings, the rural poor would like to make more money, live more comfortably and be free from want. It is not asking for too much, surely. It is supposed to be guaranteed under the Constitution, though more than 300 million people, I dare say, have never heard of it despite what our elders and leaders can claim. When facilities and opportunities for satisfying fundamental needs simply do not exist, it is quite pointless referring to this document. When *Munsif* Magistrates and police officers and revenue inspectors at the sub-divisional level are tearing the articles of the Constitution to shreds almost every day, and we have to remain silent because the system demands it, then where do the rural poor stand? In fact, the profile of any delivery system, be it law and order, the revenue or the judiciary, will show how mercilessly it is used to keep the Scheduled Castes and agricultural labourers poor, how shamelessly it is exploited to keep their backs broken. The credit system, as it is today, is another powerful tool.

Shouting from the rooftops and claiming otherwise is not going to change the situation where the action is.

'CREDIT' – THE MAGIC WORD for the socio-economic transformation of the rural areas. In rural development, regrettably, credit is the password for tongues to wag irresponsibly. Everyone with pretensions to being a big shot talks of credit and what needs to be done at the drop of a hat; how much the development of rural areas depends on it; how it must reach the common man, the underprivileged family and help out. All the right noises. The disbursal of loans is rural development. Once a loan has been given, the problems are all solved! By everyone's reckoning – the plan says so; it has been calculated by experts; the economists are convinced; even the World Bank is satisfied – once a loan has been given, from being a nobody the Scheduled Caste man becomes a yesbody; he can claim to be a citizen. His family will rise in social status. They will no longer be harassed by the moneylender. His wife will no longer be exposed to the dangers of rape. He will cease to be bonded labour. A loan will immediately ensure proper education for his children and adequate medical attention when he needs it desperately, and it will guarantee that his house will not be burnt down as and when some debauched landlord fancies it.

All this, a loan is supposed to achieve. The Scheduled Caste's life has been planned out on paper by those who know all about it. The high-powered London- and Harvard-returned whizz-kid knows what it is like to be a small and marginal farmer, a rural artisan, a Scheduled Caste and an agricultural labourer just by reading about them. He then starts talking about them as if he knows them like the palm of his hand. Easy. No problem. Give that chap there a couple of goats; in two years, he has got it made. And that chap, twenty head of sheep … an open well … a pump set – and his problems will be tikki-ti-boo. If he does not make it in two years, he is not worth saving.

What can one expect out of an illiterate, you tell me. What does he do for the two years? How does he eat? What happens if someone falls sick, or there is a wedding in the family and customs have to be observed? Those are not the expert's problems; the human challenge is absolutely insignificant to him. His problem is how to make an ARC (agricultural refinance corporation) scheme for minor innovation, i.e. the digging of open wells, a viable proposition, a bankable scheme.

After wading through unreadable muck full of meaningless statistics and God knows what else that only the writers can fathom, we are told that so many *lakhs* of rupees will be spent to install so many hundreds of pump sites and construct so many wells; that so many thousand acres will be brought under cultivation and – that's it, gentlemen. That's rural development for you.

WHO READS BETWEEN the lines? Which marginal farmer can afford the construction of an open well or the installation of a pump set? Certainly not 78% of the total farming population in this country. Who do those thousands of acres belong to, pray? Minor point. They belong to the agricultural labourers who have been allotted land under the land reform effort of the government, land which was never in the possession of the rural poor because the law saw to it. The acres belong to the marginal farmers who never had the money to cultivate the land properly and they did not have the influence to get a loan because the adjoining rich farmer saw to that – an arrangement on the sly with the bank manager you can say– the loan never materialised. If you want this observation confirmed by a respectable source and my word is not good enough, have a look at the 'Asian Survey of Agrarian Reforms and Rural Development' (ASARRD) sponsored by the FAO.

THE LIFE, SOCIAL STATUS, mental attitudes and economic security of small and marginal farmers, rural artisans, Scheduled Castes and agricultural labourers totalling over 300 million apparently hinge on the fate of a loan form. In any case, it is not worth more than twenty heads of goats or sheep, a bullock cart, an open well or a pump set because, more often than not, the loan is never paid back (such people are illiterate and ignorant – remember?) and until that is done, they are not entitled to get a second one. They graduate to sinister categories, which evidently mean something serious in bank terminology – they are non-viable, non-creditworthy, bad debts, and so it goes on.

When the chips are down, all this talk of 'weaker sections' is for the birds. On the one hand, we hear the banking system claiming that its policies are to help the weaker sections, and on the other, that this section is classified non-viable, not bankable and an A1 non-commercial proposition. Heads I win, tails you lose. But, of course, if some smart Alec was to churn out a massive scheme for the weaker sections in which a couple of *lakhs* were involved and many hundreds were to benefit on paper, all of a sudden they would become bankable. Guidelines would be set; terms and conditions would be laid out. Everyone would pat themselves on their backs for such a remarkable achievement. But that is where it always ends.

When Bhagwat Nandan, the priest from Bhojiawas village, goes to the bank, he does not fit anywhere, so he cannot get a loan; when Jamuna Bai, a *dai* from Hamara who can just about sign her name, wants a loan for a buffalo, she is not eligible; when Madan Singh from village Ladera, five miles away from Tilonia but in the adjoining district of Jaipur, wants a loan for a dairy, he cannot get it because the scheme for weaker sections only covers Ajmer district, it does not say anything about Jaipur; Sugani Bai from Chota Narena village in the same block, in the same district, cannot get a loan because the bank she knows in Tilonia has not 'adopted' her village. She has to find out which bank has 'adopted' it and then send for the loan form. This goes on.

Institutionally, there are schemes galore that cover all categories of the rural poor; individually, at the village level, the poor either do not exist for the manager or they are treated like dirt. The leather tanner, the carpenter, the blacksmith and the agricultural labourer, each is guilty when he walks in through that door. No objection certificates from other credit institutions and a character certificate from two members of the rural rich (the exploiters, the moneylenders) make him innocent. This unfortunate man, to get his loan form processed, literally has to sell his soul away to complete the formalities. Then the policymakers up in the clouds are concerned (only concerned? I ask you) about why the weaker sections are not using the banks more. Maybe because there are not enough banks?

Conclusion: open more banks in 'unbanked' areas – which means every block which does not have a bank should have one. We must educate the rural poor more, illiterate and ignorant that they are, more by becoming better crooks. It is the way of the world. There is nothing wrong with the procedures, the system is foolproof: it's these natives in the villages, they are creating problems. This is the gratitude we get after all the trouble we have taken to open a bank for them. Imagine.

TO MANAGE TO GET A LOAN is to be a lucky man. In the rural areas, a loan is given as a favour. It is the last thing that can be taken for granted. There are wheels within wheels which need to be greased to keep the system running and in which every conceivable official and non-official is implicated. When the loan finally matures, the Scheduled Caste is told in no uncertain terms that the system has done him a favour. The final amount quoted for the loan is never given; expenses have been deducted on the way. Tell this to the big shots at the top and they are far from scandalised; they know it is happening, but they haven't the courage to do anything about it. Instead, they have two reactions: (i) they will laugh it off. These things happen, they will say, they cannot be avoided or checked. But at the same time, they will froth at the mouth and insist that the bank is for helping the rural poor. But some help: (ii) they will trace the source and take it out on the bank manager who happened to lower the image of the bank for speaking the truth and making it public.

EVERYONE KNOWS that the rural branches supposed to cover bankable areas are actually punishment posts. Undesirables are posted there to cool their heels – union leaders, troublemakers, incompetent people. Big shots with petty minds use this power of transfer to juggle the staff as they like. Little do they realise how much damage it is doing to the idea of accepting the banking system. Mini-Siberias, these rural branches are.

The first question any branch manager is asked is what he has done wrong to be posted in a rural branch; which one of his bosses does not like his face? Hardly the best way to start a rural branch because, from the very beginning, the impression is created that this manager does not carry much weight with his superiors. He is a cypher. He has been sent to the branch to fill up a vacancy, not because he is needed. His word does not count, his work will not be appreciated and his superior is not going to back any initiative he takes. That is the unwritten understanding, the term of reference for almost every one of the 9,356 (June 1977) rural branches in this country. For every circular demarcating the manager's powers, there are two taking it away. The result is that he is left to use his own discretion, and he would use it in favour of the bank. By trial and experience, he knows that to do no work is to do good work. The rural branches have the worst selection of managers that can possibly infest the rural areas. The idea of helping the rural poor is furthest away from their minds. Processing forms is considered one big headache because they see visions of their confidential reports being spoiled further – in fact, beyond redemption.

Publicly, the post is advertised as a challenging one because rural credit is an entirely new field; in private, no one in banking circles believes it. Conceptually, the rural branches are committed to assisting the weaker sections. In practice, a form of institutional exploitation is evident in which the bank manager, the money lender, the rich farmer, landlord, pump dealer, co-operative inspector, executive engineer of the Electricity Board, all have a hand. The gullible public is told that the criteria for selecting schemes are no longer only that they should be commercially viable. They should be socially acceptable, also. But please note the trend even today. Every bank manager would gladly rather give a Rs.50,000 loan for a tractor to a filthily rich landlord than process a Rs.1,000 loan to 50 leather tanners or handloom workers. He would prefer a powerloom factory to a handloom unit; a massive uneconomical leather tannery to the construction of individual tanning pits; the installation of electric pump sets in open wells to giving loans for the purchase of animals to draw out water with leather buckets.

HAS ANYONE GOT a rational explanation for this senseless strategy? In the name of rural credit for the poor, how can all this fun and games be allowed to continue, and no one take the responsibility for trying to improve the situation? If someone has the impertinence to suggest that one has to be careful in selecting the loan for weaker sections, whether because (i) it might turn out to be a grant instead of a loan, (ii) they might misuse it for other purposes, or (iii) they are ignorant and illiterate (the standard complaint), my answers to these ludicrous reasons are (i) there is something called the Credit Guarantee Corporation of India (knowledge about which bankers keep tucked up their sleeves) which has been established by the Reserve Bank of India to cover all bad debts, especially those of the weaker sections, none of the nationalised banks lose if the identification is faulty in some cases; and (ii) what guarantee is there that the rich landlord will pay back the loan he has taken from the bank?

Studies have shown that the weaker sections are more regular in their repayments than members of the rural oligarchy. In fact, this is a point in favour of the weaker sections being patronised more. We give the rich farmer the benefit of the doubt; why not the rural poor? Is the extent of misuse less? Whoever says so does not know what he is talking about. In the ultimate analysis, it is substantially more. By giving loans for high-yielding varieties of seeds, chemical fertilisers, electric pump sets – inputs not within the means of 352 million marginal farmers, we might be putting more land under cultivation and increasing our food production; but it also means that less land is available to the poor: development (?) at the expense of social justice (the Constitution, anyone?)

THE BANKING SYSTEM has its quota of self-styled visionaries. A classic tale that needs to be mentioned in despatches, one that sounds good but means damn-all, is the one claiming that rural branches are there to rival the interests of the money lender in the village. Whoever thought of this one must be writing fiction stories in his spare time. Do a survey and find out who is behind the establishment of most of these 9,000 rural branches all over the country: politician, farmer, gentleman thug (there is such a thing, we manufacture them in the rural areas), with money lenders as a side business. It is not a coincidence that only the loans to those weaker sections who are already heavily in debt to the money lender are sanctioned. We all know what happens after that: the Scheduled Caste person is obliged to the money lender and, in due course, is harassed by the bank. His replacements are looked after by the money lender. Next time, a bigger loan, a bigger debt. If this is not institutional exploitation, what is?

Incidentally, these loans fall into the category of the socially acceptable, a form of social work the banks indulge in now and again just for local colour to show that they are doing something for the weaker sections. If the money lenders are not obliged, what will happen to the deposits? The sixty-four thousand dollar question.

IT IS IN THE INTERESTS of the banking system, the exploiters and the landlords that the procedures remain complicated. The trick is to keep the poor ill-informed. Puzzle them, baffle them and persuade them to sign their souls away and then convince them that they are being given special treatment. It is in the interest of the money lender in the village that the rural poor do not understand the banking system, and the frustrated, disgruntled bank manager willingly participates in this conspiracy. It means more deposits and less work. Simplify the procedures, and all hell will break loose. With forms as thick as a telephone book, there is no danger. It can make anyone blink – why not the Scheduled Caste?

He is a much-confused man. Instinct tells him that he is being taken for a ride; experience warns him that all this lavish attention is not for his benefit alone and that there is more to it than meets the eye; wisdom and practical considerations make him decide to take the risk: when a *patwari*, a *gram sevak*, a policeman, a school master ask him to take a loan in order that their quotas are met, refusal is out of the question.

The most dangerous types to cross swords with are these grass root government functionaries. They hold the law in their hands. They can run circles around any IAS officer when it comes to survival and slipping out of tricky situations. So if loan forms have to be processed to show that development is taking place, there is nothing like catching the weaker sections and 'motivating' them to take loans.

All these *crores* going into the rural areas through institutional credit agencies – look where it is all ending up. What a shame that we have the wherewithal to do something about it but lack the character, the courage and the consistency to carry it through.

© *Seminar Publications*

Don't Turn Your Back on Tradition

Bunker Roy

Originally published in *International Agricultural Development,*
January-February 1981

INDIA CLAIMS – RIGHTLY, WITH SOME PRIDE – to have increased food production from 50.8 million tonnes in 1951-52 to 125 million tonnes in 1977-78. There has been a corresponding increase in land under cultivation, rising from 116.4 million hectares in 1951 to 160 million hectares in 1971. This is described as rural development, but what has been the impact on India's 150 million rural poor: the small farmer, the rural artisan, the Scheduled Caste and the agricultural labourer?

The Directorate of Extension, part of the Ministry of Agriculture, estimates that by 1981 78% of farms will be of two hectares in size, or less. And in an FAO-sponsored study, the Asian Survey of Agrarian Reforms and Rural Development, a trend was detected of small farmers becoming subsistence farmers and then landless labourers – the effect of fragmentation of holdings and the sale of land to better-off farmers for want of resources. Technology, in the name of rural development, is playing havoc with the lives of these potentially bonded labourers. Agricultural development is not development if it results in poorer farmers being forced off their land.

That process starts when we adopt the view that traditional agricultural practices are primitive, wasteful, non-viable and unnecessary. This is a travesty of the truth. It presumes that modern practices are effective, cheap and vital (to the nation or the farmer?)

Technology and modern agricultural practices, in the present scheme of things, are being used as tools for exploitation; as levers to promote inequalities and maintain social injustices. How else can one explain the fact that 40% of India's population still lives below the poverty line of Rs.500 (about £30 a year); that a third of the country's 600,000 villages still do not have adequate, safe drinking water; that more than half of rural householders live in temporary homes made of grass and mud; that at least one out of four persons is ill unnecessarily; that 20.4 million remain unemployed, and that there are 160 million illiterates in the country?

It is because we do not have a deeper and more sympathetic understanding of field problems and the human situation that such fundamental and basic challenges still confront us. It is reflected in our inexplicable attitude towards traditional agriculture. Instead of studying it carefully and adapting our technology to the practices of the smallholder, we are literally writing the smallholder off and concentrating on the 3.9% of farmers who own 30% of the land available for cultivation.

If a marginal farmer decides to sow local varieties of seed it does not display his ignorance. He may have very good reasons for his choice. In the first place, he probably cannot afford high yielding varieties. In any case, farming a relatively poor plot of land is not his major occupation. He sells one crop during the monsoon and for the rest of the year earns a living as a rural artisan (carpenter, leather worker, weaver), as a sheep farmer or as a labourer in some famine relief camp. There are millions like him. They need help.

Perhaps as a result of our conditioning by the West, we have an inability to see the problem through Indian eyes, keeping rural realities in mind. What is taken for granted in the West – electricity, good roads, supply depots, agro-service centres – as a prerequisite to agricultural development of any kind is a luxury in many parts of India. We have also acquired a taste for agricultural research of a type that is not likely to benefit, directly or indirectly, the 200 million poor Indian farmers.

In many parts of India, the subsistence farmers see infrastructural development as just another way of taking their land away, of generating unemployment and of making them more dependent than ever before. In the name of agricultural development, electricity is often installed to drive pumps in irrigation wells. But thousands of leather workers who were employed making leather buckets are thrown out of work. Is this progress?

To understand the poorer farmer's cropping pattern requires a considerable effort; it is not enough just to conduct cursory studies. He is poor not because he lacks access to improved technology, but because of socio-economic circumstances that technology may only exacerbate.

We have a dangerous habit of waving this magic wand as if the adoption of modern practices can solve everything. In my opinion, traditional agricultural practices are being treated with too much scepticism. We have closed our minds to what has already been proved over generations. If we insist on calling such techniques 'primitive', we are only showing our ignorance. They have so much to teach us. Let us technologists start unlearning a bit. It will be a good start.

© *Research Information Ltd.*

Despotism

Bunker Roy

Originally published in *Seminar*, Issue 267, November 1981

WE ARE TREADING ON DANGEROUS GROUND NOW. All of a sudden, the peasant is in the limelight. There is not enough space on the bandwagon for those who want to be heard pleading their causes, but that does not prevent them from saying how much they have been abused over the centuries. The peasant has sweated blood for the urban types: what has he got in return? If figures are to be believed – peanuts. It is time the peasants got together and got their rights back! It is time they got their due share of the nation's resources! Why should a microscopic but dominant minority living in the urban areas control everything? Why indeed.

But this is not the crucial question. To the gullible humble public, this is very likely to receive immediate sympathy, and regrettably result in violence as well. As it has, but please note the leaders have not suffered wherever there has been some bloodshed. India believes in the caste system. It just so happens that there are some people who have been born to serve as cannon fodder when the right time comes – like the weaker sections. All for a good and just cause, our peasants will undoubtedly say.

I submit that the issues are far more serious, on a different wavelength altogether, and if the ominous signs of what is happening around us are any indication, we are facing a very grim decade in which all of us will be losers.

We must ask: who is the person shouting from the rooftops? This man calls himself a farmer. He is supposed to be a small farmer with 30 acres in Maharashtra or 10 acres in Meerut and he claims to know what poverty is like. This man claims to live in a rural area in primitive surroundings – and we believe him because we compare his living conditions with the opulent way people live in cities. This man considers possessing a TV set is a sign of success. To speak English, to have money to buy a tractor or acquire land by fair means or foul, to get an electric connection in the house, to get a job as a *patwari* or a primary school teacher – all serve as status symbols, quite apart from the power that is associated with them.

By rural standards, this man is a success. He is vocal and can whip up emotions in a crowd at the drop of a hat. He can sway public opinion in a village from one extreme to another like a pendulum, leaving the issue unresolved; but since public opinion is really the opinion of two or three people who speak on behalf of the whole village, this is not really difficult. So he can say he speaks on behalf of small and marginal farmers, rural artisans and Scheduled Castes – because no one dare oppose him, in case one day he might find his house mysteriously burnt down or someone might throw stones into that house if he dares to step over the line. I have given you the profile of a nameless peasant found in handfuls in all the villages of India. Scratch this man and you will find three quarters of him is a despot, the other quarter is a PR man.

By urban standards, he knows he is considered poor. The city types who claim to know about rural development and who unfortunately also control policy are so appallingly ignorant of rural realities that these peasants know they can get away with murder. So what do they do? They dress in tatty clothes and look bedraggled, they look bewildered and lost (just as a professor would in a rural area) and when they walk down the main street of the city looking as if they had escaped from the zoo, it is to create just this impression. Man from the Stone Age is coming into civilisation: he is at last aware that he is being victimised – Beware.

This peasant – some of them sit in Parliament and talk about poverty – is more aware of the world around him than we are. He has never known hunger but sees it around him, and what he sees leaves him unmoved and as callous as before. Even if he can do something about it, he will not, because he is actually convinced it is wrong to economically uplift the farmers and the impoverished artisans. Who will work on his land then? While he is politicking, who will look after his animals, get water to his house for him, take his child to school? He sees nothing wrong in this arrangement. This bonded labourer might well have some land of his own that he might want to cultivate, but he will never be free. He has never known what it is like to be free. But in his name an agitation is brewing that only his exploiter will benefit from. The genuinely poor farmer does not know the issues at stake: he is told to come out on a procession and he does so because his friend, the exploiter, tells him to.

I have been told if the farmers are organised and they become a force to reckon with, many of the imbalances will be corrected. Professor Raj Krishna thinks so, Dr Kurien of Amul fame thinks so, Bhanu Pratap Singh also thinks so. They do not think it is necessary to identify which farmers – the 3.9% who own 31% of the total cultivable land? But the fact that this 3.9% get away with the illegal concentration of land in their hands shows they are already organised, surely. The fact that they can bleed the co-operatives dry for their own benefit, the fact that they can break all the laws, buy up village-level government officials and monopolise the inputs available, the fact that they have their spokesmen sitting in the State Assemblies and the Parliament looking after their interests, the fact that any large-scale misappropriation of public funds in the rural areas can be effectively hushed up, all shows how well organised they are, surely? So what more do they want? They want more power to do evil, perhaps? If they are agitating to – what's the word they use? – 'regularise' this extra-constitutional power they already have and are exercising in the villages every day, I see great danger in this move.

I think it is a good thing that fertilisers are so expensive for the 3.9% when more than 78% of the farmers do not use them on their small plots because they cannot afford them anyway. Just increasing food production with alien technology for the sake of it (and showing the outside world how very great we are) while the distribution system remains as atrocious and discriminatory as ever is to my mind a meaningless exercise. For once, I am happy that we are so inefficient in our distribution of electricity and power, though it will take some time before anyone at the top realises how much damage it has done in the rural areas and how much unemployment it has generated.

Consider what this rich *kisan* has got already. He has got a deplorable delivery system at his beck and call. At his request, the *patwari* can fiddle the land records to his advantage, with the result that he has in his possession illegally occupied land totalling hundreds of acres. No-one to question him. If the SDO or the *thanedar* happens to allot his declared surplus land to a landless labourer, it is a five-minute job for this despot to get the landless labourer to refuse – on paper. If there are Scheduled Castes who have the guts to fight it out in court – and there are many thousands in this predicament – it is of no consequence if the judgement has all along been in their favour. Hundreds have come to us showing the decision of the Revenue Board saying the land is rightfully theirs – but they cannot persuade the police to help them, support them, protect them.

This rich farmer knows how weak and divided and impotent the system is and he exploits it to the full. It takes a *patwari* months, sometimes years, to measure a plot of land a mile away: it takes a *thanedar* months (sometimes never) to act on a complaint that the rich farmer has harvested a land allottee plot and taken the produce to his own house – and the way he acts is to take Rs.1500 and hush up the whole thing. When the land allottee goes to the police station to find out what happened to his complaint he gets a sound beating and is told to get lost. Such incidents are happening every day in the 600,000 villages. What are we doing about it?

Inputs. They complain they do not have enough inputs like seeds, fertilisers, power, tractors and the like. Well, if anyone looks into the village co-operative societies, and studies them in depth, the question of why this is can be easily answered. Most of the village-level co-operative societies are in the red, if not defunct, and yet we persist in propping them up with more cash. We know this system has proved a failure and that such societies are in the hands of the rich farmers but we still keep pumping money into the bottomless pit hoping against hope that it will revive. And we say that the farmers, these despots, are not organised? How else did they manage to eat up *crores* of rupees and not be questioned, not be held accountable? Who says they have been neglected? Throw this in their faces and let them dare to stand and be counted. God knows how much of this colossal amount has gone into lining people's pockets – petty bureaucrats, bank managers, co-operative inspectors, village-level functionaries who process loans for the Government (not the poor but in the name of the poor), assistant engineers of electricity boards – to name but a few.

What else has this exploiter got already? When he can afford a tractor and 100 acres of land, he has the government doctor in a primary health centre giving him free medicines and whatever else he asks for – and for services rendered, this doctor gets a status he would never get in any village, quite apart from the material comforts he will get automatically. This bloodsucker gets his children educated for free, from primary school to college, and since he knows the schemes and benefits available, he will probably get his son a scholarship. Of course, the headmaster dare not fail the son in any of the exams even if he has little more intelligence than a stone; and it is taken for granted that he will be given preferential treatment. This same boy will come back to the village to become a *patwari* or a teacher or a co-operative inspector or a clerk in the irrigation department. How's that for the wheel coming full circle? What we call exploitation, despotism and injustice – words that convey no meaning in the rural areas – is as entrenched and natural as the social system that prevails in the villages.

I do not know how they have the gall to ask for more. Every service in the cultural area is either free or heavily subsidised. They are organised enough to smother any discussion on the likelihood of the richer farmers having to pay agricultural tax. They think they are being clever when they put forward the argument that public investment has never exceeded 27% in the rural areas: that the rural sector in 1980-81 is only getting 2,266.9 *crores*, out of which 990-odd *crores* in any case is for the purchase of fertilisers – so that leaves a pittance.

But what they conveniently forget is to include the amount the Government spends to keep the allied services going (or not going, as the case appears to be) – medical, educational, revenue, law and order, co-operative, public health (drinking water) – all totalling astronomical amounts. And the contribution of the rich peasant? To hog it all up and leave nothing for the deserving and the poor: 31,000 *crores* of it in the next five years.

On what basis can they say they have been neglected and abused? The figures do not reflect the reality. The abuse and neglect of the nameless millions of marginal farmers, Scheduled Castes, agricultural labourers and artisans are shoved under the carpet like dirt. They are nobodies, non-citizens who are not allowed to raise human issues because it would be a reflection on rural India as a whole. It would only expose how much so few farmers have been pampered to the core.

It is a fallacy that the rural rich are not organised enough. They have managed to brainwash the minds of so-called intellectuals who sadly enough also control the purse strings of this country – people who have little rural exposure but who have started thinking of themselves as experts. And our rich farmers are laughing like hell behind their backs, seeing these intellectuals as puppets to be controlled and juggled around as and when they feel like it. What damage have they managed to do, you might ask.

They have managed to get this ridiculous idea accepted that agricultural development is rural development. Everything else is incidental and secondary. In other words, elementary education, adult education, the rural water supply, preventive health, training and other delivery systems are not necessary for the development of rural areas. That the rural rich give such little importance to these things is clearly seen in the way they respond to these programmes in their own areas. Shocking and disgraceful, is all I can say.

I accuse the rural lobby in Parliament, in State Assemblies, and at the district level, of successfully managing to get a warped set of priorities accepted, where the emphasis is on infrastructural development rather than on human development. Time and time again, we have had to hear that there are so few schools, dispensaries, banks, roads and what-have-you, and how much the rural people are being victimised and neglected. See the callous way, the indifferent way, in which what they have is being used, the human resources going to waste and you will understand what I mean. But the rural lobby has managed to get more funds for tangible brick and mortar development than ever before. Not organised? You must be joking.

I accuse the rural lobby of destroying rural India slowly. The wealth, the knowledge, the skills, the potential for self-reliance that the poorer communities, now numbering over 300 million, have – all this the rural rich see only as evidence of shame. They look on it with angry eyes if normal knowledge and skills are used for their own development because in the world's eyes they think we are showing how primitive we are. They are making every effort to replace traditional systems of medicine, of education, of agricultural practices, of barter which ensures inter-caste co-operation, of maintaining law and order within the village without outside interference from the police – on the grounds that we have to progress with the rest of the world. Why? What's wrong with the system already?

The rural rich lobby has been exposed to the urban way of thinking and lifestyle and is absolutely bent on urbanising rural India.

What are the implications of such a move? Without doubt, if the 300 million are not bonded already to farmers in the non-institutional system, they will now be entirely dependent on institutional infrastructures. Since the 3% of big farmers control, directly or indirectly, the grassroot delivery institutions, we all know what that means.

The rural despots have much to answer for. The track record of the facilities, the opportunities and the funds provided for the development of the rural areas that they have hijacked is so dismal that one wonders what more concessions can be made that would make life for the rural poor any better.

But let us be quite clear about one thing. The issue is not correcting imbalances and giving more rights and resources to farmers. They have far too much of that already and they are misusing it without any checks and balances. As for being divided, it is a myth because on matters that are likely to affect their interests and influence, they are ONE, and this cuts across party lines.

The issue is much more sinister and we, gullible people that we are sitting in urban comfort, are going to be selling the rural poor down the river. It is plain to see that a decade from now it is not the rural areas that are going to benefit but the rural rich, who have almost colonised all the metropolitan areas. A culture will be here to stay that will have no sympathy for the agricultural labourer and the Scheduled Caste. As yet, this is a sympathy we still have today even though we are unable to translate it into practical and positive terms in the field. When that happens, it is going to be a sad day for this country.

© *Seminar Publications*

Futile Untouchability Law

Bunker Roy

Originally published in *The Indian Express,* 17 March 1984

(This article is reproduced entirely in its original form.)

THE VILLAGE OF RAMNER DHANI in Panchayat Samiti Srinagar, one of the eight panchayat samitis in Ajmer district is like any other village in India. Maybe it is a bit more developed than others because it has a post office, electricity, three tractors, one middle school, five small shops, a co-operative society, nine hand pumps and two open wells supposedly open to the community.

Of the 350 houses in Ramner Dhani about 35 houses belong to the Rajputs, 60 to the Jats, 60 to the Regars, 30-35 to the Balais, 10 to Khatiks, 60 to Harijans and five to Muslims. It is a multi-caste community where power has been unequally distributed among the dominant castes.

Rural setting

The sarpanch Bhagurath Chowdhury is a Jat. The up-sarpanch, Narayan Singh a Rajput. The members of the Village Panchayat of Ramner Dhani include Amar Singh (Rajput), Ram Karan (Jat) and Rampal (Regar). The other smaller and more vulnerable groups–Balai, Khatik, Harijan and Muslim–do not have representation in the gram panchayat.

This would have been acceptable if it were balanced by the village level government functionaries coming from other castes. But this is not the case. The postmaster is Jagmal Singh (Rajput), the patwari is Brijraj Singh (Rajput), the group secretary of the Co-operative Society is Bachan Singh (Rajput). All three tractor owners in the village are Rajputs. Out of the nine hand pumps installed by the PHED there was only one working in the Rajput area; the rest were out of order. The thanedar of the nearest police station which is Gegal is Mool Singh (Rajput).

Enter Dharulal Khatik son of Ram Karan in this typical village setting. He is the son of a sheep farmer with 150 animals with four brothers and five sisters who own nine bighas of dry land in Ramner Dhani.

On September 21, 1983, on his way to Kishengarh he drank from the community well close to the road. This was noticed by a member belonging to a higher caste. That same evening at 9 p.m, two Jats, Bhagirath and Ramkaran and a few others came to his house and demanded that he present himself at a meeting being held near the village temple. On asking the reason why, he was forcibly dragged to the meeting where about 200 people had assembled. After being publicly humiliated, Chitar Singh (Rajput) asked Dharulal how he had the temerity to drink from a well meant only for higher castes.

In a public show of raw power Mangus (Jat), Ramchander (Jat) and Gopal Singh (Rajput) threatened the Scheduled Castes with dire consequences should any member of the lower caste dare to drink from that well again. And just to teach them a lesson in front of the whole village Dharulal was fined Rs 51. He was not in a position to pay the amount. He was threatened with death and had not some of his family members rushed to his aid he would have been seriously beaten up. Fortunately Sarwan Jat paid the fine on his behalf.

Among the prominent people of the village who insisted on the fine being paid were Ramchander (Jat), implicated in a number of cases for dishonesty at the disrtict courts, and Bhopal Singh who has already spent two years in jail for embezzling co-operative society funds but improved his standing and stature by contesting an election.

Letters of complaint

On September 22 Dharulal sent letters to the District Collector registered a/d (No. 5336), the Superintendent of Police (5339), Dy. S.P. Ajmer (5337) and SHO Thana Gegal (5335). On the 23rd the acknowledgement came back from the Collector's office but he received no reply to his letter nor was any action taken for over a month. In the meantime on October 4 Dharulal went to see the

Collector to follow up his letter. The Collector and SP assured him action would be taken and on their advice he submitted another application.

By this time word had filtered down to the village about Dharulal's complaint. On October 13 Bhopal Singh Narpat Singh, Mangu Jat and Ramchander Jat called another meeting in the village. They went around with loudspeakers summoning everyone and once they assembled threatened Dharulal with his life after severely manhandling him in public. Dharulal apologised in front of the villagers for having taken village issues at the district level.

On October 18 Dharulal went to Jaipur and got the Home Minister to forward his petition to the district to take action against the people he had named. He also asked for protection. The Additional S.P. Ajmer sent a guard for protection. The Circle Officer from Ajmer, Sumer Singh, also arrived on the scene and both the up-sarpanch Narain Singh (Rajput) and Bhopal Singh (Rajput) flatly denied ever having taken Rs 51 or threatening Dharulal. By this time Dharulal knew he was fighting a lone battle and the district administration was powerless to take stronger action. But, he was still hopeful.

More humiliation

On October 22 the Sub-Divisional Officer, Ajmer, newly appointed to the service came to the village. Bhopal Singh publicly stated he would not allow anyone to drink from the baori (community well) come what may. The previous night someone defecated near the well and accused Dharulal of doing this. The SDO did what he could under the law: He arrested Bhopal Singh, Rawat Singh, Ramchander Jat, Hamir Teli and Mandu Jat under the Protection of Civil Rights Act 1955 and took them to Ajmer. Four days later they were released on bail. In the meantime, on the SDO's instructions that Dharulal be allowed to fill water from the same well in his presence, on the 25th the patwari (Rajput) took Dharulal at a time when no one was present, made him fill water and then sign that no one had prevented him from so doing.

Dharulal has lost more than a case. It is not likely to lead to the conviction of the five people arrested, not if the patwari, the thanedar, and the gram panchayat members have anything to do with it. By appealing for justice Dharulal has lost the support of the village. The Scheduled Castes have warned him not to take water from the Baori on the road because they will all have to face the consequences. At night Dharulal's house is stoned and he can do nothing about it. Word has been passed round that his family will not be allowed to graze sheep on village land. On November 15 the Scheduled Castes were forced to write on a paper saying they had no objection to others using their land for grazing—while many of them take their animals outside the village boundaries.

Government land around the Baori (community well) has been ploughed by the Rajputs and they have staked claim to it. With the patwari being a Rajput no one has raised a voice. The sarpanch is petrified. To top it all on November 25 Manmal Dahima now Collector Sadarsingh in Mandla (Madhya Pradesh), a member of their caste came into the village and spoke to the community pleading that they cease to press the case. It would not help, he said. It is only a question of time before Dharulal is harassed into submission.

There is much to be learnt from this tragic real life incident. If we must have a law let us not play to the gallery but give it tooth and claw. It should have deterrent value. This happens when enlightened law makers with absolutely no rural experience sit down and draft an act based on their civilised Western upbringing. Only if we put ourselves in the place of the Scheduled Castes is it possible to understand why the PCR Act 1955 will neither protect nor support a Scheduled Caste and untouchability will remain to be practised openly.

Real answer

We consider murder, rape and dacoity serious. Why not untouchability? If finally we want social action groups, voluntary agencies and other citizens to help remove this evil, the law must be strengthened. This can only be done if it is made a cognisable offence, is non-bailable, and if the onus of proof is on the defaulter.

The PCR Act 1955 as it exists today is virtually useless.

Reprinted from THE INDIAN EXPRESS,
with permission of The Indian Express (P) Limited ©1978-1996.
All rights reserved through the world.

Due Process of Law

Bunker Roy

Originally published in *The Indian Express,* 27 May 1984

(This article is reproduced entirely in its original form.)

KALU S/O SUKHA AND SOLA S/O NANDA, both scheduled castes (Balai), together owned 55.8 bighas of land (Khasra No 127) in village Bandersindri, Kishengarh Tehsil, Ajmer District, in Rajasthan. The land was in their possession in 1951. Their families have been ploughing it since. Records show on March 15, 1951 they had requested the State to dig a well on their land and on August 11, 1951 the permission was granted.

He was still paying back the Rs 9,000 he had taken as a loan for digging the well when Kalu needed some more money. So he went to Suja s/o Gopi Jat for a loan of Rs 2,000. Kalu's wife was sick and so he needed money immediately. As is the custom in this area, the girwa system, for Rs 2,000 Kalu allowed Suja access to 55.8 bighas of land for cultivation till such time as the amount could be repaid in full. An agreement was signed. Kalu Balai is illiterate. Suja, knowing this, got him to sign on what was actually a sale deed. Kalu's wife died. He was still paying back the loan to the State. He now had the responsibility of raising his two sons. Again, as is the custom in this area not to pay back for years, the transaction was forgotten.

Sale deed

In November 1976 the patwari of Bandersindri informed the Tehsildar that Suja s/o Gopi Jat had bought 55 bighas of land illegally from a scheduled caste Kalu Balai and under section 175 of the Rajasthan Tenancy Act this was against the law. In 1977 the Tehsildar served Kalu a notice demanding an explanation of why Kalu Balai had sold his land to Suja Jat.

This was the first time Kalu had realised that Suja Jat had got him to sign a sale deed. He also realised why Suja had all along refused to take the money back when he had tried several times to return it.

Kalu was willing to return the amount: he was now in a position to do so. But when this gesture was again met with hostility, Kalu filed a case in the Munsif Courts at Kishengarh – just what Suja expected him to do to destroy himself totally.

On May 3, 1977 the Tehsildar Harbhajan Singh said in his statement to the court that the sale deed allowing the sale of scheduled caste land was illegal. But, he stated, the transaction took place in 1963 and since it had expired beyond the period of limitation, Kalu had no right to appeal under section 175. It was wrong for Kalu, the Tehsildar said, to raise this issue after 14 years. The case may be dropped.

On June 15, 1977 Kalu appealed to the court of the Additional Collector in Ajmer.

On May 10, 1978, nearly a year later, Kalu was given a date for a hearing. He found he was 10th on the waiting list of cases to be heard that day. His lawyer, Ved Brath Purillaha, told him to wait outside and that he was going to the Revenue Board but would be back in time. Kalu's turn came earlier than expected and their names were called in public. No one appeared. The Additional Collector dismissed the case in default.

On April 23, 1979, again nearly a year later, the restoration application of Kalu s/o Sukha was accepted by the court of the Additional Collector, Ajmer.

On March 31, 1981, nearly two years later, the Additional Collector's court passed a judgement on Appeal No. 58/77 (File No. 14/77) against the Tehsildar's decision on May 3, 1977. He ruled it was wrong of the Tehsildar to disregard the patwari's report. The Tehsildar had no authority to pass judgement on Section 175 of the Rajasthan Tenancy Act. It was not for the

Tehsildar to say the period of limitation had expired. He overruled the Tehsildar's order.

On May 12, 1981, barely 2 months later, Suja s/o Gopi Jat filed a counter appeal, this time at the level of the Revenue Board. Under section 230 of the Rajasthan Tenancy Act he appealed against the judgement of the Additional Collector dated March 31, 1981. The court of the Additional Collector had directed the Tehsildar of Kishengarh to begin proceedings against Suja Jat. In the application to the Revenue Board, Suja Jat said the proceedings under Section 175 were barred by limitation because in 1963 the period of limitation was three years. The court of the Additional Collector had no powers and it had wrongly exercised jurisdiction.

Tenancy revision

On November 11, 1982 Suja s/o Gopi Jat died and an application under Order XXII Rule 3 read with section 151 C.P.C. was submitted mentioning Smt Galku (widow) Jiwan (son) Hagami (daughter) Ohhoti (daughter) and Kani (daughter) as his heirs and legal representatives. This was accepted by the Revenue Board on December 13, 1982.

This Tenancy Revision No. 127 of 1981 at the Revenue Board will continue endlessly. Suja Jat's death has not changed the situation one bit. Kalu Balai has spent over Rs 12,000 on lawyers' fees. He has changed his lawyer to Kishen Singh Mehta B.Sc. L.L.B. from Kishengarh and the lawyer is, as could be expected, hopeful and optimistic. Kalu Balai since 1977 has been fighting this case on his own resources and in the process has got heavily in debt. Suja Jat, in the meantime, has been harvesting two crops a year and earning a comfortable income. Suja Jat claims to have dug the self-same well Kalu Balai took a loan for in 1951 and spent over Rs 20,000 deepening it further and making pucca water channels.

Suja Jat has been engangjng a battery of lawyers, all experts in delaying cases, confident that justice will continue to be denied. Kalu has been hounded out of Bandersindri and has been warned that his life is in danger. He lives in absolute penury in village Kalyanipura in Nava Panchayat cultivating 15 bighas of land with Badri Maharaj on a 50/50 share basis.

Kalu came to Tilonia beaten and broken. Sola s/o Nanda somewhere along the way went mad.

Semi-literate lawyers

Kalu's case is not extraordinary. Such cases are being fought in thousands all over the country and ill-prepared semi-literate lawyers earn their bread and butter from such suits. There is little chance of scheduled castes ever getting a fair deal. The law is on their side, but in the interests of "order" the Government is prepared to remain silent. Suja s/o Gopi himself admits in his petition dated May 12, 1981 to the Revenue Board in Para 12 that there was no sale of land dated May 30, 1963. Kalu is prepared to return the amount of Rs 2,000 he took from Suja Jat. The sale of land belonging to scheduled castes to upper castes has been declared illegal period of limitation notwithstanding. Without government collusion the registration of the land in the name of Suja Jat would not have been possible. It is the Government's responsibility to see that the land is returned to Kalu Balai. Since this land is disputed and it is in physical possession of a Jat who is illegally occupying the land Kalu is entitled to government protection and support.

The Governments at the Centre and the State are well aware of these problems and strong circulars to this effect from the Ministry of Home Affairs have been sent to the district and sub-divisional levels. It has not made any significant difference. The problems that scheduled castes face over their land still remain.

In a letter written by O.P. Joshi, Deputy Secretary to the Government of Rajasthan No. F.3/3 (34) Home-5/81 Home GR.V Department dated March 25, 1981 addressed to Mr A.J. Bahadur, Director (PCR), Ministry of Home Affairs in response to the Union Minister of Home Affairs' letter dated March 10, 1980, Mr Joshi says, "The Revenue Department has already undertaken detailed survey through the agency of the patwaris in regard to land disputes." Kalu Balai could not have been classified as a land dispute because the Government forced him to go to court.

Effective possession

In Annexure R-2 of the same note giving pointwise information about the implementation of suggestions from the Union Home Minister under Sub heading Precautionary and Preventive Measures A.1 (i) "that all these disputes should be resolved quickly in a manner which is fair to the scheduled castes who have long been exploited and denied their due" the Government of Rajasthan's response has been that they are collecting more data. On (iv) (a) that "scheduled castes be put in effective possession of lands belonging to them or allotted to them and enabled to carry on cultivation whenever there are disputes and obstructions," the State Government has replied, "Instructions were given to Collectors to ensure that the allottees of land are allowed to cultivate their land peacefully and anti-social elements should not be allowed to disturb them… It is felt that except such cases where people have gone to court of law it has been ensured that the possession is enjoyed by SC/ST allottees."

Kalu was provoked by the Tehsildar to go to a court of law. The notice should never have been served on him. Being a scheduled caste and illiterate the Tehsildar should have known that Suja Jat was taking advantage of the situation. Kalu was ploughing the land from 1951 to 1963. He needed money immediately and there was no bank or government scheme he could get it from so he had to fall back on the system that prevails of giving his land in security for a temporary loan taken. Even if Suja Jat tricked Kalu Balai into signing on a sale deed the Government should never have allowed the registration to take place and Kalu should have been advised properly. In any case he was ignorant of the existence of the sale deed until he got a notice from the Tehsildar. It is very likely that the lower government officials must have advised Kalu Balai to approach the court of law thus absolving the Government of any responsibility in the matter.

Why must a scheduled caste fight for the right to his land using his own meagre resources for an error committed by the Government–in this case quite deliberately and callously?

Reprinted from THE INDIAN EXPRESS, with permission of The Indian Express (P) Limited ©1978-1996. All rights reserved through the world.

Beware of Educated Man

Bunker Roy

Originally published in *Mainstream*, 5 May 1984

IF THERE IS ONE SINGLE INPUT that has retarded the development of the rural areas and is in fact responsible for destroying the will and confidence of the rural poor, it is this peculiar and dangerous breed we call the Educated Man. Quite apart from the fact that we have yet to recognise the difference between literacy and education, the experience of those people working in the rural areas has shown we are inclined to take labels for too seriously. We presume that a person writing 'IAS' against his name is enlightened, is broad minded, is intelligent, is willing to listen to reason, is sensitive and has common sense. More often than not this is hardly true. We presume a person who claims to be an MSc or a PhD in his subject is resourceful, believes in improvisation and has no hesitation in working with his hands. We like to think he is an asset in the rural areas because he has something to contribute or at least has the ability to listen and learn. Again, this is far from the truth.

We have seen them all. We have seen doctors licensed to kill, teachers trained to use their knowledge and skills in learning actually misusing them as tools for exploitation and how little they care for the students. We have seen them all in varying degree making free money from the very people they are supposed to serve, courtesy of the Government which pays them their salaries. When 'educated' people set such a fine example of honesty and show their integrity by doing what they do with government funds, is it surprising when the rural poor stay away from primary school, dispensaries, co-operative societies, government schemes and the like? There could not be a better way of showing disapproval than the rural poor have done in these cases.

It is the educated man with his narrow views and blinkered approach that has given a new interpretation to the concept of self-reliance: now, there are as many views as there are experts on the subject. In the name of development it is the educated man who has devised alien norms of who is progressive and who is backward, who is rich and who is poor, who is developed and who is primitive. As if this is important, as if this labelling is crucial to our understanding of the rural areas.

It is the educated man who is arrogant enough to tell us what development is: he has no time to listen to others he considers mentally and ideological inferior. Without having been directly involved in the process he pontificates on the simplicity of the approach, how easy it is to get government funds, how absurdly elementary it is to secure subsidies from the village level government functionary, and attributes any delay or inaccessibility to the ignorance of the intended beneficiary. This 'educated' man has the audacity to explain how to measure poverty without having missed three square meals in his life. He goes on to explain how to remove poverty and unemployment without having been in either state but he has basic human imagination, vision, sympathy and feeling, so he should jolly well know.

In fact what all this proves is that this so-called 'educated' man invariably rises to the level of his incompetence with the greatest of ease, where he can do the maximum damage to the rural poor.

In the village for the last 15 years we have had to live with the worst types but, regrettably, they matter because in the final analysis they have incredible control over government attitude, government thinking, government funds, government policy and government opinion. By government reckoning the educated man is a 'change agent' but his (almost) sole purpose of being there is to maintain the status quo and see that his uncles, brothers and members of his caste do not suffer from any progressive ideas the Government may have about uplifting the socio-economic condition of the poor. He uses his education effectively to sabotage any move remotely threatening this position. He monitors the impact of any such move and selects what should reach the outside world – for which he has explanations ready in advance. Between them, at the village level, by virtue of their being so-called educated, these men presume to speak on behalf of the whole village. Any development programme that does not further their self-interest, that does not strengthen their hold on the poor and is likely to hit out at the system of patronage will be virulently opposed and subtly squashed.

We like to think that government schemes and programmes for the poor actually reach them. It is the educated man in the village – the primary school teacher, *gram sevak*, co-operative inspector, *thanedar*, *patwari*, and doctor – who effectively scuppers these schemes, preventing most of the funds from reaching the poor. Laws that the poor should know about are hidden from them, loans and subsidies from village level co-operative societies are embezzled in the name of the poor, salaries are drawn from non-existent primary schools by teachers, government medical supplies are used to generate private income and land records are tampered with while land reforms on paper continue. Please note, this is not a list of irregularities committed by primitive, ignorant and illiterate people in the village. This is the contribution of educated men to rural development.

Any effort to help the people help themselves, to encourage them to stand on their own two feet and to make them aware of their rights, causes panic in the ranks. The move to support voluntary effort and organisations over whom they have no control and who follow their own code of conduct has disturbed the village level functionaries immensely. To counter the likely impact of such a strategy from causing incalculable harm to their own interests at the village level we see schemes that are making the poor more dependent than independent of government. No Collector or Commissioner or Secretary of State or Central Government has thought it fit to apply his mind to the gradual surrender of power, and how to influence the loosely educated men at the village level.

Bureaucracy, we are told, is full of educated men. But a culture has somehow developed where it is not considered fitting to be seen too often in the villages mixing with the masses; there must always be a table in between. In any case there are others to do that and since they are from the field they know best. Hence the Revenue Commissioner rarely questions a *patwari's* report; judgements and orders are actually written by underlings and the Member, Board of Revenue, just puts his thumb-print to them; a village policeman's impressions become the views of government, especially about groups that threaten that policeman's apparent invincibility; the *gram sevak's* choice of IRD beneficiaries decided in consultation with the village élite is rarely questioned.

These village level functionaries are supposed to be impartial. They are obviously labelled 'educated' and thought to be objective enough not to be influenced by the politics of the situation. Only educated men who have no choice believe this to be true. People at the receiving end are more realistic in these matters.

It is not that no one knows about all this going on in the villages. What amazes me is the total inability of the system to respond strongly to obviously deliberate cases of corruption and embezzlement of government funds. Secretaries of village-level co-operatives who have run away with fund are still free men. Who allows these cases to lapse but educated men? The very people who break the law are the people who make them and those who are supposed to enforce them – all educated men.

We have a Protection of Civil Rights Act, 1955, which is supposed to protect Scheduled Castes against the practice of untouchability. A case should be registered within 14 days of any written complaint. How many cases have been brought to notice, and how many have been registered? How many have been prosecuted? Untouchability is still being practised openly in villages, and who are the ones wanting it to continue – why, educated men. There are Acts for the well-being and development of the poor, like the Minimum Wages Act and the Child Labour Act, but who are responsible for not observing them? – all educated men in the village who know they are breaking the law but also know they can get away with it.

If the rural poor do not want loans from the Government they are called ignorant. If they do not want land from the Government it is because they are backward and illiterate. If they are not interested in getting electricity connections in their wells and houses it is because they are primitive and need to be 'educated'. If they want to stick to traditional ways of farming and not go in for high-yielding seed varieties and tractors, our 'educated' extension workers say it is because they do not know what is good for them.

The rural poor have seen the way the educated man in the village has swindled the Government. They have seen intrigue, manipulation and harassment; and because of them the poor are never free from fear and, owing to circumstances beyond their control, are often party to shady dealings (for which they are subsequently blamed). They see indifference, insensitivity and sheer callousness in the faces and actions of educated men and the poor cannot comprehend what is so special about being 'educated' if this is what it finally descends to. It is an open question really who is backward, who is primitive. But they keep silent over such issues. They do not have the ability to communicate and neither is plain speaking conducive to peaceful co-existence.

On the last rung of every delivery system where the buck stops is a degree or diploma holder who personifies the worst combination of greed, selfishness, nepotism, caste feeling and ambition to get on in life at the expense of others. It must be conceded that not all village-level government functionaries abuse their positions, but the few left who do not do so operate in an atmosphere that makes them ineffective and non-functional. The wonder is that they keep their balance at all, because pressure is put on them to toe the line by people who should really protect them. Instead they face ridicule. It is a sign of the times not to value or appreciate the honesty and integrity of truly educated men.

Where this hang-up of being 'educated' and therefore automatically superior comes out in its worst form is when the 'educated' come face to face with a member of a rural poor family, who by civilised standards is, for want of a better way of putting it, a Developed Man. This man is educated without being literate. He has the courage to question what he does not understand. He has the intelligence to ask sensible, practical and thus awkward questions, keeping the welfare of his community in mind. He has little time for stupidity and shows it publicly, much to the horror of those present who look at it more as a slight than a welcome indication of independent thinking. He will treat everyone as equals – the educated and the uneducated – and judge them by their worth, not by their status or background. Such an example should in fact make us feel proud because it is the outcome of our development schemes as stated in the objectives of our Five Year Plans – to make people aware, to create an opportunity for them to demand their rights and share of the spoils; to promote social justice rather than depend on Government for everything.

But the educated man calls these people troublemakers. He is horrified that this impoverished (but enlightened) person should be so forward and impertinent in his way of thinking and talking. That this Man should scorn protocol, expose village level officials for what they are and how they behave – in the eyes of the village level degree holder this automatically damns him as anti-social and suspect. Once word spreads, reports of his indiscretions pile up, file on file, until his reputation at district headquarters could not be worse. If he pressurises the system to move it is called intimidation. If he demands an answer based on facts and is willing to go to any lengths for justice and truth he is branded as a Naxalite or an activist.

It is a fact that we educated men and women have yet to develop and accept tools to identify and classify the Developed Man. The so-called educated man would be the last to conduct such an exercise. It would mean cutting his own throat. He would hardly like to be instrumental in phasing out his own usefulness (or irritant value) in the village. More such liberated persons would mean the system would have to adapt and adjust to changing times. It would mean the rural poor would become more independent, and not look up to the system as they do now.

Indeed it is strange how we go about digging holes and filling them up again. We expect the illiterate but educated poor from the village to pressurise the system, we look forward to our adult education programmes making him more aware of his rights, we give him information about schemes, subsidies and projects meant for his welfare and we give him land through the Revenue Department. And when he grows through all these efforts and from being a non-person becomes an actual human being, we use the police and the magistracy to discipline him and put him in his place. It requires educated men to be so devious and cunning. We say: this is not what we mean by development, this is not what we mean by awareness, this is not what we mean by self-reliance. For the educated man something must fit into preconceived patterns and boundaries, or else not be accepted at all. We do not want human beings; we want robots who respond predictably within reason – as defined by the educated man.

Study the specialised functions of farmers, potters, weavers, leather workers, barbers, shopkeepers, priests and puppeteers; they are the last word in integration, professionalism and self-reliance. But what have we educated men done? Compartmentalised each function in the name of professionalism and better management to the extent that the poor have become more dependent, and self-respect has taken a back seat. Where basic services were available to all before the educated men stepped into the picture, now they are available to a few through a few – at a cost prohibitive to the poor. Understanding, compassion and patience are called for, but these are intangible tools with which the educational system hardly equips those who pass through it. Indeed, to be modern, progressive and pushing the educated man acquires different skills to deal with the rural poor. The issue of demystifying knowledge, resources and skills is out of the question. It is more a question of overkill in relation to them all. The agricultural scientist who fiddles with computers is incapable of doing a simple soil and water test with simple instruments. The MBBS man who runs a primary health centre knows quick cures through dangerous drugs, but precious little about preventive health and the traditional medical systems more often used in villages. The management expert thinks district level is grassroots, and anything lower is a waste of time.

Again I say: if we want to develop the rural areas and give the rural poor a chance, keep these high-powered people away from the village. If they are willing to learn, by all means send them to sit and listen. But that, perhaps, is asking for too much.

© *Reprinted courtesy of Mainstream*

3: The 7th Planning Commission: Pathway to Consultancy

Heather MC Malcolm

From the early to the mid-1980s, Bunker devoted much time and thought to how voluntary groups might better serve India's poor. Believing that disparities in attitudes, aims and particularly authenticity among the 'motley, ostensibly disorganised crowd' were slowly killing an NGO movement that was losing its moral authority, he saw an urgent need to sort out the different types of non-profit, non-government organisations that were often jumbled together in the public mind. In placing voluntary agencies in relation to NGOs, he made it clear that while some NGOs undertook social service work and others rehabilitation, voluntary agencies came within the group of NGOs that were committed to rural development.[1]

He was confident that energetic young groups would redefine the roles of NGOs, moving them away from a charity-oriented approach. For this to happen, he believed that (since the rural rich would never want to give up their hold on the poor) the pace of change would have to be forced – and it was the young, 'full of zest', who were willing to take on the challenge. For his part, he saw a fivefold role for such groups: to 'act as the eyes and ears' of

---

[1] Bunker was writing on this subject in the 1980s, and since then, nomenclature in the voluntary sector has undergone many changes. Now, for example, there are not only NGOs and CBOs (Community Based Organisations) but also People's Organisations working for constitutional rights and civil society and aiming to demarcate development and human rights work. Social work has been subdivided further, into professional degree-holding social workers and those who work without degrees for social welfare. The term 'social activism' often defines people/constitutional rights-based politics. Interestingly, Ghandiji divided public action into three kinds: *sewa* (service), *nirman* (development), and *sangharsh* (struggle).

the rural poor, test the existing delivery system, help them move away from dependence on Government and generate resources to further this distancing, as well as promote a degree of professionalism. They were flexible and innovative enough to work in a broad spectrum of activity beyond social welfare, including environmental and ecological work, moving as needed between formal and informal learning processes. But they needed a forum where they could exchange ideas, as well as some form of monitoring system to strengthen their professionalism.

The idea of clear roles and accountability stayed with Bunker as time went by, and he stated his views in increasingly forthright terms. They raised many hackles, to put it mildly. But they also led VC Pande, Member of the Planning Commission, and D Bandhopadhyaya to recommend Bunker as Consultant to the Seventh Planning Commission, and in 1984, he became exactly that. From 1984 to 1989, as Planning Commission Consultant heading the group on voluntary agencies, he was placed to bring about real change.

Among other things, he succeeded for the first time in history in securing government funds to support voluntary agencies: his involvement in writing a chapter for the voluntary sector in the Seventh Plan influenced the Ministry of Development in its allocation of Rs.150 crores (a crore is ten million) to the sector. This was the first time that development action was publicly acknowledged as connected to rural development – before, it had been viewed as a part of public cooperation.

An explosion of ideas followed. Speaking out forcibly for the independence of the voluntary sector, Bunker emphasised that Government and voluntary agencies must work together on equal terms, and he chastised Government for inflexibility as well as sending arrogant, over-qualified specialists ('Educated Men!') with no rural experience to tackle rural problems. Of critical importance in relation to the way that Barefoot College worked, he redefined a professional as 'a product of the immediate area, the culture and the community … competent and confident in providing a service that he has learned by trial and error, by word of mouth, by sheer experience and by what his elders may have taught him – learning by doing in his habitat … He may be illiterate, but he is as educated as they come.' Bunker went on to stress that such human resources, though present, were grossly under-utilised in the villages.

Bunker's pointed criticisms kept coming. By March 1985, he was writing directly and with simple force to the Prime Minister, stressing that no voluntary agency was qualified to say what worked and what did not unless that agency possessed lived experience in the field. He urged that once methods had been shown to succeed, they should be replicated.

In addition, he argued the case for two deceptively simple things: one, a code of conduct (to be worked out and agreed on by voluntary agencies themselves) that would ensure accountability and strengthen professionalism in the agencies; and two, a national forum through which government representatives and voluntary agencies could meet and learn to understand one another. And, crucially, he pointed out that Government should fund the agencies in their work.

Bunker foresaw conflict, though maybe not as much as there was. His letter ushered in bitter years of exactly that, with the smaller rural-based voluntary agencies in favour of a code and the larger affluent groups, mainly based in cities, against. In 1989, Rajiv Gandhi lost the election, but although Bunker resigned from the Commission that same year he continued to press, over and over, for accountability and a code of conduct for voluntary agencies. It earned him many enemies, as his prophetic article 'Voluntary Agencies Twenty Years From Now' makes clear.

Being Planning Commission Consultant heading the group on voluntary agencies did not stop Bunker from writing on other issues, however, and many of his articles from this period continued to highlight the gap between rural values and the lack of understanding of rural life on the part of those in power at just about every level. Disappointment with Government and frustration that nothing was getting any better lie heavy in almost every line.

Naive intellectuals holding degrees from Western universities and knowing nothing about rural reality continued to impose unworkable, expensive plans (so impressive on paper) on country villages, instead of looking for ways to demystify technology, simplifying it so that the considerable human resources in these villages could be used rather than written off. Those who planned for the rural poor, Bunker stressed, had to see them as human beings and be prepared to forget what they thought they knew. He knew they would find such unlearning hard, traumatic even: he knew it because, with disarming honesty, he admitted, 'I cannot forget I was like them once.'

His frustration at the Government's lack of progress over a year is clear as he saw vast amounts of money being spent in rural areas, but not on what really mattered: *people*. It was spent, as he points out, elsewhere, on *things*, and the wrong things too, like power, irrigation, railways, defence, and even irrelevant, expensive television programmes, while people's basic needs like clean water remained unmet. Nobody listened to the poor and what they wanted, but it was vitally important that someone did, because quick fixes would not help them. Long-term commitment was needed, of the kind that encouraged new thinking, not the long-term charity that was on offer. The poor had skills and wanted to use them. They wanted the simplification of methods and technology… You can almost hear Bunker shouting and banging his fist on the table as he asks why simple solutions cannot be tried – we know the hand pump mistri scheme works! But the solutions that continued to be advocated did not work, not for India. 'We must evolve our own unique solution which, I can tell you, defies Western models,' he wrote, 'but no one seems able to tell the Prime Minister how wrong he is to listen to such poor advice.' And corruption was still rife; money was still being embezzled, people were still being harassed.

Disappointed with Government? Yes, indeed.

NGOs – Changing Role

Bunker Roy

Originally published in *Seminar*, No. 273, May 1982

THE ROLE OF NON-GOVERNMENTAL organisations (NGOs) in India has never really been understood. Nor, regrettably, has an attempt been made to clear the confusion that prevails about them in the corridors of power. The bureaucracy has never admitted in black and white that NGOs do not have a place and a role in the development process, but in practice, the response to the whole idea of the NGOs being mobilised for development purposes has been looked on with much suspicion: perhaps with very valid reason.

Not all NGOs have an unblemished track record, and neither are the people who are behind their setting up any less controversial. Has-been politicians become 'social workers' when they have nothing better to do. They form NGOs with a view to jumping into the political arena in the future, and villages have been chosen so as to nurse a particular constituency. Some NGOs are blatant fronts for political parties, though whenever the opportunity arises, they deny this vehemently. But, in the process, all NGOs are much maligned and the genuine ones suffer.

Of course, the next question is what criteria are used to distinguish the genuine from the fake: this only time will tell. When an NGO is started, the background of the people who have got together, the type of institution supporting them, the area of work they have chosen and its location (city, state, district, block, village) does give some indication to experienced people of whether a particular NGO is likely to be genuine or not. To say that all NGOs are guilty until they prove their innocence is really being quite unfair.

Perhaps the time has come to be a bit more specific. We know that there are NGOs and NGOs. For the sake of convenience, people tend to bundle them all under the one heading, with the result that anything and everything which is not within the government system falls in this category – *panchayats*, co-operative societies, youth clubs, Rotary, Lions, Inner Wheel, *Jaycees, Sarvodaya, Ramakrishna* missions, Christian missions, *bal mandirs, Nehru yuvak kendras* and other autonomous institutes, organisations and corporations.

We are such a motley, ostensibly disorganised crowd that one look at us sitting all together is likely to increase rather than lessen the suspicion, mistrust and lack of confidence between the Government and NGOs, between an NGO and its community and between the NGOs themselves. One look at all of us rubbing shoulders together should convince even the most gullible that we are not all as humble, dedicated, motivated and simple as we make ourselves out to be. The majority among us who believe that we are all humble and who at every opportunity harp on these points are actually cashing in on a much-flogged image that is dying – if it is not dead already.

This is not to devalue the tremendous work being done by many organisations in many fields, but they would be the last ones to talk about it or claim to be supermen and superwomen. In fact, if they were what they claim to be, they would be embarrassed. But in their heart of hearts, they know that the NGO movement is being slowly strangled to death, that the lifeblood of the movement – if it can be called a movement at all – is being sucked dry by leeches and bloodsuckers, leaving a shell in its place. Year by year, we are losing the moral authority that we used to have to influence policy and Government; year by year, we are losing the reputation we once enjoyed, of integrity, honesty and being just; year by year, through sheer desperation, in order to justify our existence and tell the world we NGOs are getting bigger, we are welcoming to our fold people and organisations we would never otherwise have touched with the end of a barge pole.

These self-appointed leaders of the NGO movement have lost their credibility among their own clan; they have been out of touch with the workers in the villages for so long that it is not surprising that their word carries little weight. The mantle of giving the NGO movement some direction, some dignity and some purpose in playing a crucial role in today's development world lies on the shoulders of half a dozen people who, beyond delivering the odd speeches and pontificating, have lost the will and the courage to suggest changes to the role of NGOs, to give NGO effort a new dimension and meaning. All they are worried about is themselves and the contribution they think they are making on the international circuit.

Before I come to the new role of NGOs in greater depth, a few words about the obviously long-overdue need to classify the types of so-called NGOs in India today. Unfortunately, in the minds of the humble public, all NGOs are involved in social service as against development work, which in government eyes is outside their scope. Since by 'social services' everyone means charitable work, they see little distinction between what the Rotary Club is doing by organising an eye camp or distributing clothes, and what a rural development organisation is doing mobilising people to fight for their rights. What the *Jaycees* do on weekends distributing scholarships (maybe), what the *Rama Krishna* mission does opening dispensaries and what the youth group based in a tribal area does to train village-level health workers are all one and the same thing.

By accepted definition, a voluntary organisation is supposed to do charitable work – free service to show the extent of its sacrifice and dedication, perhaps. Well, then, the largest charitable organisation today is the Government of India because all its services are free. Education is free; medical services are free; agriculture is heavily subsidised; the setting up of cottage industries is done on a concessional basis; drinking water is free; the construction of roads in the villages is free. It sounds ridiculous, especially when the rural community is in a position to pay for all these services – which is what many NGOs are trying to make happen, in the face of terrific opposition from the Government and political quarters.

A classification is necessary. Not all NGOs wish to be treated alike. Rotary Club members would not want to be seen dead with simply clad, Hindi-speaking, *Sarvodaya* workers, nor I dare say would the *Sarvodaya* workers like to be seen hobnobbing with 'Old Spice'-smelling, prim and proper pucca-type, jet set social workers – a breed that is fast becoming common these days. It is necessary to classify them under three broad headings: (i) social service

NGOs, (ii) NGOs involved in rehabilitation work and (iii) NGOs committed to rural development.

A large number of NGOs fall into the first category, among them the Rotary and Lions Club types, well-endowed, never short of money for the weekend for the philanthropy they practise, harmless, non-controversial and providing just the sort of service acceptable to Government. Now comes the twilight zone, where there is much overlap and confusion. There are traditional agencies with a long past: Christian missionaries, followers of the *Rama Krishna* mission and *Sarvodaya* workers, basically the Gandhians known for the work they have done not only in the field of social service but also in rehabilitation. During natural disasters – recall Morvi and the Andhra Pradesh cyclone – they were the first to reach and mobilise relief.

But there is another type of rehabilitation which these traditional NGOs have never been good at – the rehabilitation of more than 300 million people living below the poverty line, which requires an entirely different approach and strategy altogether. To bring marginal and small farmers, rural artisans, Scheduled Castes and agricultural labourers to a socio-economic level where they can contribute constructively and positively to India's development as citizens of this country is basically a rehabilitation programme, but we like to call it development. In a way, of course, we are involved in development: the development of the human being from a non-person to a citizen. The sheer magnitude of the task is itself mind-boggling.

Here, again, we enter a twilight zone where there is very little difference between rehabilitation and the third category of NGOs committed to rural development. It is this category which is most misunderstood, perhaps because it does not fit into any compartmentalised classification, and we know that anything which does not fit properly worries the bureaucrat. I am also convinced that it is this group which will finally be responsible for defining the changing role of NGOs and, essentially, how their capabilities can be improved.

Already, this group has been responsible for an upheaval within the NGO movement. It is not obvious, but younger groups have challenged the older leadership in as quiet and dignified a manner as possible. Not many young people are joining the *Sarvodaya* and *Rama Krishna* missions, let alone the Christians; in fact, many are leaving, thoroughly disillusioned by the lack of direction and initiative and rigidity which has stifled creative work. This has disturbed the elders, but they refuse to admit that the poor example they themselves have set is mainly responsible for this exodus. In many parts of the country, smaller breakaway groups have been formed with objectives radically different from the charity-oriented big-brother image which the elders are fond of propagating. Only time will tell how serious the threat is to the leadership, but there is no question that they have every reason to feel concerned.

What makes these groups different? They are young and full of zest, for one thing. Nonviolent but militant, they know they cannot change the world overnight, but they also know that the pace has to be forced. If it has to be done through conflict, if that is the way change is made possible, then they will be the last ones to withdraw from the skirmish. They are convinced that such fundamental changes cannot be engineered through government delivery systems because these systems have been compromised at all levels. The power that presently lies in the hands of the Government and the rural rich must be transferred to the beneficiaries: the 300 million who live below the poverty line.

It is quite unthinkable that the rural rich, who constitute only 3% of the rural population, will want to give up their influence and hold on the poor, handing it over on a silver platter.

Typical Gandhians desperately cling to the weird belief that love and charity and similar sentiments can solve all problems, and can penetrate the thick-skins of hardened scoundrels. But we only have to look at the sad state of affairs of the *Gramdan* villages and the land gifted to the people to really appreciate the dismal failure of such an approach. Look at the state *Khadi* boards stuffed with has-been politicians and burnt-out *Gandhians*: some of them look as if the last constructive thing they did was to participate in the Dandi March. These very people claim to carry the torch for all NGOs in this country.

How this transfer and distribution of power can take place is the key question. Can it be done without confrontation or conflict? Increasingly, the younger groups are convinced that this is not possible, simply because the delivery system of the Government is not committed to the kind of change likely to benefit the poor – even though all the plan documents say so. At the village level, where it counts, the rural poor are exposed to pressures from quarters that should protect them rather than exploit and abuse them. Strange that there is literally no individual or organisation oriented to guide them, educate them and provide them with the necessary tools and skills to stand, with any luck, on their own two feet.

The answers that the new NGO groups have found as a result of their exposure to the realities in the rural areas have not been accepted by most traditional agencies. In fact, the old-timers think that the 'cause' is going down the drain, and with this emerging militancy, whatever is left of the NGO movement is going to disappear. Not true; they have conveniently forgotten what it was like when they were young. They have lived off the fat of the land for so long that they have forgotten what it was like to believe and have faith.

If we are to talk about improving the capabilities of NGOs, we have to define the changing roles of the NGOs today. No NGO worth its name can, or rather, should be satisfied with cosmetic changes. Because of the failure of officially sponsored institutions, the role of the NGO has become doubly important in a way few imagined possible a decade ago. The village *panchayat* and the co-operative society – so-called NGOs – have failed to protect and help the poor; they have become the political and development arm of the rich to protect their own interests. Since both these institutions have such weak accountable procedures, *sarpanches* and members openly misuse funds, knowing full well that no one is going to ask for explanations.

Here, then, I give five definitions of the roles NGOs should take:

(a) One is to do the work of MLAs without the political sanction of vote banks. It is to act as the eyes and ears of the poor in the area: report irregularities, expose village-level government officials caught in the process of misusing money, taking bribes and not doing their jobs. It is to bring to the notice of their superiors the reasons why plans failed and targets were not met. Of course, at the slightest hint of any such move, the NGO is likely to be branded as a CIA racket or be accused of conversion or of taking foreign money. There can be no answer to such ridiculous suggestions, but fortunately there are people in the Government who do not take them seriously. However, they could destroy whatever relationship an NGO might have made with the poor and it is also possible that that NGO could fade away. In such cases, traditional agencies buy the peace. They do not like to oppose anything or anyone, even when something seriously wrong is being done in front of them.

(b) The second role of NGOs, to my mind, follows from the first; it is to test the existing delivery system. The Holy Trinity that is causing incalculable damage to government credibility – the revenue, the police and the lower judiciary – has yet to be fully tested by any village-based institution. It is one of the crucial roles of a genuine NGO to bring this delivery system to breaking point, if need be, just to see how flexible and adaptable it is. How do we do this? You will notice that most of the poor living below the poverty line have land, but they do not physically possess it. Such cases need to be reported. Cases of trespass and illegal possession need to be brought to the attention of the police, and disputed cases where 'stay' orders have been obtained need to be followed up with proper legal advice. More than half the land distributed so far by the Government is useless to the rural poor because the transactions exist only on paper.

This is not the only way to test the delivery system. There are government schemes for Scheduled Castes and other socially vulnerable groups which never reach them. The NGO should do its homework and see which scheme fits which target group and then follow it up with the relevant department. But this is not being done by any NGO, with the result that *lakhs* of rupees are being swallowed up in the form of subsidies.

The Government has admitted that it cannot tackle this vast problem of development on its own. The objectives may be the same, of reaching the poor, but strategies differ and methods at the lowest levels sometimes have to be even more radical than is imagined if the ultimate goal is to reach vulnerable groups. Inherent in such a confession is Government's failure to motivate the right types of people to provide services and opportunities to the poor. All along, the human factor has been taken for granted, but it has proved a stumbling block and prevented knowledge and skills percolating from below.

(c) The third role of NGOs is to mobilise the rural poor to choose their own kind for training and equip them with the necessary wherewithal to provide technical and socio-economic services independent of Government. The identification and training of non-institutional human resources from the village itself would also be a sort of recognition of rural skills, knowledge and experience which urban professionals have much to learn from. Sadly, we conceited types think that an illiterate farmer has nothing to teach the scientist.

(d) The fourth role of NGOs is to generate resources within the area with a view to becoming self-supporting in the future. The charity approach must cease, thus decreasing the dependence of the community on the NGO. The younger NGOs believe that if the service is worthwhile, the community should pay to support it. Anything given free is not appreciated. Perhaps the rural rich should be obliged to pay the recurring costs. In any case, what the NGOs are publicly encouraging, the government servant is privately abusing for his own selfish ends. A primary health centre doctor does private practice before ten and after five; a primary school teacher makes money on private tuition; a *patwari* and *gram sevak* make money on distributing subsidy forms and get a cut on the astonishing grounds that 'We are taking government money, not yours!' To a marginal farmer, this logic is irrefutable. It is not that the resources are not available. The service that has been provided is questionable; otherwise, how can a private practitioner flourish where a PHC is based?

(e) Putting an end to the charity approach leads to the fifth role of NGOs – a role which is much frowned upon and treated with even greater suspicion: the need to promote a degree of professionalism. The NGOs today suffer from a lack of clarity of purpose and direction: resources are dissipated, workers are haphazardly selected, objectives are not clear and methods are equally vague; the services being provided are not at par and the backup equipment and support to provide techno-economic services are non-existent. All these signs and symptoms are indications that the NGO lacks a professional approach, without which, in this day and age, it cannot function. Sure, there are many NGOs without this professional touch, but my response to such an NGO is that we can admire it but it cannot be replicated.

The position of the NGOs today is hardly enviable. For three decades, we have worked in the villages, each doing our own little bit, but in the year of the Lord 1981, we still have to find a place in the sun. We still have to prove our credibility. We have yet to develop the growth pains of a movement. Scattered here and there, we have yet to form a common forum. We are constantly talking about it, that we must meet, but each of us is on our own ego trip. Every agency wants to coordinate and speak on behalf of the others, with the result that in the world around us we cut a sorry figure.

These changing NGO roles that I have envisaged for the future will not, I daresay, be acceptable to traditional older agencies. They would virulently oppose them on the grounds that we are encouraging militancy. Not so. We are convinced that, contrary to general opinion, the NGOs are more secure and stable than government programmes. We are here to stay. Our policies and strategies do not change with personalities, as is the case with Government; there is a consistency noticeable in the implementation of NGO programmes, which the Government will find hard to beat. In retrospect, perhaps the old system where ICS and IAS officers used to stay for years in districts was a good thing; at least they did what the NGOs are doing now – digging their heels in and staying, regardless of unpleasant consequences, and completing the job. Under the circumstances, it is neither unwise nor uncommon to expect hostility and opposition from vested interests; after all, we are committed to fundamental change and our policy is not to join them but beat them at their own game.

The elders are a spent force. My only quarrel with them is that they did not have the vision to look ahead and see the potential in the NGOs. If they had, they would not have allowed one NGO to grow in one place for two decades or more, but instead would have used the agency to train people and start many similar efforts on a smaller scale, and would have covered the country by now. We should have had many more of the old Gandhians like Prembhais and Mohan Singh Mehtas and Harivallabh Parikhs scattered all over the country. Incredible people as they are, it is a reflection on them that they could not think along the lines of replicating their ideas in other parts of India.

© *Seminar Publications*

Voluntarism and the 7th Plan

Bunker Roy

Originally published in *The Indian Express,* 17 August 1984

(This article is reproduced entirely in its original form.)

IF THE APPROACH PAPER ON THE 7TH PLAN (1985-90) approved by the National Development Council is any indication there is a definite role for voluntary agencies in the implementation of anti-poverty and the minimum needs programmes. Much of what voluntary agencies have been saying over the years has found mention.

While discussing poverty alleviation, employment and social justice the Approach Paper has conceded that "the objective of removal of poverty can be fulfilled in the measures in which the poor themselves become conscious, improve their education and capabilities and become organised and assert themselves." It goes on to say that the administrative machinery at the local level for implementing minimum wages for agricultural labour will have to be streamlined and measures taken to strengthen the organisation and bargaining power of agricultural labourers.

Upgrading skills

In order to do this the Government will, to a large extent, depend on the effort put by voluntary agencies at the village level. But it also depends on upgrading the skills of the rural poor through training. The Human Resource Development aspect of the development process tends to be forgotten and the Approach Paper has suggested that the existing training programmes be reviewed. In the field of social services the Approach Paper has expressed the need for a more flexible design of education to be evolved to make it relevant to local culture and environment and to the problems of community health. Voluntary agencies working in such fields for decades have long expressed such ideas to Government. Evidently their voice has been heard.

In Part Two of the Approach Paper which contains summaries of sectoral issues, to take them one by one, many ideas on forestry that social action groups in tribal areas have voiced in numerous public fora have found mention. Under the subheading Forestry the Approach Paper mentions that "In tribal areas where the tribal economy revolves around forests and forest-based produce, forest-based programmes have to be so devised as to be in consonance with the socio-economic fabric of the tribal culture and ethos, and to strengthen the linkages between tribal development and the tribal and/or forest lands with which they so closely identify themselves."

In the chapter on Rural Development and Poverty Alleviation the Approach Paper calls for "redistributive land reforms that provide a minimum level of land holding to the landless and a measure of security of tenancy essential for securing the rural agricultural poor against income fluctuations... Group ventures and collective action will have to be promoted in order to protect the rural poor. Elsewhere, the Approach Paper, almost reflecting the concerns of many volunteer agencies in the field, says, "The traditional skills in the villages and the rural areas and a not inconsiderable part of the services and goods in demand at that level – the village blacksmith, the silversmith, the tanner, the cobbler, the potter, the carpenter, the weaver, the dai and the 'vaid' – had been omitted in the sweep of development at the grassroot level. The rural occupation structure is thereby adversely affected and leads to widening the rural-urban gap. The skills existing at these base levels will need to be fully developed."

In October 1982 the Prime Minister directed that voluntary agencies be involved in the implementation of anti-poverty and minimum needs programmes. She suggested that consultative groups be formed in all the States under the chairmanship of the Chief Secretary or Development Commissioner. Soon after the acceptance of the paper on public participation at the last meeting of the National Development Council (April 1983) the Government appears to have decided that voluntary agencies might be used as the eyes and ears of beneficiaries.

Monitoring machinery

The Approach Paper contains this crucial paragraph: "A monitoring machinery will have to be created and strengthened to establish that target groups have in fact received the benefits, assets and items of social consumption that are being provided for them as part of the national effort for significantly reducing poverty levels. Voluntary organisations will have to be associated more closely and actively than hitherto with programmes for reduction of poverty and with efforts to make minimum needs available to the population for improving the quality of life. This will be incorporated as part of the overall strategy for augmenting such programmes meant for the poor, and also as an alternative feedback mechanism for ascertaining whether the target groups have received the benefits meant for them."

The Government has realised that voluntary agencies have a role to play in professional areas other than social welfare like in forestry, agricultural research and education, rural development, alternative sources of energy, non-formal education, housing, urban development, water supply and sanitation, women's development, development of Scheduled Castes and Scheduled Tribes, science and technology, environment and sociology. These fields require an entirely new sort of voluntary agency.

The Approach Paper on the issue of energy says: "There are reports of growing scarcity of fuel wood in the rural areas. This is a matter of concern. While intensified efforts should be continued in the field of social forestry and bio-gas to meet the energy requirements of rural communities, it will be necessary to take up a minimum needs programme in the seriously affected areas covering social forestry, bio-gas, solar energy and other forms of energy to meet the requirements of the rural community. Efforts have to be made to develop and popularise efficient chulas to reduce consumption of energy for domestic cooking. All these additional rural energy programmes will need to be implemented in an integrated manner. Help of local bodies, voluntary organisations, women's organisations, schools and other decentralised grassroots agencies will also be taken."

Appropriate technology

The accent on appropriate technology, to develop better designs of ploughs, carts, yokes, harnesses and other appliances also finds mention in the Approach Paper.

The various educational experiments being carried out by volunteering agencies all over the country seem to have had some effect on changing policy. Over and above the established regular schools run by traditional voluntary organisations the accent this time in the Approach Paper seems to be radically different. "The emphasis should be on innovation, on low-cost alternatives and societal involvement, all aimed at linking education effectively to the needs of the people, to employment and to development ... the content, method and timing of education will have to be related to local needs and detailed block and school level planning introduced with specific targets."

Quite obviously these observations are directed at voluntary agencies which are in a position to be flexible and involve the community in the education of children, at least more than the Government can. Since many voluntary agencies have done a fair amount of work in this field already the Approach Paper says, "Measures will need to be adopted to impart some formal respectability to all types of learning, especially of informal learning, and learning by doing: the resources of mechanics, artisans and craftsmen of all kinds will have to be utilised for the purpose by involving them in the educational process."

Much has been written on the traditional areas where voluntary agencies have always been expected to take a leading role like in health, family planning and nutrition, social welfare and women's development. If at all, the Approach Paper has invited greater participation of voluntary agencies. But where there has been a significant departure from the previous Plans is in the unusual invitation for voluntary agencies actively to participate and take a greater share in the dissemination of suitable technology for the development of rural areas. There is a specific and direct recommendation in the Chapter on Science and Technology inviting the "involvement of voluntary agencies in several field level S&T programmes and provide adequate support to them for carrying out the application-oriented S&T tasks." Later there is a plea for the "popularisation of science and development of scientific temper to make sure that S&T reach the grassroots."

Finally, in the Chapter on Environment and Ecology it says, "Non-governmental organisations, voluntary bodies and the private sector will be encouraged to take an active role 'in' the long-term conservation of our different ecosystems as also of floral, faunal and micro-organism diversity."

New awareness

Some people will say all this is nothing new. It has been said before in all the previous Plans and yet the problems facing the voluntary agencies remain the same. To a considerable extent this is true and that is because there was no established forum where Government and voluntary agencies could meet. Now with the idea of the consultative group at the state government level catching on misunderstandings due to poor and irregular communication will at least be minimised. It all depends on State Governments of course. In spite of clear guidelines from the Planning Commission to identify and involve grassroot agencies living in the villages, the perception of many bureaucrats of what is a voluntary agency is dangerously superficial. To many, apart from Rotary Clubs and Lions Clubs, there are no other voluntary agencies since the Government is doing everything.

Reprinted from THE INDIAN EXPRESS, *with permission of* The Indian Express (P) Limited © 1978-1996. *All rights reserved through the world.*

For Prime Minister, a Word of Advice

Bunker Roy

Originally published in *Mainstream*, Special Number, 9 March 1985

Prime Minister

A word of advice on behalf of voluntary agencies working in rural India.

Thousands all over the country are providing basic professional services, generating awareness, mobilising people, professionalising volunteerism and making people help themselves in a small but significant way – a new breed of young men and women who are convinced that the Government and urban-based experts alone cannot tackle India's vast problems. We have watched – and commend – the steps you have taken to throw up fresh ideas on how to reach the villages, make the Government more responsive to the needs of the rural poor, make education more relevant, develop wastelands and promote social justice, but more perhaps by accident than design you have left out of your deliberations, your committees, your think-tanks and expert groups the very people who will eventually, hopefully, deliver the goods at the village level, the gut level where it counts.

The same mistakes seem about to be made as in the past. We are depending on the same people who were consulted earlier but who have little new to contribute because they are not from the field. Let not the Thinker, the Armchair Radical, the Impractical Man control you, influence you, sway your balance and judgement.

They may know the problem theoretically, but they do not know the people and their practical problems. This specimen called the Expert, hiding behind his degrees and qualifications, is a dangerous breed. This man who speaks smoothly, answers glibly and knows all the solutions is going to be the death of us. It is a wise move to de-link degrees from jobs. We need someone who does not mind dirtying his fingernails.

You need workers around you with actual field experience. There are so many all over the country. Why haven't you consulted them? Someone who knows what it is like to be on the other side of the table? Someone who has felt the traumas and the frustrations and knows what needs to be done to improve the system from below – small, insignificant changes that mean a lot.

It's time you listened to these ordinary people, the very stuff India is made of. Let the so-called experts listen for a change to how changes from below can make a world of difference. It is at that level where the buck stops, where it actually counts and directly affects the lives of over 300 million people living below the poverty line. These people have much to tell you. New ideas, new projects, new programmes, new approaches and methods have been tried in the field. These have worked in spite of the corruption we hear so much of, the indifference of the bureaucracy we have to live with, the hostility of the vested interests that is taken for granted. These ideas and methods and projects have not only survived, but in spite of such occupational hazards as have been noted above, voluntary agencies have translated them into action with an impact which we can see and learn from. What is stopping the Government from learning from these experiments?

The professionalism with which these voluntary agencies are going about implementing new ideas at the village level indicates a seriousness and consistency that the Government would do well to learn from. But what is even more significant is the fact that all these experiments have been carried out in co-operation with State and Central Government, in which the Government has played a supportive and secondary but vital role.

These are not projects that are being implemented in isolation. Surely, this means such projects can be replicated on a much larger scale? So why are we not trying? Why are we not allowing such simple, inexpensive and effective ideas and methods to be tried more widely? Instead, we are setting up high-powered committees and groups, rehashing the same issues all over again. Do we have the time?

It's time such efforts were given the attention they deserve. The Government has much to learn from the *Lok Adalats* in the tribal areas of Gujarat and Rajasthan; the release and rehabilitation of bonded labourers on waste lands by MYRADA in Karnataka; the promotion and construction of bio-gas plants in ten states of India through voluntary agencies like AFPRO, the science education programme of Eklayva and Kishore Bharati in Madhya Pradesh and Shastra Sahitya *Parishad* in Kerala; the installations of hand pumps by more than 25 agencies all over the country at 20 to 30% cheaper rates than the Government's; the campaign against harmful and deadly drugs by a group of highly motivated doctors of the Medico Friends Circle; the issues that started the campaign against the Forest Bill by voluntary agencies working with tribals all over the country; the experiment of the *Pani Panchayat* with such incredible results in Maharashtra; the low-cost housing schemes of the study action groups in Ahmedabad; the community-based one-tier system of repair and maintenance of hand pumps adopted by the Government of Rajasthan; the organising of women's groups to fight for their rights through a SEWA in Gujarat; the low-cost preventive health programmes through voluntary agencies in Gujarat, Tamil Nadu, Maharashtra, Rajasthan and Bihar where infant mortality rates have dropped sharply; the establishment of evening learning centres (often called 'Night Schools') for drop-out children in Rajasthan; the use of traditional media for educational purposes and spreading messages among the rural poor who do not and cannot look at TV or hear the radio; the emergence of small viable environmental groups producing a wealth of material on pollution and other ecological hazards; the inevitability of human rights groups providing feedback to the Government of the ineffectiveness and non-observance of laws at the village level such as those on Protection of Civil Rights,

Minimum Wages, Abolition of Bonded Labour, Equal Remuneration, etc.

What's special about these methods, approaches and experiments? The fact that they have all been exhaustively documented, professionally researched and thoroughly tested in the field.

Second, all of them show how within, and using the same system, it is possible to reach the poor simply, inexpensively and more effectively.

Third, contrary to the image voluntary agencies have in the eyes of the Government, such efforts have shown a competent and realistic understanding of the system at work – warts and all – and how it is possible to beat it, bypass it, cut across it and, with government support, reach a larger cross-section of the poor.

But why isn't the Government listening? Why isn't anyone in the Government saying, Come share these ideas with us? Tell us how we can help spread these tested ideas in the field? What kind and extent of support do we need to change the system from within so that it can respond to the new methods better? What rules need changing?

How come no one has asked these voluntary agencies how they accomplished what they did in spite of so many hurdles? What can these experts tell us from their books and reports that the voluntary agencies do not know already? They can only suggest cosmetic changes when it is fundamental reform that is necessary – not at the top, where it does not really matter, but at the *tehsil* and block and village levels, where nothing seems to change. Strong circulars are not going to ensure accountability. The threat of transfer is not going to stop teachers, doctors, thanedars, co-operative inspectors or *patwaris* from being less corrupt, or desisting from indulging in illegal and unlawful activities. They know no one bothers about them at the village level and they are safe. It is only the work of voluntary agencies that is a threat to them, and that is why they use every means to discredit it.

How can the Government help? In many ways. First, listen to what these voluntary agencies have to say on the very same problems that you have expressed your concern about in public. The experts will only tell you how it cannot be done; they will make simple issues look complicated and expensive – that is their job. In contrast, the simple, ordinary but highly professional people in voluntary agencies will tell you how the problems can be tackled without too much fuss.

Second, at the national level, form an independent, autonomous council of voluntary agencies to establish a code of conduct for these agencies that is acceptable to Central State Governments. This is because, as we all know, there are so many frauds that need to be exposed. This sector needs to be kept free of politicking. No one engaged in party politics in the last four years at least should be on this council, or it will be a non-starter. This needs to be done fast because now that many aspiring politicians have lost their election, they will become social workers and start volunteering agencies in the name of the poor. Just like the Press Council, the Bar Council and the Medical Council, voluntary agencies need such a body.

Third, as the late Prime Minister suggested, there is the need to institutionalise a forum through which state government officials and village-level voluntary agencies can meet regularly. This idea needs to be revived and fully supported. Even if it is a forum where we agree to disagree, it should exist so that voluntary agencies have a place where they can bring field problems to the notice of planners and policymakers, where the exchange of experiences and views can break barriers and remove suspicion and doubts about the work and functions of voluntary agencies. Now, voluntary agencies are being victimised on the hearsay evidence of fictitious reports, and there is no forum where they can explain their points of view. The rule today seems to be that they are guilty until they have proved their innocence.

Fourth, the Government must provide funds to voluntary agencies. Why should they have to go to foreign sources to implement ideas, new methods and approaches? Government money, which is public money, should be accessible to the citizens of this country, and allocation of funds to voluntary agencies with professional and managerial expertise should lead to a greater impact in the right places. At least, then, we would be able to set an example for others to see and follow. But, sad to say, there is resistance to this idea in some quarters within the Government.

This just shows how necessary it is for some fresh thinking in the Government and to weed out those who cannot accept that voluntary agencies can be progressive, professional and competent.

Fifth, make information accessible to the people. The government documents, reports, studies and surveys ostensibly meant for the enlightenment and development of the people and the rural poor are marked 'For Official Use Only', 'For Private Circulation Only', as if they should not be discussed or criticised. After all, if a document is public, there should be a system of feedback. Only then can any realism seep into development planning. Circulars on subsidies, government orders and new schemes take months to obtain and only after great difficulty, as if the Government is doing the voluntary agency that wants to read them a special favour. Surely all the secrecy is unnecessary and pointless?

I have said my bit, Prime Minister. Can we expect a response from you?

© *Reprinted courtesy of Mainstream*

Participation in Development

Bunker Roy

Originally published in *Seminar*, 309 Symposium,
The Faces of Reality, May 1985

THE TWO MOST WIDELY ABUSED WORDS that may mean so many different things to so many people are 'participation' and 'development'. What they mean so far as the rural areas are concerned has been discussed so often that, at the outset, I must strengthen my case with a quotation from George Orwell: 'We have now sunk to a depth at which re-statement of the obvious is the first duty of intelligent men.' It's time for a re-statement because so much has been said on the subject that it has lost all meaning and sense and has come to the stage of gross misinterpretation.

The person who looks on development as a game of numbers, and the only reality he faces is what he has read on paper: what does he know about participation? The urban-trained whizz-kid who thinks the world owes him something: what does he know about the problems of the rural poor never free from hunger, want or fear? Are these people really necessary in the world of development? Could we not do without their participation? Would the village/slum be a better place without their fancy ideas and cock-eyed theories and preconceived notions?

I am inclined to think so. 15 years ago when I started working in the villages of Rajasthan, I thought it was necessary to professionalise volunteerism, bringing more urban skills, managerial expertise and other inputs. Now I am not so sure. I have changed my definition of professionalism. I have found urban skills to be counter-productive if, more often than not, they are not linked to other qualities and values more important than service. Degrees I have found to be irrelevant: the more qualified, the more chances there are of the person doing greater harm than good. This is because he comes with high expectations, preconceived notions and an arrogance which is unhealthy.

Very few are prepared to go through an unlearning process, to start from scratch as human beings and look on those in the village with different eyes. They lack patience and have no way of coping with the slow pace in a village. They expect results in double quick time, expect gratitude, love and affection and expect to be considered one of 'them' – while never missing an opportunity to mention how much they have sacrificed to live and work in a village.

They do not have the ability to listen silently, act quietly and show respect for other people's views, whatever the source. They have lost the ability to improvise and work with their hands: they need machines, equipment and God knows what else to be effective. Ask them if they see a difference between literacy and education and they will not know what you are talking about. Actually, they have been taught to make simple things look complicated and inexpensive appliances to look costly, formidable and inaccessible.

There is no doubt that the biggest threat to development today is from the breed we call the Educated Man. He is in fact literate, but totally uneducated. He should be enlightened, open to new ideas, believe in the rule of law and want to help the poor raise their standard of living. In reality, the person who passes off as an educated man has a vested interest in keeping the poor poor. Who embezzles funds, writes fictitious reports, plays with figures, breaks the law at the village level and gets away with it? Only those who call themselves educated. Who grabs land and takes the poor to court and uses the power of the word for their own ends? Or draws subsidies on non-existent persons and makes others pay, breaks the law for their relatives but enforces it to preserve their status, but the educated? The doctor misuses medicines and starts private practice on government time and money; the teacher draws a salary but never comes to school; the policeman breaks the law he is supposed to enforce.

In the eyes of the world, they are all supposed to be educated. Why blame the poor, then, for keeping away from Government, for not taking loans from banks, for not filling in subsidy forms, for not wanting to send their children to school and for not going to government dispensaries? Under the circumstances, the poor are being more sensible and practical and definitely showing more wisdom than we ever credit them with. They see the corruption, feel it every day and keep quiet because no one is prepared to listen to illiterate people: they have no standing in society. They want to read and write but would not want to be educated if this is what education meant.

When we talk of participation, we propose a condition or environment of equality of choices, of opportunities, a situation in which there is mutual respect for one another. Instead, we find one side looking down on the other in sheer contempt. The village-level government functionary, the rich farmer and exploiter are not willing to be considered as equals to ordinary village people, not prepared to share knowledge and skills and experiences as human beings, are not open to considering the resources in a village for development purposes. In the village, what we call charity and patronage equals development. Where is the question of participation?

Government has its own views on participation and development. Voluntary agencies in many parts of the country practise it. But there are voluntary agencies and voluntary agencies. Where participation has been institutionalised it is artificial, but where it has been allowed to grow slowly, gently, naturally and with a great deal of spirit and solidarity, people have been known to call it uncharitable names. Participation in development hinges on trust and on decentralising responsibilities, administrative and financial. It presumes the growing importance we must give to the political process of changing attitudes and opinions and giving people the tools to become effective pressure groups.

The role of voluntary agencies in this case is to provide institutional support, the staying power to sustain people through difficult times and rally around them when the going is rough and where there is general misunderstanding of the aim and purpose of small groups fighting non-violently because what they are fighting about is generally considered unimportant. It is all very well to talk of participation, but we must have a little knowledge and even more practical experience to be able to notice participation when we are in the middle of it. We have not yet developed the tools to identify the process of participation in development, and that is why this whole issue is so sensitive. We have not been able to compartmentalise the process and put it in a convenient slot: experts, planners and bureaucrats have been trying for years but evidently without much success. One way in which they have been dubiously successful is the creation of a post for it in the UN: they call the incumbent a 'community participation officer.' To the UN, that is a major step forward.

Leave it to the urban experts and this is what happens. At the village level, where it counts, the problem of participation remains. The involvement of the community in decision-making and in being a party to its own development has become increasingly important because of the growing indifference of bureaucracy at the lower level in responding to the felt needs of the community. Someone has to test the system from below, some pressure groups have to be created or developed or encouraged to make the system move and some individuals have to be identified who could prod, provoke, activate and possibly initiate the existing structures to change from the grassroots.

This obviously takes time. The pace cannot be forced. It would be absurd to fix targets and conduct ludicrous time plan exercises. The change that we hope to see will be intangible. But if we notice a community or a group growing, always asking questions, not being intimidated by the presence of officials and politicians and with its members speaking their minds and not prepared to be suppressed or subjected to humiliation of any kind regardless of the caste or class they come from, that will indeed be the first sign of participation.

Under the circumstances, the bureaucrat's role is to preserve law and order. But you will notice he goes much further than his brief. If he is mediocre – 90% turn out to be ordinary – he will opt for order even though the law may be on the side of the Scheduled Caste or the small farmer or the rural artisan. The bureaucrat has scant respect for this whole idea of participation. It undermines his position, threatens his social status and, what's worse, it means losing control over the funds that he can distribute at will without asking questions or even answering them. Since there is no effective system of accountability at the village level, since he has made himself inaccessible to his superiors and inferiors by being his own master and interpreting laws and schemes to his own convenience, he would be the last to allow himself to be questioned by people he has always considered to be lower than human beings.

When we expect the Government to start initiating a process of participation in development, then the trouble starts. Urban-trained whizz-kid economists seem to forget that there are deliberate built-in obstacles in the bureaucracy that make participation in development a mockery and virtually impossible from within. The development of human resources essential for the sort of participation which we would like to encourage has low priority, and the lower one goes in the delivery system the more of a non-issue it becomes.

Seen from the village level, it is difficult for a variety of reasons.

1. In practice government policy seems to be to make rural communities more dependent on, rather than independent of, the system. Until no-objection certificates are obtained from often corrupt officials, a poor man is considered guilty and likely to 'run off with the money'. In actual fact, it is the corrupt official who issues the certificate and who indulges in such practices in the name of the poor.

2. Any mention of social justice or equality in thought and practice is interpreted as impertinence and indiscipline, as not knowing your place, and strong steps are taken by the village-level government functionary to suppress/squash it.

3. Policy is less important than personality. The bureaucrat looks for servility, total obedience and no opposition to what he considers right: he is neither civil nor does he think he is a servant. Anyone who talks of participation he considers an enemy and a threat. Whatever the policy might be, he goes entirely by personal impressions and interprets the policy accordingly. He is not impartial, objective or non-aligned.

4. The government functionary has not been trained for development work. He is basically a maintenance man/woman supposed to keep the system working. He is not expected to be creative, imaginative and responsive to the felt needs of the poor. He believes more in order than in law.

5. Government is convinced that order, discipline and rules can be enforced only if a distance is maintained and barriers are given respect. The two barriers that keep mediocre civil servants at some distance from the people are qualifications and hierarchies. These barriers give them importance, make them look invincible and allow them a social status of sorts which they crave. Any move to devalue the importance or undermine the necessity of these barriers so that distance is reduced and participation is possible is strongly resented, and no explanation is acceptable. The village-level functionary will fight tooth and nail to see that distance is preserved and barriers are not broken down.

If the only significant way of getting the rural communities and the ultimate beneficiaries to participate is a greater awareness of the need to develop human resources, how we go about it is the crucial question. Government, with its class bias, its fetish for standardisation, its arrogant stand of being the know-all and its paternalistic and impersonal way of going about reaching the poor, is hardly the answer. Alternatives have to be tried and tested and allowed to grow in this democratic society of ours, and it is here that the role of voluntary agencies needs to be emphasised. The role is not of middleman but of midwife.

Government has a lot to learn from voluntary agencies. The hundreds that are working in the rural areas all over the country have shown what results can be produced even under pressure from vested interests, from indifferent village-level government functionaries and from unscrupulous politicians. They have shown how new ideas can be tried out with varying degrees of success in spite of such pressures and how the implementation stage can be kept inexpensive, simple and at the same time yield results. The key to success is investment in the human being.

To voluntary agencies, the development of people is more important than the development of infrastructures like roads and buildings. Development is the process of changing non-citizens, non-people, completely impoverished, down and out zombies, into human beings who can think and act independently, who are aware of their rights and know where to go when those rights are violated. But they cannot reach this stage on their own. They need to be assisted, they need to be provoked, they need to be supported: the process has to be participatory from the very beginning.

What makes it different from the government approach to development?

1. The development of people cannot be time-bound or target-oriented and squeezed into one financial year. It is ongoing and there are suitable indicators, but mediocre government servants would shudder to accept them.

2. The use of village resources, skills, knowledge and experience for development ensures the maximum participation. Why get it from outside when it is right there in the village? Substituting village people in place of imports is the answer. The doctor,

engineer, lawyer, banker, ANM, are basically alien and important resources not really interested in participation. In any case, they represent overkill. They are not really needed in the strengths in which they have been deployed.

3. The mobilisation of financial resources from within the community is one way of promoting dignity, self respect and self reliance in due course. The tendency in Government is to dispense charity in the name of development – give everything free, or subsidise it.

4. In order to make urban tools, skills and appliances accessible, in order to give the human touch, one major role of voluntary agencies is to demystify processes, appliances, technologies and skills. Make them simple, make them replicable, make them inexpensive so that the rural poor are not overawed, not intimidated and do not consider them as yet other tools for exploitation.

5. Change only comes from conflict of ideas, of attitudes and approaches in interpretation. Such conflicts at the village level are not only good but desirable, and as and when they occur, voluntary agencies use them for human development purposes – to instil confidence, to show that institutional support is forthcoming when needed at critical times, to make it all a learning experience and set an example for others to emulate.

In the ultimate analysis, we have to ask ourselves whether we do in fact want communities to participate in their own development. If it means having to contend with so many critical issues, if it means changing lifestyles, do we want to upset the cosy arrangements of the status quo as they are?

Participation in development is hardly as easy as it sounds. The tragedy comes when participation of the sort that we look for and need to encourage is taking place but we cannot recognise it.

© *Seminar Publications*

Let Voluntary Agencies Plan Their Own Schemes

Bunker Roy

Originally published in *Kurukshetra*, October 1985

The author, who is a dedicated social worker and the Director of the well-known Social Work and Research Centre at Tilonia, in Rajasthan, feels that the voluntary agencies are closer to the rural people than the government functionaries and are, thus, in a better position to bring about community participation in schemes of rural development. The participation of voluntary agencies in rural development has been far from satisfactory. There are many factors responsible for it. One of the most important is that although the voluntary agencies have expertise and skills to plan and implement development schemes, they do not have the independence and authority to do so. 'We are given watertight handouts and offered a take it or leave it option,' the author laments.

THE BIGGEST OBSTACLE to understanding and accepting the role of volunteerism in development is the urban-trained literate (as opposed to educated) person. He still equates voluntarism only with charity, welfare and rehabilitation, which in their own way are as important as they are necessary, but he refuses to concede that the changing times could define yet another role for voluntary agencies in development. For years, voluntary agencies have been known to be involved only in welfare work in the non-controversial areas of health, education and relief, and traditional voluntary agencies have set an example (good or bad remains to be seen) following the dictates of Government. This attitude, this inclination to do good, this feeling of wanting to help the helpless and reach the unreached, this desire to give without strings attached may have been the right 'tool' for welfare work, but it is disastrous for development work of the kind we think is necessary and long overdue. Why?

> We, in India, need social service on a very large scale and in the wide sense of the term. There is no lack of problems, no lack of work, and what is really needed is a body of social workers who will devote themselves in a spirit of service.
>
> – Dr. Rajendra Prasad

Development at the expense of social justice is not development: the role of voluntary agencies is to see that the delivery of social justice is considered as important and crucial an input as seeds or fertilisers and pumps. Right now, the question of rights, the enforcement of the law and the protection of Scheduled Castes, Scheduled Tribes and minorities are non-issues, insignificant and secondary to the issues of increasing food production, getting combine harvesters, extending power to the villages and pampering the rural rich. The tools for welfare work will hardly stop a rich farmer from grabbing the poor man's land or paying less than the minimal wage. They will not stop a rural industrialist who owns power looms from exploiting displaced handloom weavers, or an upper caste community from practising untouchability in temples, wells and public places. A welfare approach will not stop the almost total exploitation of rural women in the house, in the fields and in society. So distorted have been the views of planners, experts, bureaucrats and the *kulak* lobby of what we mean by development that consistently the first casualty has always been the rural poor. It has not helped that this distorted view is also the Western view of development based on Western experience in the First and Second Worlds. The rural poor in India are the guinea pigs on whom various experiments and models can be tried. The fact that they themselves may have some ideas to offer, they themselves may have some models to try on themselves is not a point worth considering. After all, they are illiterate, they are impoverished, they are without house and home and vulnerable – what ideas can they have?

The tragedy is that they have much to teach us, and one of the crucial roles of voluntary agencies in development is to show HOW and WHAT Government can learn from them. This applies to everyone, all along the line from the top to the bottom. They practise self-reliance – because they have no choice – and see what a good job they do of it! But we urban-trained literate people cannot see beyond our noses. An integrated approach to development is something new to our urban-trained expert; he would, of course, be horrified to learn the low-cost/no-cost way the rural poor have managed to integrate lifestyles, skills, knowledge, experience and services modestly, quietly and with a great deal of dignity and understanding. A shopkeeper is a doctor, extension worker, keeper of contraceptives, seeds for social forestry and basic provisions, writer of applications and odd-job man. Where integration is necessary, the Government is compartmentalising. Where a man with common sense and an open mind is required, the Government sends a specialist with degrees and qualifications who is totally unnecessary and often harmful, because he is ignorant of local conditions and requirements. The role of voluntary agencies is to show by practice how the rural poor, with a bit of training and support, can well look after themselves and decide for themselves what they need for their own development. This fact cannot be comprehended by our urban-trained expert. In these matters, he is uneducated.

The need to professionalise volunteerism has been felt in the development of rural areas. The immediate reaction among the traditional agencies is that this is tantamount to commercialising volunteerism and bringing in an alien element. The traditional agencies would rather depend heavily on dedication and sacrifice than competence and consistency. The urban world is coming to the doorstep of the villages with all sorts of strange and ugly appliances designed to destroy the livelihood and lifestyle of rural India in the name of progress and development. If those traditional voluntary agencies had their way, they would prefer to let the rural poor see themselves be destroyed silently, nonviolently and totally, rather than do anything about it. It is time to understand the evils of science and technology left in the hands of unscrupulous and unthinking people who believe their indiscriminate application in the villages of India would change the face of this country. Indeed it would – for the worse. The role of volunteering agencies in development is to demystify science and technology – make it understandable, accessible and easy to accept. The only way this can be done is to professionalise.

By 'professionalism', I do not refer to the end products that come out of urban-based training institutions which have hijacked the word 'rural' for their own ends, but to a product that the urban and educated person would find hard to accept as a colleague. He/she is a product of the immediate area, the culture and the community. The person is competent and confident in providing a service that he has learnt by trial and error, by word-of-mouth, by sheer experience and by what his elders may have taught him – learning by doing in his habitat. He not only believes in what he is doing, but in turn the community has faith in his powers. The community uses his 'professional' services and skills and also looks after his creature comforts and supports him. He may be illiterate, but he is as educated as they come. He commands respect in rural society. He can influence opinion – as and when he wants to. He is the source of information and has enough managerial and administrative expertise to hoodwink the Government – as and when he wants to. In this loosely classified category of professionals fall many people we call quacks, frauds and exploiters – water diviners, traditional midwives, priests (as teachers), puppeteers (as communicators), *hakims, vaids*, bonesetters, guinea worm extractors, hand pump *mistris*, smokeless *chula* trainers, rural artisans. (The actual frauds and exploiters in the villages are the degree holders who flaunt their qualifications and call themselves doctors, teachers, engineers and social workers.) These human resources are grossly under-utilised in the villages, and the role of voluntary agencies in development is to see that they are given respectability and credibility, and treated as professionals. Going by the current way of thinking, this is too much to ask.

The other words for this process are 'community' and 'participation'. Voluntary agencies are known to be closer to the target group than they are to government functionaries. If this is true and universally accepted, then Government must also accept, however reluctantly, that we have tested these human and financial resources that are available for developmental purposes under pressure, and found them to have stood up to the tests.

Then why the hesitation? Why the resistance? Why the involvement of voluntary agencies only with strings attached?

If there is a role for voluntary agencies in the development process, then it is time the Government started accepting a few realities:

(i) the voluntary agencies in development can plan for themselves. We have the expertise, the knowledge and the skills to plan and implement schemes

(ii) there is no need for Government to take for granted that the voluntary agencies need to be spoon-fed. The voluntary agencies have not been given the independence, the autonomy or the authority to plan schemes for themselves. Instead, we are given a watertight handout and offered a take it or leave it option

(iii) Government must make a clear distinction between non-government organisations (NGOs) and voluntary agencies. NGOs are trade unions, co-operatives, political parties, *Khadi* boards – structured, organised, politicised – but outside the government sector. These are not voluntary agencies

(iv) there is more than one approach to developing rural areas. The Government has one, voluntary agencies have more. Such approaches/models/methods can coexist, can supplement each other so that in the final analysis the rural poor are the ultimate beneficiaries

(v) it is only as partners that voluntary agencies will co-operate with Government. We refuse to be identified as contractors and touts, but we are prepared to be intermediaries and catalytic agents. The question is of co-operation. We should not and will not enter into any agreement as if a government is doing us a favour. Equality, interexchange of ideas and experiences, sharing of resources and a degree of openness is what voluntary agencies look for.

Where it has been possible to get the Government to meet us halfway, encouraging moves have already taken place on both sides. Clarity on paper is all very well but its interpretation and practice at the village level, at the cutting edge level, is what matters. The education of bureaucracy at this level on the role of voluntary agencies in development is long overdue, and that will only come from conflict in attitudes and ideas. Regrettably, we have seen that when such situations have arisen, Government has allowed vested interests to take one-sided decisions on its behalf. Perhaps if the senior bureaucrats of State started showing a bit of courage and defended these agencies, at least on paper, it would help. Now, is that asking for too much?

© *Yojana/Kurukshetra, Publications Division, Ministry of I&B, Government of India.*

Raw Deal for Rural Poor

Bunker Roy

Originally published in *Mainstream*, 15 February 1986

IT IS TIME SOMEONE SPOKE OUT against the lopsided and distorted way we are going about tackling the problems of developing the rural areas. There must be some method in this madness that I cannot see. Here we have the third largest supply of human and technical resources in the world but by the looks of it we are still far away from providing for basic, minimum needs – safe drinking water is still not available in nearly 200,000 villages; there are still thousands of primary schools in this country without basic amenities like roofs, blackboards, furniture and good (not necessarily trained) teachers; at the last count nearly 20 million families did not have roofs over their heads; primary health centres are lying deserted or understaffed because doctors consider it a punishment to be posted to them; co-operative societies are in the red by the thousands in villages and basic provisions are available only through the *banias*. Because of petty corruption and collusion, we are not in a position to guarantee 100 days of employment to the poorest of the poor in spite of the colossal delivery system at our disposal. And no one is raising a voice against questionable practices or taking action when they are reported because we do not want to demoralise the bureaucracy. The Government seems impotent to respond to absolutely simple requests: stop trees from being cut, stop victimising tribals for living off twigs, give genuine *pattas* to the small and marginal farmers who are tilling the land, provide protection to Scheduled Castes against the terrible practice of untouchability. But there is no change in the attitude of the village-level government functionary, no fear of severe action for non-performance and no urgency in district or state officials to make the Government work a little faster.

These are the problems that need to be tackled immediately, and we have it in us to change this dismal state of affairs dramatically and in a fundamental way. But who is listening? Who thinks such insignificant matters are important? The answer is that we are sanctioning more money this year than last and we have recruited more staff – as if doing this is solving the problem. High-powered economists in the corridors of power dole out recipes which make it sound as if they are desperate to urbanise rural areas. Peel off the jargon in which they pontificate and it sounds as if though improving the industrial base, removing controls and flooding rural markets with inexpensive, good quality consumer products will solve the unemployment problems in the rural areas, prevent migration and the slow but deliberate destruction of rural skills. The magic words seem to be 'management' and 'professionalism' – as though these do not already exist in the rural areas and someone from the urban areas is needed to tell us about them. It just shows how ignorant we are of the tremendous resources already present in the rural areas.

I cannot forget I was like them once: born and brought up in almost the same environment, cloistered and protected and exposed to a world light years away from poverty, hunger, exploitation and injustice. We were told about our rights but never about duties. We looked at the brighter side of life but with one eye closed to the misery around us. That was someone else's problem. Ours was to lead, to think big, to take on the nation and the world, and never look back – certainly not to the village, which in any case was as alien to us in school and college as to any foreigner in the First and Second worlds.

Now, almost two decades later, looking at the rural development policies designed and planned by the very people who were once colleagues of mine in school and college, I cannot help but be disturbed, ask basic questions and question their competence to decide the fate of millions of families living below the poverty line. For the first time in the history of independent India, the people have given a mandate to a government to use its awesome power to reform the administrative system from below, bring about a fundamental change in attitudes, provide a more competent service, make the unholy trinity (the revenue, judiciary and police) by force or fear more responsive to the needs and expectations of the poor at the village level. But we see, instead, a year of inaction in these vital areas; we see and feel neglect.

I am not against acquiring the best technology, attracting the best brains and taking on the world on equal terms. I am all for a policy that shows that India, as a nation, should not be taken lightly or taken for granted. This language the West understands and is applauding. But let us hasten slowly. Let us not lose our balance and lose sight of our pressing priorities at home. Let us set our house in order first. But when it comes to providing money for meeting basic needs – and more money than ever before will be needed if we are to complete the task before the 21st-century – we are told there is none. It has all gone into power, irrigation, railways, defence and other such sectors.

In the interests of national self-reliance, for the good of the country as a whole and for industry to prosper, village self-reliance must suffer (there is absolutely no justification for this absurd policy). Reading between the lines, it appears there will be more government interference and official influence in the lives of the rural poor, and the policy is to make communities more dependent on Government because the feeling is that *we*, the educated, scientific and intellectual community in India, know best what is good for the rural areas. Well, the rural areas need disoriented and indifferent and badly trained doctors, teachers, engineers and economists like we need a hole in the head. Keep them in the cities to which most of the rural population is migrating anyway. There is no doubt that the biggest and most serious threat to the development of the rural poor is the so-called Educated Man. Keep him away if you want human development to take place, if you want community participation, if you want rural skills to be upgraded and to grow and mature and be used for the communities' own development. The point is: is anyone listening or even prepared to listen to some sound advice? A position of power makes you arrogant, and arrogance arising from ignorance is the worst form of tyranny.

The tragedy is that we have the power to take strong decisions and change the face of rural India. But this government has more time for long-term fiscal policies for industry, and lessening controls, and providing concessions, than it has for 80% of India's population, out of which more than 300 million live in dismal impoverished conditions. For them, we have cosmetic Band-Aid solutions. It seems no one in the Government has any idea of where and at what level the problems need to be tackled. Surely anyone with any rural experience should be able to tell you that the first point of attack should be the block and village-based institutions? The functionaries of these block and village-based delivery systems personified in the teacher, the co-operative inspector, the *gram sevak*, the *patwari* and the *thanedar* need to be shaken up. Someone has to put the fear of God into them. Presently, they are almost above the law and not accountable to anyone because they enjoy political protection.

It is all a question of perceptions, and they are naturally influenced and conditioned by their environment and experience. If you are surrounded all your life with gadgets, machines and impersonal systems, and your friends and acquaintances have lived half their lives in the First and Second worlds, naturally the Western model of development and the way the West thinks that rural poverty should be tackled will have some influence. There can never be a technical and management solution to what is basically a social problem involving people of different castes and class. We must evolve our own unique solution which, I can tell you, defies Western models, but no one seems to be able to tell the Prime Minister how wrong he is to listen to such poor advice. He should lean on people he may not understand, but trust. He may not be a believer but he must have faith. He must have someone objective around him who thinks of the rural poor first and his party interests later.

If funds are an immediate problem, then take steps to stop the leakages that are running into *crores* of rupees. A surgical knife through the Electricity Boards, the PWD, the Irrigation and Cooperative Departments at the block and district level is necessary. But in the year that has passed, leakages continue, and the Government is silent on the issue. The Comptroller and Auditor General's (CAG) report of 1983-84 lists in detail the financial irregularities in almost every development department, but such a listing has become a regular feature that no bureaucracy has taken seriously, and no action is ever taken against senior officials. But true to Parkinson's Law, if irregularities run into thousands this is discussed in the Cabinet and the CBI is asked to enquire into it. Witness the infamous Kudal Commission, which is costing the Government more to maintain than it is managing to expose, in spite of its using unfair and unjust means. While voluntary agencies are being harassed for mere thousands of rupees or perhaps *lakhs* over decades of hard work and sacrifice, *crores* are allowed to be embezzled every year by district, block and village-level officials.

My one-time acquaintance who has now become the Prime Minister of India will always receive my support, but at the same time, he must know that I consider his track record for the first year in tackling the problems of the rural poor dismal and disturbing. His urban bias is showing. A couple of village visits to rural areas will not do. It is insufficient, inadequate and incomplete. He must tackle the real problems that I mentioned earlier, now. Listen, for once, to someone who knows this area far better and in greater depth than do many of your party members who have axes to grind. Many of them would not like such drastic steps to be taken, but it is the only way out if we want the basic needs of the rural poor to be met by the turn of the century. That, indeed, would be a phenomenal achievement.

© *Reprinted courtesy of Mainstream*

Action is Called Right Now to Avoid a Rude Shock!

Bunker Roy

Originally published in *Yojana*, 15 August 1986

With this poor perception of rural realities; this tragic pattern of land ownership; this fondness for borrowed models and this so-called strategy of raising families above the poverty line, we are, says the author, heading towards a rude shock. And, he adds, if we do not act right now and 'hasten' to reverse the process, our rural scene in 2001 will see a sea change, yes, for the worse.

IF PRESENT TRENDS CONTINUE the rural scene will change beyond recognition—for the worse. The urbanisation of rural areas, which seems to be the answer given by all the urban based experts to all the human problems in the rural areas, is going to have disastrous results by the turn of the century. If we keep looking at it – as we do – as basically an economic problem, keep giving importance to viability and balancing of the books, keep designing schemes to raise families temporarily above the poverty line and then expect them to stand on their own feet, we are in for a rude shock. We have not yet developed confidence enough to come up with Indian models that are typically and uniquely ours: we have become slaves to what the West says, as was bound to happen since we have voluntarily surrendered ourselves to years of subtle brainwashing.

It takes a long time for damage to be felt because this country is so large, but I imagine that by 2001 we will have realised our mistake. But that will be too late.

Mahatma Gandhi and all the sensible things he said about the development of rural areas will have long been forgotten. Already what he said about village self-reliance, about rural communities depending on each other, of production by the masses instead of mass production is falling on deaf ears as if he were outdated. In 1967, when I started working in the villages, I used to think he was a bit of a crank, and without knowing it I looked down on what looked like alien ideas. Now, in 1986, I cannot help but wonder at the vision of the man. He will remain relevant in 2001 – but only to those who know what rural India is like, what lives the people lead, what problems they face and where the solutions lie. But the number who feel Gandhi to be relevant in 2001 will be very few. Unless people, experts, policy planners and others who think they know how to develop rural areas actually start living with the people and seeing for themselves, solutions will be hard to find. In 1986, you find very few such people living and working with the rural community. In 2001, they will be extinct. Because distance planning is already a fashion. Playing with machines and designing schemes for the rural poor in an antiseptic atmosphere is reality. The smell of mud, dung, 'of goodly rain on dry ground', of dust and the homely dirt of teashops; the environment of pain, insecurity and exploitation; the conflict of ideas, approaches and methods; the exchange of experiences, lifestyles and ways of thinking and acting; the tension that precedes change and results in a feeling of liberation is all a part of a process which cannot, indeed must not, be short-circuited. With the coming of the impersonal expert who does not believe in this process of learning and unlearning, does not believe in not forcing a pace that the rural areas are not used to; who shows an arrogance and confidence that comes from acquiring a degree in rural development at a foreign university and feels he has 'arrived'; this breed, we are going to see more of as we get closer to 2001. And it is going to be the death of us.

This TV Onslaught!

One indication is the growth of television, the impersonal medium that allows no feedback, no exchange of ideas and no questioning of the information being disseminated. By 2001, more than 400 million people in the rural areas will be forced to look at programmes that have no relevance to their daily lives. They will be forced to urbanise – or perish. It is the middle class that will control this medium and who are already planning for the rural poor. By 2001, I suspect they would want the rural identity to completely disappear. Programmes costing between Rs.30,000 per hour to Rs.15 *lakhs* per hour are being designed for audiences whose total earnings do not exceed Rs.3,500 per year. One hour of entertainment costs the equivalent of three hand pumps providing safe drinking water or the cost of running ninety primary schools for one year. What they call programmes for education, family welfare, rural development and women's welfare supposedly designed for rural audiences are so useless that they only serve to give employment to someone's relative, foreign-returned with a degree on rural communities.

I see a trying time for the rural poor. Already forces heavily against them are developing themselves. Government is supposed to help them with schemes, subsidies and programmes but, on the other hand, the poor have been made so dependent on the system that I very much doubt if the intention ever was to allow them to stand on their own feet. By 2001, the dependency will be total – and on a mere handful of people. The 3% of the rural rich who own 30% of the total cultivable land will see that technology becomes a tool for exploitation. Already there are indications of the law and order system in the village being used in favour of the rich, and although land-grabbing cases are on the increase, they are not being registered by the police. If 35 million households or about 45% of the total number of rural households own no land at all, or less than 0.4 ha, by 2001 the future will look bleak indeed. Two thirds of the agricultural labour households in this country are already in debt and things are not likely to get better, by the looks of it. I am quoting government figures so the situation must be much more alarming than it has been made out to be.

Poor Delivery System!

Delivery systems today are nowhere oriented towards making the rural areas better places to live in. The educational system has ensured that four-fifths of the doctors coming out of universities live in urban areas where only one fifth of the population lives, while in the rural areas five million die every year of exposure, poor nutrition, non-immunisation and lack of proper medical attention. The educational system has made sure that the literate, the more literate and the even more literate (receivers of what we mistakenly call higher education) never come back to the village. Looking the other way – Jaipur, Delhi, New York – is supposed to be looking ahead. Coming back to the village after receiving a degree (NOT an education) without getting a government job is doing something wrong. Wanting to help communities develop themselves without your taking a secure salary means you have not received a good education. The new Education Policy (1986) has suggested a way out, through de-linking jobs from degrees, but again people are interpreting this in a narrow, conventional and limited sense and equating it with employment.

Since most people have never lived and worked in a rural area, I do not suppose educational planners realise the significance of implementing such a policy. If it is implemented as it should be, by 2001 it will have far-reaching repercussions in the rural areas. It will allow village resources, village skills and village knowledge to be used for the first time to render services for development purposes. This will enable village para-professionals such as *dais*, village-level health workers, *hakims, vaids*, water diviners, bone-setters and hand pump *mistries* to provide services without having to get paper degrees certifying that they are qualified to provide such services.

As I have said before, the biggest threat to development is the Educated Man who flaunts his degree and thinks he is indispensable in the development of rural areas. But it is the doctor, the engineer and the teacher who uses his degree to exploit the community, misuses his qualification for corrupt practices and abuses his knowledge for his own advancement at the expense of the community. If and when services (jobs) are delinked from degrees, his hold on the community will be minimised, the place in rural society that he has found for himself will be devalued, and genuine community involvement where people can depend on each other can take place. The resources and skills of the community so far have no place in government planning and implementation. The community is only supposed to act as recipient, its people takers and not givers; and such one-sided systems will eventually make beggars of them all.

And the Crucial Issue!

The issue is where the limit to government interference and involvement should be. There must be a limit beyond which it is uneconomical for Government to transfer people or provide a service. Already, according to the late Raj Krishna, every rupee of input was costing the Government Rs.5. Provision of government services is not only becoming prohibitively expensive but proving to be inefficient, and from a management point of view that makes it totally unacceptable. But the argument being put forward is that the rural community is a bunch of crooks, so in order to ensure better accountability of public money, recruitment of government personnel is a must. So instead of the community making money, it becomes the government functionary who makes money in the name of better accountability. The hard decision will have to be taken that beyond a certain point, the responsibilities of planning and implementation, of collecting resources and providing a service, must rest solely on the community, with Government playing a supplementary role – like providing training, equipment, hardware and so on. As things stand, government machinery has become a monster out of control.

This is one of the reasons why the role of voluntary agencies has become so important, and I am certain that by 2001 these agencies will be a force to be reckoned with in the rural areas. When seen collectively, the social action groups in villages today all over the country are no longer a drop in the ocean. Because it is Government's job to see that public money is used more effectively, because we notice the importance of Government in controlling and enforcing discipline on the system from below and preventing leakages, because we see that government interference and involvement has led to poor involvement of communities in the planning and implementation of their own programmes, because we see little or no accountability within the system either to the community or to the Government, the role of voluntary agencies has assumed tremendous importance. Government has started to see the wisdom of channelling funds to voluntary agencies for antipoverty and minimum needs programmes. But voluntary agencies have been suspicious of government motives for such a long time – and with good reason – that it will take time for some of us to unbend. But there is no doubt that the atmosphere is right for sitting across the table and negotiating an understanding on our terms, on the basis of which we shall take government funds.

If there is any hope of introducing progressive ideas in the development of rural areas by 2001, it will depend on the extent to which the social action groups will want to be involved. Forums for removing deep-rooted misunderstandings will have to be created and procedures to make funds more accessible to smaller groups will have to be simplified. Institutional support when smaller groups clash against vested interests while introducing progressive ideas will have to be forthcoming without reservations, so that the rural poor have a say in their own development. 2001 will see the tangible results of such processes taking place now.

© *Yojana/Kurukshetra, Publications Division, Ministry of I&B, Government of India.*

The Rural Self-Employed

Bunker Roy

Originally published in *Kurukshetra*, October 1987

The author seems to be very much disappointed and disillusioned with the results of the various programmes of development for the rural poor and the way they are being implemented. He feels, 'We have lost the ability to reach people in our own way, reach them with our own knowledge, resources and skills, and instead have succumbed to alien models from outside the country which has done more harm than good.' And asserts, 'In the name of the rural poor and the self-employed, we are planning more for the Government and less for the people. After three decades of effort, the self-employed in the rural areas are still denied basic needs.'

WHAT THE WESTERN-TRAINED EXPERTS IN INDIA call the unorganised, informal, marginal, unregulated, peripheral and residual are actually the self-employed workers in rural India.

But far from being marginal, peripheral and residual, they are an integral part of the rural community, and unless policy planners go through an unlearning process they are doing this 'invisible' sector a grave injustice. This workforce of over 300 million offers a living profile of how all development efforts have failed to reach these poorest of the poor. We have lost the ability to reach people in our own way, reach them with our own knowledge, resources and skills, and instead have succumbed to alien models from outside the country. This has done more harm than good.

What have we done for the 300 million? We have allowed systems which are ostensibly designed to serve and assist the rural poor to grow monstrous. We have delivery systems in health, education, law and order, agriculture, rural development and social welfare that are so colossal and so astronomically expensive that it costs the Government almost Rs.10 to deliver a service with Re.1. In the name of the rural poor and the self-employed, we are planning more for the Government and less for the people. After three decades of effort, the self-employed in the rural areas are still denied basic needs.

On average, women have to spend three to four hours fetching drinking water from sources getting deeper and further away; they have to spend half a day collecting firewood for their *chulas*; they still have no option but to use primitive tools for agricultural purposes. And the removal of drudgery from these strenuous operations is still a distant dream. Where innovation is the need of the hour, we have been found wanting, which is one reason why we still spend a huge sum for primary schools on only 30% of the school-going children India: the other 70% cannot afford to go to school in the mornings because they're involved – and rightly so – in the economic activities of their parents, all self-employed. Our experts have shot down the idea of starting schools in the evening because they are not convenient for the teacher.

The self-employed, the poor, the impoverished and the vulnerable believe in education in a very broad sense and also practise it every hour of the day: the experts believe in literacy but like to call it education.

The self-employed believe in the integration of many functions and services in a few people: the Government believes in compartmentalisation in the name of management and professionalism.

The rural poor believe in people and human beings: the Government in systems, the more impersonal the better.

The poor believe in using their own skills, and demystifying processes, methods and approaches thus making them less expensive: Government calls this quackery and is convinced that development needs experts with paper qualifications.

Why are we making simple solutions complicated? If the rural poor are to be involved in their own development and be a part of the decision-making process (as they say is the objective in the first place) then why is it not possible to form groups of beneficiaries of 20 women to work on a given plot of land during famine relief operations, and at the end of 15 days an engineer comes and measures the work done and then makes payment accordingly? Why do we need a mate system at all? Such a system is undesirable because the mate can fiddle with the attendance register, add the names of fictitious people and institutionalise dishonesty with the support and contrivance of the petty officials. Under an NREP, wheat can be siphoned off at source so that the self-employed do not get their rightful share. If we can only ensure the payment of minimum wages to the self-employed workers, make that the one and only point out of all the 20 points, to be adopted as a strategy for tackling the problems with unemployment poverty, and redeploy the entire machinery of the Government to see that it is done. The problems of the report will have been solved. But what do we see today? People (and the figure runs into millions) work for eight hours a day but they do not get paid for months: they live on credit and get indebted to the local *bania* who in any case looks after wheat distribution for the Government. There seems to be no break in this vicious circle.

The self-employed have their own skills in road building, in building their own houses to last with local materials, and repairing and maintaining their own water supply (hand pumps), diesel and electric pump sets. But we are just not giving them a chance.

Village women can grow their own nurseries and plant trees in their own plots and construct smokeless *chulas* in their own homes without excessive government supervision and control. Rural youth can be paid part time to to run evening schools in their own villages: they would do a far better job than government teachers. Carpenters can make appliances for the handicapped and blacksmiths can produce basic simple agricultural implements. What is getting in the way?

Lack of trust and faith in the community to be able to accomplish the task. We do not trust traditional midwives even when there is ample evidence of their skills: most of the Honourable Members of Parliament over 40 and coming from the rural areas were delivered by *dais* and not by ANMs! Why are they still looked upon with suspicion and mistrust and not given the dignity and self-respect they deserve? Is it because they do not conform, they do not fit in, they do not follow rules? If the community has more faith in and shows more respect to water diviners than to the geologist or geophysicist, it is a reflection on the credibility of the latter. To the rural community, these people – community assets in human terms – are not peripheral or residual, but extremely important and respected members of the village community.

Perhaps this version of self-employment is too advanced a concept for the urban-trained expert who in any case believes in wearing blinkers for his own protection. But definitions and concepts can only change if pressure is applied from below. There is ample evidence to support a move to re-define self-employment and what it means in the non-institutional sector of rural India. In fact every group, whether it be rural women, Scheduled Castes or Scheduled Tribes, rural artisans, marginal farmers or agricultural labourers, has a product or a skill or a service to sell. But again, two standards are applied. The doctor should be paid but the *hakim* or *vaid* or homeopath should do *shramdan*. An ANM should be allowed to ask a professional fee but not a *dai*. A teacher is allowed to receive a salary from the Government without accountability. But ask a priest to run a class in the evening and the Government must check, 'supervise and monitor', his progress. They all perform a vital service and they are workers for and with the community. But the self-employed are guilty until they prove their innocence.

Consider the case of the hand pump *mistri* (HPM). The repair and maintenance of hand pumps is supposed to be a very technical and sophisticated business. State Governments maintain huge departments with engineers, trucks, jeeps and equipment deployed for the maintenance of hand pumps running into crores. There is a way of demystifying the technology of repairing and maintaining hand pumps through the HPMs. The HPM is trained for three months under TRYSEM. He is trained more in practice than in theory and is made to dismantle and put together out of order hand pumps already installed in villages.

The HPM is then allocated 30 to 40 hand pumps within a radius of 5 km from the village he lives in; he has a stake in working there because he has no choice. If his training is good, he can perform all major and minor repairs on the pump. It will not require engineers to waste precious fuel and time coming from district headquarters 50 km away just to repair a few pumps. This will cut the cost from Rs.700-1000 per hand pump per year, which is what it costs the Government without using the HPM system, to Rs.250-300 per hand pump per year, which is what it would cost the Government within that system. It will save *crores* of rupees, hand over maintenance to the community, make the HPM accountable to the community and allow him self-employed status because he will not be a government servant.

The greatest resistance to this idea comes from the engineers themselves, who are not prepared to see the advantages.

The hand pump *mistri* is one profile of how the Government could use village knowledge and village skills for development purposes if only it listened to the voice of the people. The HPM provides an example of developing people without compromising on human dignity, self-respect and social justice.

In Uttar Pradesh, by the last count over 20,000 villages were identified as problem villages. After this severe drought, there are bound to be many more. If the idea of the HPM is implemented in Uttar Pradesh there is scope for generating over 20,000 jobs in the self-employment sector for village youth. They could be trained under TRYSEM to repair and maintain the traditional shallow depth locally-manufactured hand pumps, the cost of which must run into millions in a state where water is available between 30 to 80 feet in the Indo-Gangetic plain. In Rajasthan, the HPM is paid Rs.200 per hand pump per year. In Uttar Pradesh, the HPM could be paid Rs.300 per month per village just to look after the 600 locally-manufactured hand pumps. This would be a part time job. It would save the UP Government *crores* of rupees which it currently spends on maintenance alone.

What will it take for the Government to start looking at the problems of the self-employed in the rural areas with a bit more understanding? Lip-service will not do when time is not on our side. When local solutions to local problems are staring us in the face and we can generate employment where it is needed the most, then what is stopping us from acting?

This country is not short of ideas or people with vision. The system is in a position to absorb innovation of any kind, provided the people behind it have courage, are capable of being consistent and have adequate staying power to carry it through regardless of opposition. We need to invest in such people.

© *Yojana/Kurukshetra, Publications Division, Ministry of I&B, Government of India.*

Voluntary Agencies: Twenty Years From Now

Bunker Roy

Originally published in *Mainstream*, 23 July 1988

THE VOLUNTARY SECTOR has been through turbulent times. The fact is that there will never be a time when it will cease to be controversial because it provides support and protection to all and sundry.

Ever since I started working in the voluntary sector in 1967, over 21 years ago, I have seen and met a wide cross-section of people and groups who claim to be voluntary agencies. I met a close adviser of the present Chief Minister of West Bengal who told me that only people who do not manage to get government jobs start voluntary agencies. I could not help responding by saying that only people who fail in the voluntary sector get into politics. Tragically, this is true because there are living examples to be found in almost all the States of India. People have cashed in on the confusion that reigns in the voluntary sector. Since Independence, no one has made an attempt to give the sector direction and meaning, depth and substance, identity and credibility. It was too small to attract attention, thus everyone could claim to be an expert on the subject.

In the absence of any long-term dialogue or discussion at any level between voluntary agencies themselves (they only get together when they think they are being threatened), and in the absence of any forum where critical and sensitive issues affecting voluntary agencies could be discussed, this sector has provided refuge to a galaxy of has-been politicians, people with criminal records, armchair radicals with nothing better to do, intellectually dishonest thinkers, Gandhians who Gandhiji would have disowned on the spot and various types of power-brokers who love playing politics with gullible mediocre bureaucrats who have outdated ideas of what the voluntary sector as a whole should be doing.

By sheer default, such people have gained prominence and importance, and have entrenched themselves in strategic places, wary of any moves that might affect their power and influence over others. They are quick to use (or rather, misuse) the power of the written word against any step that could make them vulnerable, expose their misdeeds and question their mythical authority. They have never had it so good. Lots of funds from India and abroad, a comfortable lifestyle in the city, the acquired image of being activists without having to do much about it except write sensational stuff, and go abroad, and give speeches and lectures on how lousy a country India is to live in because Rajiv Gandhi is Prime Minister. Though they write as if their own lives depend on it, on their own farms, these very voluntary agencies do not pay their workers minimum wages. They practise untouchability in their own organisations, believe in hierarchy and centralisation in decision-making and, in their own way, are as unjust, exploitative, chauvinistic and inhuman as the people and organisations they write against with such virulence.

I see all this changing 20 years from now. The first steps have been taken to set this disorganised house in order. The ones who held supreme for over three decades are now having to find out where they stand, and instead of accepting it gracefully, they are sharpening their claws. They will fight to the finish, even if it means taking a part of the sector down with them. They will not think twice before doing it.

Fortunately, 20 years from now, they will be nobodies. A new generation will emerge – more knowledgeable, more competent, confident and professional with grassroots experience and contact that India will not be able to do without. They will call the tune: they will influence and dictate policy and they will produce results at the same time. This new generation in the voluntary sector will be more vocal and will have more skills to communicate at all levels, and thus will make its presence felt.

The voluntary sector got high visibility for the wrong reasons with the appointment of the Kudal Commission in 1980 – a gift to the nation by one set of Gandhians who did not get along with another set. As a result, nearly 1000 voluntary agencies had to appear before it. Everyone recalled the enquiry into the *Bharat Sevek Samaj*, which carried on for 17 years, and Justice Kudal was well set to enter the 21st century. It was fortunate for the voluntary sector that Rajiv Gandhi's government was elected in 1985. A sustained campaign to wind up the Kudal Commission yielded results when – in 1986-87 – it ceased to exist. Regrettably, the role that the Gandhians, the old traditional voluntary groups, played in the campaign for and against the continuation of that Commission is not a chapter in our history that we should be proud of. Suffice it to say, rare but expected Gandhian qualities were displayed on both sides. What the Kudal Commission did illustrate was the passing of an old order and that it was time to look for alternatives, new approaches and new faces. The old guard have done enough harm to the voluntary sector by surrendering their independence, their autonomy and their identity.

In spite of political pressure to continue the witch-hunt, the fact that younger non-aligned and vocal groups in the voluntary sector collectively managed to wind up the Commission is the first indication that a fundamental shift in power within the voluntary sector has taken place. There is every indication that the older social service-oriented groups will no longer carry so much weight. This new-found confidence will be increasingly obvious 20 years from now. The emergence of non-aligned apolitical groups in their thousands all over the country establishing identities of their own is a post-Kudal Commission phenomenon.

If the winding up of the Kudal Commission gave the newer village-based groups some confidence, the opening of a dialogue with Government gave them some credibility. Voluntary groups realised it was no longer possible to work in rural development in isolation, and the sooner an attempt was made to institutionalise a dialogue with Government at all levels, the sooner it would lead to mutual understanding and respect. Three decades of mutual hostility and suspicion at the village level could not be wished away in a few meetings, and a regular dialogue was long overdue.

From 1982, an effort was made at state level to establish consultative groups of voluntary agencies with the chief secretary/development commissioner as chairman. Through the deputy chairman, the Planning Commission wrote letters to all chief ministers suggesting that such consultative groups should be established immediately, but only a few states responded positively. Not one followed the suggestion that this group should meet once every three months, so this effort was a non-starter.

This indifference to voluntary agencies was nothing new. Other ways had to be found to get State Government's attention. If the direct approach proved futile, maybe direct financial and administrative support from New Delhi would wake them up and at least get a reaction: it was necessary to think in the future.

In more ways than one, the Seventh Plan document on the involvement of voluntary agencies approved by the National Development Council in 1985 gave momentum to a series of moves that should yield tangible, positive results 20 years from now. Containing many controversial statements on issues never debated before, in any forum, it was the first attempt at clarifying the roles of voluntary agencies working in the rural areas. It was the Government of India's most widely and hotly discussed policy document, and its impact will be felt in the future.

It stated that not all non-governmental organisations (NGOs) like co-operatives, trade unions, and *Panchayati Raj* institutions were voluntary agencies, and it was time that voluntary agencies acquired an identity of their own. It stated that voluntary agencies had the professional skills to plan their own schemes and, in future, they should be consulted before schemes were approved by government – a far-reaching observation that is going to lead to change in government attitudes and thinking in the future. In fact, all the roles it envisaged for the voluntary agencies will contribute to changing civil service attitudes, right down the line. This is one reason why the roles have not been accepted fully, especially at the district and block levels. To be the eyes and ears of the people; to set an example; to test the system and see if the laws are responsive to the needs of the poor; to disseminate information; to demystify technology; to organise support and demand a community system of accountability for grassroot government functionaries – these are roles that vested interests at the village level will never allow the Government to accept.

The time is not right for all these roles to be accepted in totality, but the first significant step has been taken by Government to formulate a policy for the future. It is now left to the voluntary agencies to see that it is implemented. The way it is going, the discussions that have already taken place with the bureaucracy and the mileage that the voluntary sector has already received in changing policy to suit the role gives me tremendous hope for the future. Let us not forget that the roles have been so conceived that maximum impact at the village level will depend on voluntary agencies receiving funds directly from the Government of India. Had it been mandatory for funds to be channelled through State Governments – as was the case before the Seventh Plan – the roles would have been very different. Now, with pressure on the State Governments building up from below to support voluntary effort (or get bypassed), ten years from now, I imagine many of those Governments will see the wisdom of supporting village groups more for political and social economic reasons. By then, voluntary groups will have trained a new generation of leaders from the backward, minority and other socio-economic groups who are going to be in a position to use the ballot box to take over village-based institutions – the *panchayats* and co-operatives – for socio-economic development of their own communities. Twenty years from now, this is not unthinkable. The new generation of leaders will be a force to reckon with and cannot be taken for granted or subdued or bribed to accept what is going on today.

What should give traditional social service-oriented voluntary groups based in cities sleepless nights is the step that the Government has taken, for the first time in history, of committing a considerable sum of money to be spent through the voluntary sector. This amount will be spent only through those agencies based in rural areas, thus disqualifying big institutional so-called voluntary groups based in cities who have all along misused their influence and connections to take funds from government on behalf of the rural poor. Even now, some urban-based groups continue to do this by applying political pressure, but gradually this is going to change. Already, since the Seventh Plan chapter on voluntary agencies was approved, many urban-based groups have shifted to the rural areas and established their bases. Twenty years from now, this reverse migration will have been completed. The so-called all-India organisations (AIOs) operating as power-brokers that do not allow their branches to develop and grow at their own pace, with their own identity, will be forced to give them more independence and autonomy – and their own registration. On their own, these organisations have refused to promote volunteerism. On the contrary, they have encouraged dependency. With the policy of the Government taking such a sensible and practical turn to support only those groups based in rural areas, these AIOs will have to decentralise – or perish. Twenty years from now, these monoliths with no financial discipline or community accountability will disappear from the scene totally.

In the last few years, voluntary agencies have started meeting with each other more often on a number of issues. More than ever before, the Government has facilitated some of these meetings, when 20 years ago such support from Government was unthinkable. Twenty years ago, people did not question where the funds came from to organise meetings, because foreign donor agencies were the only source. Now, that is no longer true. Village groups have started asking awkward questions and bigger groups can no longer afford to remain silent in open forums and get away with weak explanations.

The free, open and frank debate on the Draft Code of Conduct, which attracted a great deal of attention to the state of the voluntary sector as it exists today, has done the sector a world of good. The debate brought the divisions within the sector out into the open, and for once no one could be indifferent to what was being discussed. Much to the discomfort of many groups, positions had to be taken in public, *tamashas* had to be arranged, sensitive issues had to be thrashed out face-to-face and access to the press had to be exploited to the maximum. The likelihood of a National Council of Rural Voluntary agencies being formed by an Act of Parliament sent many groups based in urban areas into a frenzy, and many armchair radicals found it a golden opportunity to get a bit of glory and contribute their own tuppenny bit for mankind. The idea in the first place was to divert attention from the need to have a National Council of Voluntary Agencies that could speak with Government with a common collective voice on everything from the Foreign Contribution Regulation Act and changes in the Income Tax Act to why a village group was being harassed in a particular State. The urban-based group with the most to lose started a campaign with foreign funds to kill any discussion on the Draft Code or a National Council, and the extent to which it went is now history. But what did the debate on the Draft Code finally achieve?

It started a search for alternatives within the sector, which was, to my mind, a significant achievement. People began discussing the need for a forum of some kind, the need for discipline and accountability and the question of what makes the voluntary sector different from Government (if at all). Parameshwara Rao may not agree with me, but if the debate on the draft Code of Conduct had never taken place, his Common Action Programme

(CAP) may not have got off the ground or assumed the importance it has today. One hears of sporadic attempts all over the country to establish regional forums, just to provide a common front and speak with one voice to Government and other interest groups. Twenty years from now, these efforts will bear fruit. However, the search for alternatives will continue as priorities change, and a new generation of voluntary workers will start emerging from this process. Because it is an area of darkness, it is believed that any effort to get closer to Government will lead to co-option, loss of independence, imposition and controls. Twenty years from now, it will be considered as co-operation leading to mutual respect and discussion on equal terms.

There is no doubt that the Government has taken steps in the right direction to meet the voluntary agencies halfway, if not further. To lead to a better understanding of the work that voluntary agencies are doing in the rural areas, on a regular basis, representatives of this sector are being invited to interact with probationers and serving civil servants during training programmes so that a generation from now there will be less suspicion and hostility. Probationers have to spend at least ten days of their training with voluntary agencies based in backward rural areas as part of their exposure to the real problems being faced by the poor. If there are any officers who want to be deputed to voluntary agencies on a regular basis, according to the Department of Personnel, this is also possible. As a result of a meeting with the Prime Minister in December 1987, a group has been appointed under the Department of Administrative Reforms to suggest ways and means of simplifying procedures for giving grants to voluntary agencies. All the ministers dealing with voluntary agencies have been invited to be a part of this group. Twenty years from now, these steps will lead to the voluntary groups working in the rural areas coming closer to Government and establishing a working relationship on a long-term basis.

I see a great future 20 years from now for the voluntary sector. Within a decade, new ideas, new approaches and new methods now being tested in the field will be ready for replication on a larger scale, and by that time, the voluntary sector will be well entrenched to influence policy at different levels and see that these ideas are given a good try. The trust and faith that is missing in the community's ability to solve its own problems will once more be revised, and dependence on Government will be reduced.

> *We shall not cease from exploration*
> *And the end of all our exploring*
> *Will be to arrive where we started*
> *And know the place for the first time*
>
> T.S. Eliot, Little Gidding

© *Reprinted courtesy of Mainstream*

4: And So It Goes On

Heather MC Malcolm

Plus ça change, plus c'est la même chose.
[The more things change, the more they stay the same.]
Jean-Baptiste Alphonse Karr

TIME PASSED. GOVERNMENTS CHANGED. Major events rocked the country; in mid-May 1991, Rajiv Gandhi was assassinated. If, following this, Government thought that Bunker's criticisms would stop, it was wrong. Throughout the 90s, the attacks kept coming. In 'The Wages of Sin', the Minimum Wages Act came under fierce fire. Not only was it pointless, having no 'teeth', but it lacked credibility coming from a government that, in Gujarat, saw nothing wrong with reducing the already low wages paid in a time of drought, causing hundreds to die of starvation; a government that failed to acknowledge corrupt practice on the part of 'mates' who were supposed to allocate and measure work done fairly, but instead defrauded workers so that in practice they had no right to work at all. Bunker's contempt for the Act is clear: 'The punishments under this Act are so absurd that I dare say there has been no conviction in its history.'

It wasn't simply the Acts themselves that came under fire, however; so did their implementation. Bunker expresses equal contempt for the way that Government allowed fair price shops to be run by 'suspect' co-operatives and private traders in ways that were anything but fair. He had sympathy for district collectors, though: people who had no choice but to cope, somehow, with the mess created by others through committee piled on committee working to different definitions of poverty. Unsurprisingly, this produced a muddled superabundance of plans and led to confusion, overstaffing, and the absence of useful information.

Nor did Bunker forget the need for a code of conduct and accountability. By 1994, he was looking back rather sombrely at his years of starting out in the voluntary sector, to a time when a simple lifestyle was the essence of volunteerism, and – as you will notice as you read this book – several of his articles contain pointers to his unease at India's importation of Western models, which he saw as costly, top-heavy and damaging to the environment.

This unease grew over time, and Bunker became increasingly critical of foreign, Western, funding agencies, through which a lot of easy money had changed everything, and not necessarily for the better. Although financial support for Barefoot College was always welcome, Bunker was happiest when it came from within India itself, using Indian money, and took the form of investment in people rather than charity.

Indeed, the influx of Western cash into India that began as a trickle in the 1970s and had grown to a flood by the 1990s prompted him to issue a wake-up call, warning that India was growing over-reliant on the foreign funds pouring into development programmes. In 1966, he pointed out that organisations such as the World Bank and United Nations were driven not by goodwill but by economic expediency and correctness, and warned voluntary agencies that depended heavily on such funds that they sailed in dangerous waters. Reliance on funding from the West required India to shape its ideas of what 'development' was in accordance with Western ideas, so that, in effect, an element of control over Indian development was being subtly exercised. Not only that; India was also left vulnerable if and when funding coming from abroad was to be withdrawn. Voluntary agencies should take heed and learn to discipline themselves. And as ever, accountability and transparency remained issues. Some voluntary agencies, Bunker writes, did not allow audits of their accounts, and others refused to make their audits public.[2]

---

[2] Bunker's own commitment to accountability was amply demonstrated in July 1997 when, facing down critics who had not expected him to do it, he opened ten years of SWRC's financial records including bank

None of this, however, is to suggest that Bunker was anti-Western. His many Western friends can attest to that. But with his strong belief in the Gandhian idea that traditional village cultures and self-sufficiency went together, and needed no great input from outside to manage very well, he was and remains pro-Indian, which is a very different thing. Use local skills; work with what you have; restrain your greed; live lightly off the land and respect the environment. At a time when the world is slowly waking up to the consequences of the high-tech life on which Western invention embarked in the late 18th century (starting with Britain's industrial revolution and enthusiastically adopted by many other countries on our planet), Gandhi's message speaks especially loud. Barefoot College, putting his message into practice, offers a path out of the morass in which the world is currently floundering. Its model for living, one that has been tried and tested for over 50 years, has been found to work – not just in Rajasthan but in other Indian states, as well as other countries. Can the rest of us really afford to ignore it? Can we not learn from this model?

The Wages of Sin

Bunker Roy

Originally published in *India Today*, 30 June 1990

AN INCREDIBLE 90% OF THE 600,000 villages in India have a population of under 2,000. And, after four decades, they still remain the personal property of a handful of village-level bureaucrats who openly exploit the rural poor; they know they have the power to get away with breaking the law, twisting rules, ignoring government orders and sabotaging anti-poverty schemes. No one questions how it is that important government circulars

---

passbooks, accounts, files and even his own personal and travel documents to public view in the *panchayat* (village council) of Buharu.

supposed to protect the life and property of the rural poor end up in village tea-shops used to wrap *barfis* and *puris*.

Even as experts in New Delhi agitate only about changing policy and making new laws, the system is on the verge of collapse with no accountability at any level. The last time they worked in villages (if they ever did) was over two decades ago, and they think villages have stayed the same since. The issues they are getting worked up about sound tragicomic.

A rash promise about the right to work, and this Government has gone into a coma. However, this right can only be ensured if the Minimum Wages Act is given teeth, and there is no indication of this being done. But what is the point of anyone demanding a right to work if he or she has no right to a decent wage? The Government is the worst offender in respect of this law. In Gujarat, during the worst drought for years, an ordinance brought the minimum wage down from Rs.17 to Rs.11. There were hundreds of 'starvation' deaths, which village-level bureaucrats classified as 'poverty deaths'.

While people were dying, a casual debate was on among well-fed policy-makers about which should be given more importance: waged employment or self-employment. These people ought to be classified as criminals because their indecision has led to many deaths.

Today, under the Minimum Wages Act, one has no right to work. This right comes at the pleasure of the 'mate' who looks after the roster to give you work, strike you off the rolls, and measure the work you have done to ensure that you always get less than is rightfully yours. The punishments under this Act are so absurd that I dare say there has been no conviction in its history. This Government certainly does not have the guts or the vision to amend it. So the right to work is going to be a non-starter.

Linked to the right to wages is the problem of availability of food and essential supplies. We are experts in deflecting the issue by saying we should be proud the country is producing 170 million tonnes of food grains. But whether it is reaching the rural poor, and how, are questions no one is prepared to face. Of the 350,000 ration shops ostensibly functioning, 29% are run by suspect village-level operatives and the rest by private traders. These very traders run their own private shops in the same village. Under the Public Distribution System (PDS), a fair price shop is supposed to stock seven essential items: wheat, rice, edible oil, sugar, kerosene, soft coke and controlled cloth. Over 90% of those in rural areas will not be stocking these because the initiative to run the PDS remains with the co-operatives or private traders, and not with the Government. Only after a demand draft is deposited with the Civil Supplies Corporation can the co-operative lift the supplies.

Since most of the fair price shops are grossly mismanaged, the rural poor are forced to depend on private traders. There is a strong case for linking the PDS with the banking system. This will enable shop owners to lift their quotas and introduce a credit system for all ration card holders. Also, there is a distinct urban bias at the expense of the rural, hilly, tribal and coastal areas.

The Food Corporation of India has been forbidden to procure coarse grain even though it is the staple food of the poor. This Government should allow it under the PDS immediately.

The time has come to think in terms of food subsidies. If the fertiliser industry and rich farmers can be subsidised to the tune of Rs.4,000 *crore*, if electricity, irrigation water, seeds, public transport and tractors can be subsidised by several thousand *crore* rupees, there is no justification for the 200 million families living below the poverty line to be denied the basic right to receive food at subsidised rates. Numerous calculations of the cost of doing this have been made and all of them are below Rs.1,000 *crore*. The previous Government was too full of World Bank-returned experts with no rural experience to appreciate the political advantage of introducing such a subsidy. But by taking this one step, the Government could guarantee its remaining in power for the next two decades.

It is over crucial issues such as these that planners should be burning their midnight oil today, rather than showing their personal kinks for non-issues like cutting down centrally sponsored schemes, as if that were going to improve the lives of the rural poor.

© *Courtesy India Today magazine*

Required: A Code of Conduct

Bunker Roy

Originally published in *Deccan Herald*, 24 January 1994

WHEN I WAS ASKED TO JOIN THE PLANNING COMMISSION by V.C. Pande in 1982, it was the first time any grassroots voluntary agency had been asked to influence and decide national policy for the Government.

The mandate I had been given was simple: draft a policy statement on behalf of village-level groups that could be included in the Seventh Plan document which would make Government at all levels understand the functions of such groups.

National Debate

The behind-the-scenes manipulations that were required to get this policy statement accepted need not be mentioned here. Suffice it to say that after strong resistance from conventional policy planners it was finally included in the Seventh Plan. Included in the policy statement were two harmless lines to the effect that voluntary groups needed to get together to decide on a code of conduct for themselves, with a view to improving financial discipline and public accountability.

It started a national debate that generated more heat than light. Foreign funding agencies with many of their representatives based in Bangalore and Madras opposed it vehemently. From 1984 to 1987, hundreds of meetings were held to discuss the implications of agreeing to a code of conduct. Most of the village-based groups welcomed it because they were, in any case, already following a strict code.

The 'power brokers' based in the urban areas, with enormous budgets running to *crores* of rupees, did their best to sabotage the entire process. Adopting an extravagant lifestyle in these cities and speaking on behalf of the rural poor suited them. Becoming self-appointed spokesmen for the Scheduled Castes, Scheduled Tribes and other backward classes with massive foreign money backing them, some even felt that they were only accountable to the people – the ones they themselves exploited. Neither the Government nor other voluntary groups could look into their account books.

In the name of better management, they could get fantastic salaries and perks and no one had any right to question their ethics. Among other things, they were not obliged to pay minimum wages to their staff.

They were against any code of conduct that believed in openness and a democratic way of functioning. They said they did not need a code when the strength of the voluntary sector was self-discipline and self-control; that this was just a Rajiv Gandhi plot to control and destroy the voluntary sector.

Now, in 1993, what does the scene look like from the outside? Is the Code still necessary? After five years of silence on this issue, has the spirit of volunteerism taken a beating? More than ever, it is obvious that this sector has been destroyed by too much money, resulting in a colossal waste of manpower and financial resources. For this, the blame lies entirely with foreign funding agencies who have flooded the sector with easy money.

Where is the sacrifice and dedication associated with volunteerism? It can be found only in small village-level voluntary groups which show tremendous courage while facing formidable odds – all working with very little money and no security. When they should actually be supported, they are being told there is no money.

Will Do Much Good

It will be good if the funding agencies cut their support in half, to those receiving over Rs.3 *crore* a year. They have produced several megalomaniacs in the South who have started business concerns in the name of voluntary agencies. It will do the voluntary sector a world of good if these collapsed. In public forums, they talk of self-reliance when they are totally dependent themselves.

The tragedy is that these multi-*crore* organisations have done little that is new and fundamental. Yes, they have shown they can deliver services at a lower cost than the Government; they can plan and implement projects with more community involvement; they can develop waste land, install hand pumps, run adult education classes, build houses and protect the environment better and more inexpensively that the Government can. Does that make them voluntary?

Not Voluntary

If their lifestyles remain the same, if they think of their rights before their duty to society, if they think of their own security and are insensitive to the insecurity of the poor, they are certainly not voluntary.

Should the foreign funding agencies decide to cut their support in half to these groups in the Global South, what will happen?

Since by reputation I am supposed to run a multi-*crore* operation in Tilonia, in Rajasthan, I will answer that question myself. If in the last two decades, these vast groups have not lined up an income-generating activity large enough to support their running costs they will collapse like a pack of cards. If they have mistreated their staff, encouraged hierarchies, discriminated against the majority at the expense of a few favourites, then once the members of the organisation know that funds are drying up, they will bite the hand that fed them because they have nothing to fear.

If grants are drastically cut to these organisations and rumours spread, very few would have the will to rally round and survive. They have had it too easy for far too long to know what it is like to be insecure. The outcome will be a spate of allegations and counter-allegations aired in public. Maybe for the voluntary sector such a painful lesson is necessary.

Will the communities miss them? We all know how they can be manipulated to send petitions with hundreds of signatures of the rural poor protesting against the foreign donor agency for having taken such 'high-handed' and 'undemocratic' decisions without consulting the 'partners'. Protest rallies will be organised, but when the stamina for such demonstrations has been exhausted then the *real* information will start coming in from the field. For every person who may have been assisted there will be ten who will state that they have been cheated, exploited, discriminated against and treated unfairly.

Is this a sign of failure? Of course not. This can happen to a small group with much less money as well. The only difference is that the small group has the staying power to survive. It knows what the odds are like: it works close to the ground. But the affluent groups will go to the press and the courts and friends in Government. However, it will not help.

Will the Government miss them? Will the Government ask them to stay, or write a letter to the foreign donor agencies asking them not to cut the funds because they are doing such good work? I cannot imagine any government official doing so for anybody.

Because easy money is available, these groups have refused to approach Government for funds when funds would have been easily available, because taking government money would have compromised their independence and their flexibility, and their organisation would have been subject to government rules and control.

Undignified

Thus, they would never agree to any code that was monitored through a body that received official patronage. Fair enough. But look at the undignified position they are in now – wholly controlled by funding organisations not on Indian soil. Where is their self-respect?

@ Courtesy Deccan Herald

Bane of Foreign Funds for Volunteers

Bunker Roy

Originally published in *The Indian Express*, 16 February 1996

(This article is reproduced entirely in its original form.)

INDIA IS A CLASSIC EXAMPLE of how foreign money can infiltrate and subvert an old movement where the spirit of volunteerism was sustained by service and sacrifice, not money. Today several thousand voluntary organisations all over the country are totally dependent on foreign funds, among them several hundred Gandhian and Sarvodaya organisations.

Like the sacred cow no one is talking about how 90% of all the voluntary groups can disappear if foreign funding groups decide to call it a day. Since the '70s India has been a success story of sorts and there are, as a result, a rash of foreign funding agencies with their offices in metropolitan cities overseeing and reporting how their money has been spent. There is no objection to that. What is objectionable is how they deliberately conceal their expensive failures. Whereas it can be a learning process, their fear is that the public contributions might fall and their jobs will suffer.

But who in the voluntary sector in India are questioning the role of foreign funding agencies? Where is there any debate on how they should function? On whose word do they accept or reject proposals of grassroots groups? With the professional and commercial culture coming into the voluntary sector through the NGOs, the cancer is spreading to the grassroot groups as well. There is little thought being given to reducing dependency on outside. Whatever is foreign is neither good, necessary, nor desirable. Indeed it has been proved to be a threat to the self-respect of rural communities.

Yet, because so much money is flowing into this sector no one is ringing the alarm bells. The World Bank, the UN and other donor agencies have identified this sector not because they have any sincere feeling or compassion for the welfare of the rural poor. It is economically viable for them and politically correct to divert funds to the NGOs. They are supposed to be closer to the poor: the NGOs are supposed to convey the voice of the grassroot groups as they know what is happening on the ground.

The two critical issues before the voluntary sector are financial discipline and public accountability. The debate on agreeing to follow a code of conduct needs to be revived and it should be applicable irrespective of whether the organisation accepts Government funds or foreign funds. A transparency form has to be filled by all organisations applying for government funds. Foreign donor agencies should also use that form when considering grants. This has also something to do with public accountability. Some voluntary agencies do not allow audit of their accounts; some refuse to make it public. Many organisations have skeletons in their cupboards (indeed like all foreign funding agencies) they would rather keep hidden for fear of ridicule.

If we cannot put our own house in order, if we cannot come to some agreement on how we should conduct ourselves because we are too weak and divided, then the State has a duty to step in. With a general election coming and political parties looking for issues that will look good in their manifestos, there cannot be a better opportunity for quick Government intervention to attract the common voter. On the Indian side, what restrictions need to be enforced on the foreign funding agencies? There should be an upper limit to what one voluntary agency can receive from foreign sources. Today several hundred organisations receive over Rs five crore every year for rural development work and they are totally dependent on them.

Whether it is the UN, the World Bank, the Ford Foundation or any other funding agency, the collective amount should not exceed Rs five crore. This will at least curb megalomaniac tendencies and make so-called leaders with massive chips on their shoulders behave like human beings. It will force them to create small groups with a small budget and work in a smaller area. The splintering of massive organisations into small registered independent groups is long overdue.

No foreign funds should be allowed to be received by any voluntary organisation which has no capacity to raise resources within the country. The source could be Government, private industry or the community they work with. This has to be reflected in the financial statements before any foreign funds are received. It would reduce dependency, make organisations try harder to get Government funds and, as a result, perhaps change the policies and schemes of the Government to suit voluntary agencies. The move towards becoming self-sufficient is hard and difficult. But for voluntary groups working in difficult geographical areas that is the only long-term solution.

Reprinted from THE INDIAN EXPRESS, with permission of The Indian Express (P) Limited © 1978-1996. All rights reserved through the world.

Barefoot College, new campus entrance

Villagers and small bullock cart

Villagers gathered at the well

Woman grinding grain

Outdoor life

Women working in fields

Looking after goats

5: The Elephant in the Room

Heather MC Malcolm

IT'S A DEPRESSING THOUGHT THAT PERHAPS, since self-interest lies in the hearts of so many of us human beings, corruption as a way of furthering that self-interest may well be an inbuilt feature of the human condition. Societies try to build in checks and balances to curb it: we have laws, moral codes, feedback systems. But what happens when the laws are ignored or twisted, moral codes laughed at, and feedback systems don't even exist, as in rural Indian villages?

This is not to suggest that India is the only country to suffer from corruption. Daily, the world's Press is packed with scandalous stories revealing this politician's venality or that policeman's turning of a criminally blind eye, to the extent that even the most optimistic of us tend to feel despondent. But this book has an Indian focus, and though India is a long way from being the most corrupt of countries, it is also a long way from being the least, sharing a ranking of 85th out of 180 according to Trading Economics' 'Corruption Perceptions Index Rank' [tradingeconomics.com, accessed on 20th April 2022].

What can the world do to help? Acknowledge that corruption is a real barrier to development, for a start. Its presence – the elephant in the room – sits in many of the articles in this collection. Here, we present a somewhat shocking account of an incident at a symposium held in Oslo in 1998 as part of the United Nations Development Programme (UNDP), at which Bunker drew delegates' attention to the fact that corruption was a real and huge barrier to development. And got nowhere. Would it be any different today?

But there is a ray of hope. There's the MKSS (Mazdoor [Labour] Kisan [Farmer] Shakti [Strength] Sangathan [Organisation]), which was formed in May 1990 to stand up for ordinary people, using tactics that Gandhiji would have recognised. The story of how it set up fair provision shops run the way they were intended to be run and fought for the proper payment of wages and against government mismanagement, terrifying officialdom in the process, is told in an article which makes clear the power of the public hearings that were held.[3]

Among the Eyeless in Oslo

Bunker Roy

Originally published in *The Telegraph Calcutta*, 20 October 1998

A CRUCIAL SYMPOSIUM ON HUMAN DEVELOPMENT called this month in Oslo by the United Nations Development Programme and the High Commissioner for Human Rights was meant to discuss and agree on how best to link rights with human development. It was hosted by the Government of Norway with its good track record of honouring the agreed UN target of 0.7% of gross national product for development purposes. It was considered a good time for all heavyweights to be present to acknowledge Norway's commitment at a time when other developed nations were suffering from donor fatigue.

So Gus Speth, UNDP administrator, Mary Robinson, High Commissioner, and Norway's Hilde Johnson, Minister for International Co-operation and Human Rights, were present along with a host of others (evidently all luminaries in their subjects) to conceptualise and probe ways and means of operationalising the indivisible link between human rights and human development.

With a view to showing how important these issues are, several independent experts on the right to development – India's Arjun

---

[3] The full story of the MKSS and its successful campaign for ordinary people to have the right to information is told in *The RTI Story: Power to the People* by Aruna Roy with the MKSS Collective, published in 2018 by Roli Books, New Delhi.

Sengupta – and extreme poverty – Belgium's Anne Marie Lizin – have been appointed. They are supposed to give direction and focus and provide practical answers.

It was all a great disappointment. After one and a half days of baffled silence with almost everyone waffling and making the right noises, I stood up to speak to nearly 100 so-called "distinguished" people.

Tilonia State of Mind

l started by saying that after listening to them for one and a half days I was convinced that what I am doing in the small village of Tilonia in the State of Rajasthan in India is more important and crucial than what was being done by all the people collected in that room. The UN has obviously lost complete touch with reality. For the reality is like what Rajiv Gandhi confessed as Indian prime minister nearly a decade ago: out of one rupee of development expenditure only 17 *paise* actually reach the rural poor – and even that was an understatement. Where did the 83 *paise* for development go?

None of the speakers had mentioned the words "corruption", "embezzlement", "wastage" or "leakages" – as if these did not exist and were not problems worth mentioning. How is it that they could be so smug when the reality was that development aid was being wasted on the ground and all they could talk about was of global aid getting less – and rightly so if the money was not getting to the right people?

Much more important than the right to development (which is impossible to operationalise) was the right to information. Not access to, or freedom of, but the right to information on the ground at the village level. There was no need for consultants, surveys and studies or to waste thousands of dollars to establish the extent of corruption.

Final Account Down

What was needed was for someone with a bit of common sense to walk into the villages and ask the villagers two simple questions. Do you know how much money is coming for development in your village? Do you know how the money has been spent? It was far from easy to collect this information because there was resistance all the way from the petty bureaucrat, the grassroots elected politician, engineers and touts to moneylenders. Once questions were answered, the information was shared in public hearings with thousands of the poor people most affected by such corruption.

In silence, the experts and distinguished people heard of the power of public hearings and how many corrupt officials and politicians had even returned in full the money they had embezzled. The poor had the right to demand and receive funds to be spent on the development of their own village. In the process of exercising their collective power, they had acquired a dignity no law could possibly give them.

The ultimate fallout of the movement was good. In a moment of anger, the Chief Minister of Rajasthan – pressured by the mass movement – asked in a public meeting if the Barefoot College of Tilonia would open its account books to the public. In the first public hearing of its kind in the history of the voluntary movement in India in July 1997, this was actually done.

The astonishing response of several UN officials to my intervention was that they could not talk about corruption and embezzlement of public funds. It was not in their mandate. Which world is the UN living in?

© Courtesy of ABP Pvt, Ltd.

Villages as a Positive Force for Good Governance: The Right to Information

India's Struggle Against Grass-Roots Corruption

Bunker Roy

Originally published in *United Nations Chronicle*, Volume XXXVII, Number 1, 2000

(This article is reproduced entirely in its original form.)

INDIA IS THE LARGEST DEMOCRACY IN THE WORLD. Despite a bewildering variety of religions, cultures, languages, food habits, customs and traditions, the ballot box keeps this country together.

Immense problems such as extremes of wealth and poverty still prevail because of the caste system in rural India, but there is respect and fear for the power of the vote. However, there are still millions today in the nearly 600,000 villages who are not yet on the voter's list and have no rights. The economic planners, policymakers and the so-called experts sitting in Delhi and the State capitals are ignorant of ground realities and hopelessly out of touch with the situation in the villages.

Strange are the performance indicators of government officials, whose buzz words are transparency and accountability. Anyone who manages to spend the money budgeted and allocated is considered efficient, so the mad rush to show that the amount has actually been spent at year's end is simply solved by falsifying receipt vouchers and muster rolls on a colossal scale. Thousands of schools, dispensaries, roads, small dams, community centres and residential quarters have been shown to be complete on paper, but in reality are incomplete, inhospitably unutilized and abandoned.

There is no transparency and no accountability at the local level where it counts the most. Poor citizens cannot go up to the lowest government functionary and ask how much and for what purpose money is being spent in their village. They have no right to ask for detailed information on expenditure because that is where the corruption begins—making false receipts and vouchers running into millions of dollars.

The general conviction among the over 300 million living below the poverty line is that the public exchequer is being looted, and that the money earmarked for development is going into the pockets of the rich and the powerful. From the highest echelons of Government to the lowest village functionary, the law makers and law enforcers are often also the law breakers, and no one in the Government can touch them. Rajiv Gandhi, as Prime Minister of India, once lamented helplessly that out of every rupee spent for development only 17 per cent actually reached the poor.

It takes years for donors and policymakers to wake up and realize what what is happening. What is needed is not stronger laws, stricter punishment or more visits to the villages to supervise officials and look into accounts books. Nor will recruiting more experts and re-employing retired bureaucrats help when too often they have been the problem in the first place.

However, a powerful answer has been found by a grass roots movement operating in one of the most backward regions of India. In the early nineties, a mass-based organization calling itself the Mazdoor (Labour) Kisan (Farmer) Shakti (Strength) Sangathan (Organisation) (MKSS) started working in one of the most neglected areas of Rajasthan. Meeting their basic needs with modest public contributions from the community, the core group started living in a small mud hut in the village of Devdungari. Just off the national highway to Udaipur, the villagers could well have been living in the nineteenth century—the way millions of poor people still live in rural India.

The MKSS prepared no project proposals, received no foreign funds, recruited no staff and attracted no visitors, thus making it difficult to classify and slot them. All they did was walk from village to village asking simple questions: did the people know how much money was coming to their village for development and where it was being spent? These were simple questions the poor could understand but had not dared to ask.

The MKSS went to the Government Block Office, which administers development funding in about 100 villages, to request detailed information on development expenditure. They were told they had no right and there was no government rule allowing any villager to demand such information–and get it. At the national and state levels, planners, politicians and administrators, all out of touch with reality, were claiming there was total transparency. At the village level, however, vouchers, bills and muster rolls that showed who was receiving payments or wages were kept secret.

To perforate the "Iron Curtain" between the community and the Government, the MKSS launched a people's campaign, the like of which had never been seen or experienced in Rajasthan since the Freedom Movement in the 1940s. The campaign included several public hearings where cases of misappropriation and corruption of public funds were shared with several thousand people. Sit-in protests and strikes forced a Chief Minister to make a commitment in the State Assembly and then publicly dishonour it. It enabled the establishment of a Committee on Transparency to study the feasibility of supplying photocopies of bills, vouchers and muster rolls. But when the Committee recommended that it was practical, the State Government declared the Committee's findings secret.

The staying power of the MKSS in organizing a 53-day strike in Jaipur, supported and sustained by contributions from ordinary people on the streets, baffled the Government, which refused to yield to the demands of the MKSS. This was strange, because all the MKSS wanted was for the Government to honour what the Chief Minister had already committed to on the House floor.

The strike ended finally when the Deputy Chief Minister revealed that the State Government had already conceded more than what the MKSS had demanded six months before the strike had been called! No one in the Government, from the Chief Minister and Chief Secretary (senior-most bureaucrat in the State) downwards, was aware of this *Gazette* (government order) until it surfaced by sheer accident!

The MKSS took the extra ordinary *Gazette* back to the villages to see how effective it was. It was one thing to pass a government order; it was quite another to see how seriously the village officials and *sarpanches* (elected village representatives) honoured the order. First, everyone pleaded ignorance: they had received no such *Gazette*. So after the first month, every MKSS member kept a copy in his or her tatty pocket to be produced at an instance should any village official claim not having seen it. When applications were submitted at the Block Office and *Panchayat* (Village Council) headquarters, the village officials refused to act on it.

What was the experience of the MKSS trying to have a written government order implemented?

The orders are meaningless as long as the village officials are strong enough to flaunt and abuse them, knowing fully well that no action can be taken against them. What eventually made them act was the tremendous grassroots following, and indeed moral authority, of the MKSS.

Two months after applying pressure to implement the government order and get the critical information from the *Panchayats*, the MKSS held its first public hearing in a small village called Kukarkheda. The idea was to share its experience with the people. The MKSS backed its claims with written evidence and documentation extracted from the Block Office, which they shared with in front several hundred people who first listened in puzzlement and then with collective anger. So great was the pressure from the people and so complete was the public humiliation of these officials that even before the first hearing started, the woman *sarpanch* of the local *Panchayat* had returned Rs 100,000. In a second public hearing held in Surajpura (Ajmer District), the *sarpanch* of Rawatmal publicly returned Rs 147,000, while the *sarpanch* of Surajpura handed back Rs 114,000.

For the first time since the *Panchayat* movement was founded in the 1950s under Nehru, village representatives began to return the money they had embezzled from their constituencies. It was not fear of the law or arrest or departmental inquiry or suspension that made them act this way. It was fear of the people through the public hearings that finally humbled them.

© United Nations 2000.
Reprinted with the permission of the United Nations.

6: Bunker Roy and the 50-Year Pilgrimage

Heather MC Malcolm and Aruna Roy

In both the west and the east, the 1960s were years of change. US President John F Kennedy was assassinated, an event that shocked the world, but it was also at about that time that the Beatles came to India in search of music and mysticism, and India's young people looked westward, wanting to study at universities abroad. In the east of the country, however, there was unrest as tea garden workers wanting better wages organized themselves into a political party.

At Delhi university in 1965, in response to a call from Jaiprakash Narain, a Gandhian *Sarvoday*,[4] a young man, Sanjit 'Bunker' Roy, volunteered to help with humanitarian work during the famine in Bihar, now Jharkhand. Bunker was then the sportsman of the day. Not only was he India's National Squash Champion and his University's Tennis Captain, but he also represented his college in swimming and cricket. But his privileged background, which included education at the Doon School and St. Stephens, had sheltered him from the realities of India, and when he walked into Bihar's Palamu district, Bunker entered another world. Here, he saw people and dogs fighting over scraps of food, and witnessed hunger and poverty on a scale and intensity he could not have imagined. Those eight weeks changed him forever.

His M.A. behind him, Bunker disappointed his widowed mother by refusing lucrative jobs and abandoning his phenomenal sports career. Instead, he went searching for ways in which he could work for the less privileged. Quoting Robert Frost: 'Two roads diverged in a wood, and I – I took the one less traveled by. And that has made all the difference', he walked on.

---

[4] A member of a movement aiming to uplift the people of rural India by peaceful and co-operative means.

His journey took him to work as a driver for Tibetan refugees, and later for missionaries who sent him as a team leader to blast out and dig open wells for water in arid Rajasthan. This was unparalleled hands-on learning about the real India, through which Bunker came to understand that the people knew what their own development should be and would be able to craft it themselves, but were denied opportunities to do so by top-down approaches from government and administration.

'Development' was the buzzword of that decade, and under the starry Rajasthani skies, Bunker dreamed of the ways that development could relieve and lift the misery of his less fortunate brethren. He dreamed of an India that would recognize the existence of knowledge and skills beyond the imagination of policy makers and planners, and those who designed others' destinies as they sat in air-conditioned offices in the UN and Delhi and other national capitals. He imagined a partnership between the farmer and the city professional, one that would build a better India. In his understanding of "development", he stood unflinching and resolute with people. Ordinary people.

Bunker met Aruna in the 'class of '65'. Although their concerns about poverty and inequality were shared, they differed in their views of what the solutions should be, and while Bunker travelled to rural India, Aruna qualified to become a civil servant. After seven years in the service, however, she left to join Bunker and Barefoot.

Gandhi spoke of *sewa*, *nirman* and *sangharsh* (service, development and struggle) as the three important modes of public action. While both Bunker and Aruna embraced service, Barefoot worked with development, and after nine years in Barefoot College, Aruna went on to work with struggle, fighting for basic rights for the less privileged. With others, she founded the Mazdoor Kisan Shakti Sangathan (MKSS) collective, out of whose work evolved India's Right to Information Act.

Meanwhile, word of Bunker's unusual experiment in development got around, and many reporters and other media representatives sought him out, curious to know what he was doing. His work was no flash in the pan: he stayed the course, and before long, the excellence of sound practice and shared wisdom ushered in an immense vision of what people could achieve by walking together, offering solutions to the world. Out of all this was born the concept of the 'Barefooter', which is now known the world over.

For 50 years, Bunker has remained constant in his values, persistent and determined. This chapter offers a selection of articles which give glimpses of him at different stages and from the perspectives of different writers. But the last article, 'Why the Millennium Goals Won't Work', shows Bunker consistent in his concern about plans that are made without involving the people who will be affected by them, and illustrates not only how firm he can be but also his continuing concern for the future.

Portraits of an Era
(excerpt from chapter 8)

Tara Ali Baig

Published by Roli Books Pvt. Limited, 1988

PERHAPS IT WAS THE POLITICISATION of many national organisations that created a new mood in the country. With Government's increasing centralisation and more and more control on every aspect of life, individualists as we are as a people subtle changes were taking place among us. Highly educated and highly motivated young people were going to grassroots areas and setting up new services. All over the country, this became an increasing phenomenon. Among the most visible was the work of Sanjit (Bunker) Roy at Tilonia. Bunker was only 26 when he started on his chosen career. He came from a distinguished family, many of whom had been in the Indian Civil Service and were patriots, like C.R. Das. As Bunker came from what is called the élite class and was the product of Doon School and St Stephen's College, his success in pioneering rural work on a scale hitherto not attempted naturally caused considerable excitement. What is more important, however, is the inspiration that he has provided to many young people who would not be prepared to live lives of luxury in a mad scramble after wealth when there were so many glaring inequalities as yet unresolved all over the country.

When you see a handsome young man dressed in the chic homespun fashion of the modern Indian male, coming out of the Planning Commission where he is currently an Adviser[5] on the rural voluntary programmes, you would never suspect that he was bald, dark and had hair in his ears when he was born! Described thus inelegantly by his mother, Sanjit (Bunker) Roy came into the world in 1945 in Burnpur, where his father, Nogie Roy, worked for the Indian Iron and Steel company.

Bunker's mother, Aruna, brought up her two boys Shankar and Bunker in so original a fashion that they could quite easily write a book to rival Gerald Durrell's and call it 'Mother and Other Animals'. Bunker's first train journey by himself was at the age of five. At four, he boarded a tram in Calcutta and went by himself to his grandmother's house across the city. Mother followed in a car, but he was taught very young to fend for himself. At six, he was already in boarding school in Patna, and then in St. Patrick's in Asansol. In 1957, he went to Doon School and concentrated on sports to such an extent that his grades were too low to be admitted to college. His redoubtable mother paid twenty-three visits to St Stephen's in seven days and got admission for him. It is more than likely that the exhausted Principal felt by then that he might as well ignore the 33 per cent marks which had held things up in the first place.

Nogie, Bunker's father, died very young, but during his lifetime it seems the conversations with his boys while demolishing breakfast eggs always centred on intellectual topics like Darwin's theories, transcendental matters, and the state of the nation. Bunker's greatest friend at the time was the sweeper's son, Kedar, and they used to spend hours in the servant's quarters or sprawled on the grass smoking *biris*. Bunker still sprawls out on anything remotely sprawlable but does not smoke any more. Perhaps the formula of starting everything early in life has some merit.

---

[5] Actually, his title was 'Consultant' [Ed.]

Bunker's other friend was a pet monkey called Kankar, since he felt that Shankar and he, to fulfil Darwin's theories, must have a younger brother.

While the two brothers, and presumably Kankar, went to school in Asansol, tragedy struck this young family. Nogie died suddenly and Aruna was faced with having to provide for her two young sons. Having been brought up by a grandfather who was determined to make his girls as independent as the boys, Aruna refused to fall back upon her father who had found it difficult to bring up this headstrong girl. She decided to drive to Delhi from Calcutta. One of Nogie's cousins, Subroto Mukherji, India's first chief of the Air Force, said he could get her a job. Subroto and Sharda, his wife (who later became Governor of Andhra Pradesh and then Gujarat), were a tower of strength to Aruna in her most difficult years.

Typically, Aruna set forth alone for Delhi and during the long drive of some 1,600 kilometres propped her boys on cushions and made them take the wheel for three to four hour stretches, though they were only nine and ten at the time! During the next two years, she said she moved in and out of nine different houses. Fortunately, the boys were now in Doon School and Subroto had got her a job in the State Trading Corporation (STC) for the princely salary of Rs.350 a month. Twenty-five years later, she was to be one of the top executives of STC as Commercial Adviser to our Embassy in Moscow and Regional Manager of ten countries in East Europe. The beginnings were lean years for them all but perhaps provided the best training in self-reliance a family could have had. Bunker and Shankar learned to be frugal, have few wants and concentrate their energies on more important things – like sports! In this Bunker excelled, becoming the national squash champion three times. He competed in two World Championships in Australia and New Zealand, beating the world's number two, Cam Nancarrow, in the semi-finals in Auckland.[6]

Normally in India there is little equation between academic life and sports, the usual approach being that studies are serious, and

---

[6] 1967 and 1971, in Sydney and the world championship semi finals in Auckland [Ed.]

sports are a kind of recreation. Unfortunately, all our education is geared to acquiring jobs and not to learning or to becoming whole human beings. Bunker has proved many things in his young life, and one of them is certainly that the skill, stamina and determination that championship games of any kind require provide excellent groundwork for a life of achievement based upon one's own talents and capabilities. Whatever Bunker was to create was entirely his own doing. Far from depending upon his distinguished ancestry, he started from the opposite end of the spectrum, moved by the plight of people at the bottom of the ladder, and learned in the field and on the spot how to help them change their own destinies.

For a young man in his early twenties, the task he set himself was formidable. It started with the Bihar famine in 1965, where, as a volunteer, he saw horrifying things like a man fighting a dog over food, rats and grass being eaten for want of better nourishment, and the whole hideous scenario of disaster, against which poverty has no weapons. Back in Delhi, determined to find a place to work, he joined the Catholic Relief Services in Rajasthan, and worked as a labourer in Ajmer where they were deepening wells. His descriptions of learning the art of finding water sources in desert areas like Rajasthan are graphic. He had to learn how to use explosives, go down wells in rickety buckets, blast away, get covered with dust and experience every hardship that is part of the process of boring a well.

In 1972, he heard of an old set of sanatorium buildings vacant in Tilonia, in the Silhora Block. It was here, with one colleague, that he set up the SWRC (Social Work and Research Centre) which has now become a showpiece and model for the world of development planning at the grassroots level. In fact, even if the work was an uphill task, it was never based upon loans and handouts, but on basic professionalism where villagers smilingly paid for technical services, learnt to grow better crops, make better marketable handicrafts and began to value good health and education. This integrated approach worked because Bunker and his wife, also Aruna, who had resigned from the IAS (Indian Administrative Service), lived with the villagers, not as outsiders, but as co-workers, in a classless society. By attracting young professionals, who first started the ground water surveys and identified systems of reaching water sources that have changed the face of this arid area, Bunker and Aruna did not rely upon charity, but on teachers, doctors and engineers who were young enough to rough it out and village-level workers who were all salaried.

Bunker feels strongly that the Government is not equipped to promote sound rural development or build up self-reliance and self-respect from which true progress can be generated. The key factor in this is the close identification of the activist, in other words, the personality who can make a rigid, structured group of villagers accept helpful change within the community itself. The trained rural worker sent to different places or the Block Development Officer, a peripatetic official, can seldom have the deep rapport with a poor community that the situation demands. It takes living with them and working with them to gain their gradual acceptance, confidence and trust in order to experiment with something new.

Bunker discovered through experience that real development does not need complex, expensive solutions and must be left to the people themselves. Modernisation is not necessarily development. He firmly believes that making a complete human being is true development. Tilonia has, therefore, been a genuine rural laboratory, but again it is more than that. It also represents the importance of what is called 'elite' education and background turned clearly and categorically towards creating a new kind of India, one in which young people brought up without class consciousness or prejudices have begun to confront the monumental imperviousness of an old society whose vested interests still violently resist change.

In 1985, Bunker was awarded the prestigious Jamnalal Bajaj Award, the first young person ever to receive it. Bunker's unusual dedication has become the inspiration for hundreds of other young people, equally gifted, and equally determined to contribute their share to an India which can realise its enormous potential. Tilonia models have been set up elsewhere in fifteen other centres, and all over India there are countless new projects where people with vision are battling and winning out against village hostilities, to help a community help itself.

Today, his vision is directed into the heart of bureaucracy itself. An Adviser to the Planning Commission, he is in constant demand for consultations with agencies like the World Bank, CIDA (Canadian International Development Agency) and government ministries, dealing with the non-governmental services on which he feels the administration has to depend. In 1985, he addressed an open letter to the Prime Minister and very bluntly told him that he must respond to the common people, must delink jobs from degrees, must rely upon workers with field experience, trust non-governmental workers to continue with their work despite the hostility of vested interests, and rely upon rural wisdom to act in its own best interests.

Today, Aruna more or less runs Tilonia as Bunker is constantly on the move. She also works with hundreds of rural women in other centres, taking up their problems and trying to establish sources of income for them, for female servitude is also a hard fact. She firmly believes that Tilonia cannot be managed without outside professionals and with the new self-reliance of the people themselves. She does not see eye to eye with Bunker's tilting against the windmills of bureaucracy, a view shared by many voluntary organisations and agencies who feel somehow that he is selling them down the river by giving Government a handle with which to take control over them later.

However, Bunker is still a young man with a vision of his country that no one can gainsay. He is seldom in any place for longer than a day or two. He knows a vast number of people working in remote areas of the country. He still travels in Delhi on his motorcycle, the helmet incongruous with the *khadi kurta-paijama* he always wears. Though UNESCO, OXFAM and dozens of other funding agencies have now come forward to build up Tilonia and other centres, Bunker's own lifestyle remains frugal and totally unaltered. His mother says he leaves clothes at various points all over the country and as far as she is concerned, she is simply his *dhobi* and shoeblack. What is certain is that he travels light, and is genuinely a man of the people.

© *The Baig Family*

Rebuilding Grassroots Potential

Matt Ross

Originally published in *Regeneration and Renewal*, 30 May 2003

'MANY COMMUNITIES HAVE GOT TOGETHER, fed up with professionals, fed up with Government, and done something on their own,' says Bunker Roy. 'Today the trend is towards looking in rather than looking out; looking at the strengths of your own communities. And the strengths are there: it's just that they've been eroded and demoralised by people from outside.'

Roy is one of India's leading community activists, a champion of the poor whose ideological roots lie in the thinking of Mahatma Gandhi. Like Gandhi, he's a highly educated man who has dedicated his life to grassroots action. Like Gandhi, his mission has led him to challenge the Indian establishment. And like Gandhi's, his methods are having dramatic results whose lessons are applicable far beyond India's shores. Indeed, Roy's approach is receiving international recognition: earlier this month he won the UK's biggest environmental award, the University of St. Andrew's £20,000 Prize for the Environment.

Yet this is a Gandhian approach for a modern age: rather than non-violent resistance, Roy preaches positive self-empowerment. 'People in villages, who may be backward, primitive, illiterate and poor, have technology and skills which have been tested through centuries,' he says.

Roy believes that 'paper-qualified professionals', and the skewing of development towards major infrastructure projects dependent on outside investment and expertise, have emasculated people. 'Let's start with the knowledge and skills that the people have first and if they are found wanting in some, then we get the skills in from outside,' he says. 'The competence of ordinary people to handle the most sophisticated of technologies is incredible.'

Village communities, argues Bunker, 'have the knowledge, have the skills, have the solutions: it's all low-cost, community-based, community-managed. Why aren't we using it? Because can you imagine all those consultants and World Bank people who'd be out of jobs? It's too much for them to even think. It's as simple as that to me: they have the solutions but don't want to implement them, because they're too low-cost.'

Born into a wealthy family, Roy had 'a very expensive and exclusive and snobbish education'. But, he says, 'I like to think that my real education began when I started living with the poor.' Fresh out of university, Roy began digging village wells. 'My mother was horrified that I should do something so different from what was expected.' He smiles. 'I was supposed to be a bureaucrat or a diplomat or a lawyer or a businessman.'

In 1971, hoping to give local people 'the space to be able to implement their own solutions', Roy founded the Barefoot College in Rajasthan. 'We were young and daring: we had the feeling that we were invincible, and we wanted to change the world. I still feel like that even now,' he says. 'There has to be an anger inside you, about the right and the wrong and the rich and the poor. These things should make you feel a burning inside, that there's something you can do at your level.'

Thirty years on, Roy has inspired the foundation of 20 Barefoot Colleges in 14 Indian states. The establishment, he says, is sceptical: 'No one could believe that a semi-literate woman who's passed five years of schooling can solar electrify an entire village, repair and maintain it, and treat it as a way of life; as if there's nothing extraordinary about it. This demystification of technology, putting it in the hands of ordinary people, will take lightyears for engineers to understand.'

And Roy's methods have had remarkable results. Training local people to install and maintain solar systems, the college has brought electric lighting to 100 Himalayan villages at a fraction of the cost of mains power. It has also established 150 night schools, run by an elected Children's Parliament, where 4,000 7-14 year-olds learn about their own culture. 'The current prime minister looks after ten goats in the morning, but she is the PM at night,' says Roy. 'If she happens to write me a postcard saying: 'This teacher is not working', he is fired.'

The same ethos informed the construction of the Barefoot College's own solar-powered campus, which was supervised by an illiterate local handyman. In 2001, the campus won the prestigious Aga Khan Prize for Architecture but when the Aga Khan's officials insisted on crediting the architect – whose blueprints, Roy says, were only needed in order to get planning approval – the college returned the prize.

The college has also pioneered the revival of traditional rainwater collection techniques. Rejecting expensive boreholes, water pipes and dams, it attracts children to its night schools by distributing nine million litres of rainwater annually. And by demonstrating how local people can build rainwater tanks in the mountains of Sikkim, the college has 'changed the whole water policy of Sikkim State,' says Roy. 'Now the chief minister is just collecting rainwater, and if any engineer tells him he's doing something wrong, he sends them to see our tank.'

On the campus, 70 of the buildings are geodesic domes, built from scrap metal by a villager. 'Peanuts it cost!' exclaims Roy. 'A prominent architect brings out a design, a blacksmith makes it. No hassle. You don't need to go through architectural school to do that: he just sees it and does it on his own. This innate knowledge and skill you see everywhere in the world, but you don't give people the opportunity to do it. The Barefoot College does that, and I think more opportunities like this must be created in the UK.'

The Barefoot College is empowering communities, making a real difference to the lives of thousands. And it's doing so on a shoestring budget, using as capital the energy and enthusiasm of people normally seen as passive and unskilled. So, what does Roy's mother think of his unusual lifestyle now? 'Ah,' he smiles, 'she got used to it eventually.'

© Reprinted courtesy of Regeneration and Renewal

Affirmation

By three journalists from the *First City* publication
Originally published in *First City*, March 2005

First City at Barefoot College, Tilonia, District Ajmer, Rajasthan. Following Magsaysay awardee Bunker Roy's dream, as a people-powered, internet-connected, solar-energised, rainwater harvested, drip-irrigated economy makes a self-sufficient reality.

This is the story of how a one-man interview preoccupation became a crash course in development and philosophy – beyond the jargon. How that one-man story led to many others (which in turn led back to him, full circle); each one a story of indomitable spirit.

PS: Heed the warning when Bunker says, 'In a very small way, we are in the business of changing mindsets', because 34 years later, the Barefoot College (BFC) idea has caught on. There are BFCs in the 80 villages neighbouring Tilonia, as well as beyond, in 19 Indian states, and in villages in Ghana, Kenya, Tanzania, Afghanistan, Sierra Leone, South Africa, and Senegal.

It (designated interview dates) completely, deliberately slipped my mind,' was the wry, chuckled confession, immediately followed by the near-order, 'Go to Tilonia. Then we'll speak.' Instructions to ask for a 'Vasu' or 'Laxman Singh' once there, and the zzzz-monotone of a dead exchange. Another phase in the catch-Bunker Roy-if-you-can chase.

To figure out the elusive Mr. Roy, somewhat of a legend for having placed a village in Rajasthan on the global consciousness, we take the seven-odd hours road trip to Tilonia. Some kilometres after Dudu, an hour from Jaipur, we get off the Jaipur-Ajmer highway. We expect a dirt track but it is a smooth 5-kilometre tarmac ride into the campus; the first of the surprises here, immediately followed by another. A white, geodesic internet *dhaba*. Inside, 55-year-old Noorti Bai sits cross-legged in front of a computer screen, teaching a young boy how to make water maps.

She's been in Tilonia since 1981. Ask how she picked up computer skills, instead she chooses to first tell us about more immediate (and perhaps tougher?) concerns. Among them, water scarcity and drought ('You should save water, you know a bit like you keep a bank balance,' she advises), forced prostitution, and the *mazdoor* (labourer) problem of minimum wage and a 100-workday guarantee, a case that she won in the Supreme Court, in 1982. In this context, once you've learnt to read and write, managed with Hindi alphabets like she did as a field worker while filing progress reports on the water table and the night schools, and tackled the women's development issue, computer literacy acquired in six months is no big deal really. She tells us that she has already trained 10 women in computer skills and sent them off to the field, to manage paper work, adding nonchalantly, 'I burn CDs. I also make water maps; work with the Hindi and English (keyboard) keys and I am internet connected.'

It's a validation of Bunker's (not so crazy after all) Tilonia impetus that began 'soon after leaving college, when I deepened and blasted open wells for water for five years' (1967-1971). 'That meant going down a 100-foot open well by rope, and blasting it with explosives. I lived with very poor and ordinary people under the stars. I heard the simple stories they had to tell of their skills, knowledge and wisdom, which books, lectures and university education can never teach you. My real education started when I saw water diviners, traditional bonesetters, midwives, at work... the humble beginnings of BFC.' And you can't but appreciate why, after giving up the attendant privileges that come with a Doon-Stephen's background (Bunker was also a national squash champion), he maintains, 'I have not given up or sacrificed anything.' Or get his drift, when he quotes Twain's 'Never let school interfere with your education' to back his 'There is a difference between Literacy and Education. Literacy is reading and writing and what you pick up in school. Education is what you receive from your family, your community and your environment. I see great hope in the Illiterate but Educated. I see no hope in the literate, so uneducated about rural realities. It's people with my background, my so-called educational background, my kind which has disappointed me the most. The biggest threat to any sort of development of the rural poor today is the Literate Man/Woman.'

This sentiment gets wholehearted endorsement from a reticent Vasu, who offers 'general dogsbody' managing paper work ('and I like it that way because it gives me my space') as self-description, and everything else as 'academic', when we attempt to trace his Tilonia history, and determine his place in the scheme of things. He sits behind his desk, Ancient Mariner proportions to his brooding, *kurta*-clad figure that fills the room, his tendency for unfinished sentences each time a new thought takes shape, jostling out its three-minute-old predecessor. He shows signs of testiness at the task in hand: Encapsulate the Tilonia brief for yet another Bunker dispatch of Google-age visitors. He relaxes when we say we're camping here for the night, and are not en route to Pushkar. Quick guest-house accommodation and outside-mess (dining) hours lunch arrangements are made. His 'What do you want to focus on? There's lots here,' finds answer in a tentative murmur … 'people…' and we are assigned Laxman Singh, 'trained geologist who prefers to be called a water diviner'. Laxman Singh grins, right on cue, tries the 'You're in safe hands' reassurance that Vasu gives, and then promptly delegates us to a cheerful Ram Niwas he chances upon, because 'There's nothing he doesn't know; he can tell you more than me!'

Ram Niwas, guide and translator for the city slickers, uses our campus walk, undertaken with religious sincerity, as an opportunity to make sure we get the drift of things here. 'No need for paper qualification or certificates, thus Barefoot College. ('Or maybe BFC because you have to take off your shoes before entering any room!' he jokes later). Any villager of any age, willing to work for his village is welcome to the Barefoot College to stay and learn the rural development work going on – solar engineering, drinking water, theatre and puppetry, health, crafts, education — anything that interests them. 'At Tilonia, everyone is constantly learning something new. And the greatest thing is that we work for ourselves, rely on ourselves, apply ourselves to look for solutions to the problems of our community. And if we need certain technical skills, we call people from outside and learn, but the outside experts don't dictate. We adapt it to our needs. The city always ends up as the centre, and we have to change that to keep the future in villages going.'

And at almost every corner in Tilonia, we run into the future: The geodesic pathology lab, manned by Laxman and Gopal, two handicapped boys who trained at a clinic in Jaipur. The Health Centre offers three kinds of treatments – 'mostly bio-chemic and homeopathic because there are no side-effects, allopathic in emergencies (serious cases referred to the city hospital)'. Although it serves as the village hospital, it really is a training centre for the rural youth, turning them into Barefoot health workers, supplementing the *dai's* (midwife's) knowledge with medical updates, conducting monthly family planning camps (on an average 20-25 women come). Again, at the old campus, where we meet Barefoot solar engineer Shabnam. She is explaining the technicalities of the solar cooker to her class of three – Dushmanda from Afghanistan ('Hindi *kam aati hai'* – Hindi is weak but no problem), a girl from Sikkim, and Shabnam's daughter. '*Didi*, (big sister) it is very simple, come I will show you how,' she offers when she sees us observing a young girl take a *degchi* (vessel) of hot water off a solar cooker. A similar 'it is very simple' reassurance comes from wiry turbanned Girdah Ram at the Electrical Centre, when we cannot explain how a fan works. From Killa *gaon* (village) on the Ajmer-Jaipur border 20 kilometres away, Girdha passed out from the Centre-run night school, conducted his own night school for nine years, trained in computers, and is now here to be a solar engineer. 'People lose their *jhijhak* (apprehensions) after coming here because we realise that you only learn through failure,' he says. Adds Ram Niwas: 'No one here is scared of IT.' Dashrath Kumar, the man in charge of the Electrical Centre that supplies 40-kilowatt light to the campus, has, until now, trained 60-70 men and women from Orissa, Bihar, Andhra Pradesh, Jammu & Kashmir, Assam, Sikkim, Madhya Pradesh, Ladakh, Himachal, Tanzania, Ghana, Ethiopia, and Sierra Leone. He explains, 'I have found that it doesn't matter whether someone is literate or illiterate, or what language they speak, because this is all practical training. We are able to understand through gestures, drawings and charts.'

When the frequent refrain of 'Have you met Bhanwar Singh?' finally meets us in flesh, blood and so much humility, it belies the legend associated with the Barefoot architect (and erstwhile driver). He planned and built the new campus with its pink and white bougainvillea arbour walks and drip-irrigation fed flower beds, from blueprints etched in the mud. He visualised the amphitheatre built over an underground water tank that can store four *lakh* litres of water. It is also responsible for the 'natural air conditioning' feature here, born of the ingenious use of upturned *kulhads* (earthenware) in the roofs, so the air stays trapped inside, blocked in by cement on either side, the village women's special grind of *kankari milai chuna* (gravel), and windows placed in a way that allows natural light and air. Bhanwar saw all this grow from the effort of 20-25 masons and 40-45 labourers, over two years and at an extremely low construction cost – Rs.60 per square foot instead of the market rate of Rs.100 per square foot. 'The local *karigars* (artisans) may not know how to make maps but we sure know how to make houses,' he says. 'The only problem I had, was the money ... when they told me I had to spend so many *lakhs*, I wondered what to do with it all!' Bhanwar offers a grudging respect for computer technology, next on his learning agenda. 'I think I probably could've done more if I'd been *padha likha* (literate), because I could've made notes of my ideas and kept them for future use. Like you can fit things in a computer, and even if a man cops it 20 years later, you have the information.'

We stop by Bansi's *chai* shop behind the station at Tilonia Junction (a very Malgudi Days air about it ... and there we go again with our urban distance!) Vasu and gang used to come here for the grapevine, when people in the village were still getting used to the BFC manoeuvres and asking questions like 'Why are you employing handicapped people? Nothing will get done...' Cut to The Present: The entire *Kabaad se Jugaad* (Trash to Treasure) is run by the physically challenged. As we lounge around, treating ourselves to the Tilonia special of Bansi's *kalakand* (milk cake), meticulously scraped out from blackened *kadhai* (wok) and a second round of *kulhadchai* (tea in an earthenware cup), our idle remarks on how quaint the *kulhad* (earthenware) is alerts Ram Niwas. Without realised irony, he tells us that the *kulhad* we are gushing over is actually a caste marker. If we'd come here without him, Bansi would've given us tea in the *sheeshe ke* (made of glass) tumblers that are lined up on the slab behind us. 'Bansi is not associated with the Centre. Caste is not an issue in Tilonia, but I face a lot of prejudice when I work in villages. In fact, when I went to my village with a *katputli* (puppetry) performance, people were outraged that a *Dalit* dared to go up on the *chaupal* (stage). And I was forced to get off. There are still problems today but there were more when I initially started working. And if it hadn't been for all the support I got here, I don't think I would've continued.' He heard of the Centre when they came to install a hand pump for all-caste-use, was intrigued and came looking for them. 'I applied for a *chaprasi ka kaam* (labourer), because I was really desperate, and when they told me that no such work exists, I thought it was just a way of fobbing me off. I appealed to Director Sahib (Bunker) who asked if I was game enough to be an accountant … A completely strange world for me, of paperwork and banks! I was a little scared but he said "Try *karo*"'. Ram Niwas did, and in the process, entered a way of life constantly shaped by the 'try *karo*' dictum. Like his *katputli* shows and singing while at the Tikawada field centre when he decided to switch to the communications team, which led to newer things. 'I was naturally drawn towards theatre. To use it to say what I want to … issues that need to be addressed. And it was during my time spent at the women's group training that I realised I must change my attitude towards women. Till then, I felt I was more advanced than my wife and mother, because I was higher secondary pass, and that what I thought was correct, because I was a man. How strange it was that while I was ready to revolt against caste hierarchy, there was another hierarchy inside my own house! So if we talk of changing things, we really should begin from home.' Close to two decades later, spreading the message from village to village, he admits that he will still have to wed his daughter within his own caste, but having given her the benefits of education, he will also allow her the freedom of choice of groom.

It's a small beginning nevertheless, as Bunker tells you. 'No one can be indifferent to what we are doing in Tilonia. Whatever their personal or professional opinion, no one can say we have not accomplished what we said we would, and shown it on the ground.' And here's where the tiny matter of attitude shift comes in: alternate aspirations, an alternate anthem. 'Civil society has failed Bharat, not India. They have compromised the very spirit of volunteerism. They do not know what sacrifice means. They have not set an example of simplicity, of compassion, of humility, of courage (as Ernest Hemingway defined it "Grace under pressure"). Civil society has no role models to offer. All we see is greed and materialism around us and there is nothing that sets civil society apart. The only sign of success is how much money you make or how big your business is ...' And a question still in the process of being phrased ... 'What I expect from you?' And an answer more articulate than our questions. 'I expect people, who unfortunately have the power and the money to do incalculable harm, to listen and learn. As far as the Government and the bureaucracy is concerned, the role for the BFC is to re-educate and take them through a slow process of un-learning. Demonstrate to them what is possible. They are beyond teaching and quite un-trainable in practice, but if they see what they have always considered impossible, then it makes all the difference. In a very small way, we are in the business of changing mind-sets. A semi-literate rural woman as a solar engineer or an illiterate woman feeding information in a computer is, for the bureaucrat, in the realm of the impossible.'

The spirit of innovating and adapting, constantly searching for the practical alternative, finds breeding ground in the night schools which Vasu describes as 'important because it is a space for rural working children. Since everything is in terms of crops, their animals, the grazing ground –- night schools are the only places they can fantasise in.' He adds, 'Every time we feel low, we go and hang out in a night school in progress, and without a mood instigator, we comply with the excited arrangements, only to enter a potentially explosive situation.'

Groups of four to 14-year olds sit huddled around solar lamps, the gleam in their eyes a dead giveaway to the fact that this can disintegrate into a laugh-a-riot at the slightest provocation. In our case, it was how we couldn't muster wits enough to sing a folk song ('no film songs!') after the preliminary round of introductions that began with name, age, village, class, what they did during the day (this differed from housekeeping to grazing the goats) and whatever they volunteered between muffled hilarity and camera flash distraction. It brings to mind Vasu's 'These children are really uninhibited ... so much so I sometimes find myself inhibited when I am with them! And it is really amazing to see this small girl with two three huge buffaloes meekly following her!' A deep in work but soon persuaded Gopal Singh (just taken over as night in-charge) tells us, 'Reading, writing, addition, subtraction have their place, but we also concentrate on the practical knowledge that we can give them. Once a child in a night school was asked, "Which leader would you like to emulate?" He answered, "I guess they're all OK but not really relevant to us. We are more interested in the problems of our village and in information that directly benefits us, what'll help us earn later."' The Children's Parliament at Tilonia follows from this, helping children understand the election process, 'important because when they participate in the village *panchayat* (village council) election as adults, we hope they have enough *rajnaitik samajh* (political wisdom) to not vote along caste lines but to vote along *nirdaliya* (independence) lines,' he says. Children between 9 and 13 fill in forms, campaign (there have been cases of candidates being disqualified because they distributed toffees), and the winners form a cabinet in Tilonia, and meet monthly. The feared children's *panchayat* ('I haven't been hauled up by the youth parliament, but the doctor has!' says Vasu) has managed feats. It collected Rs. 40,000 for a piped water system, at the initiative of an 11-year-old PM. For the last five years, the PMs have been girls, prompting a campaigning male candidate to ask whether he'd need reservation to be elected! 'This, in a place where women are not seen at the tea stalls,' emphasises Ram Niwas. Since we're still struggling for a non-film *lok geet* (folk song), we can leave them with, we choose to distract them with our curiosity. Like what would the voting 'uns like to change about their village? Neeta, to the collective assent of all the girls: 'We want to wear jeans, but our grandparents object. Even being allowed to wear *salwar kameez* (pyjama-type trousers and long shirt) was quite a battle.'

Vasu first met Bunker some 30 years ago at Aruna Roy's place. 'So I asked him the first logical question, "What do you do?" And he gave me his usual Buddha silence. So I asked him the next logical question, "Where do you live?" He said, Tilonia, and told me a little about the place. My last logical question was, "Can I come?" I caught the night train and reached here. And since then, there's been no looking back.' Over 30-something years later, over evening chai, bench-prophet philosopher to his audience of three,

Vasu debates if Tilonia is about ideals working out for real. 'Yes,' he deliberates, 'but when you are in this kind of a scenario – a semi-feudal status and globalisation going on hand in hand – you tend to get a little confused. And I think the moral of the story is that it's always better to be confused than clear, because then you think you've got all your answers and solutions. We've made mistakes, but we've not made the same ones again. And we have not done badly at all.' He still marvels that 'all it really took was three people to get together. Bunker, a cartographer and a typist. At that time, there were 12 or 14 other such experiments of living in a village to try and understand its problems which attracted university graduates, post-graduates, professionals, but we are the survivors.' All the credit, he feels, goes to the 'code of ethics' that helped 'certain "non-negotiables" get concretised. Decentralisation of the development process, also of technology, so it could be easily replicated, else we'd just be spare-part technicians. Taking a living wage and not a market wage, a collective decision-making process, faith in the rule of law, and a level playing field – equality in terms of gender and class. At the maximum, one can earn about Rs.5,000 and that need not be the Director, and no one gets less than a minimum wage,' explains Vasu. The rationale is echoed by Bunker, who works for a 'somewhere in the middle' Rs.2,000 monthly salary because 'Why should the Boss get the highest amount?'

Also a bit Utopian, concedes Vasu ('But we all need a Utopia. That's why I came here. It was the *adda* (haunt) of thinkers, social workers, doctors, chartered accountants…), given to the occasional rants, when tougher demands, or the inclination towards 'different processes', see many come and go, like the many who came and implemented 'successful failures' in the last 30 years. 'But,' Vasu emphasises, 'when your back is against the wall, that's when you find that people who matter will not turn away. That's when people stick (together). And that's where the difference is. And I don't get tired of saying this to anyone who comes to Tilonia – it is these people who have accepted me, put up with my idiosyncrasies. Why beat around the bush, it was people like me…' Thoughts chasing each other for an impending confession. 'When we came in the beginning, our ego got a big battering, because you know, we were *padha-likha* (literate), urban-educated professionals and all that. But the sense here is that a person's value is not in terms of his educational degree. I found it a bit uncomfortable to deal with in the beginning and it took me a long time to realise but it has had a sobering effect on me; it has in fact, been humbling. So you see, these "non-negotiables" are very important for us, because this gives us an opportunity every now and then to have a reality check, and if we are honest to ourselves, to make that 180-degree turn the other way round. This leaves you room for improvement.' And a damn good perspective to boot. 'The crazier the idea, it can be applied in Tilonia! We have no hang-ups with someone coming and saying, "This is a low cost/no cost idea, can we try this?" That's how so many things have failed, so many have succeeded. We brought in exotic Mexican beasts from Chandigarh that flew away, and the one that remained was hen-pecked by the country variety!' A bellow of laughter follows. He resumes, more serious, 'This is something that education doesn't teach you – it doesn't teach you the importance of failure. But don't make the same mistakes twice, because remember you are playing with lives.'

This Tilonia fulcrum of crazy ideas wherein workable practices are formulated gets further affirmed the next morning, when we catch the 'water diviner' who'd abandoned his assigned tour guide position. 'Do I get bothered by people? That's a strange question, but I'll try to answer it as best as I can,' he laughs. 'People come here, very curious to know about what's going on, and we always give people a heartfelt welcome, teaming them up with someone with a matching frequency. If you don't get along with me, you can meet Ram Niwasji…' sets the tone for his quirky humour (not without a bite!) Also an 'unlearner', he wears his mantle nonchalantly. 'I am a geologist as far as academic records are concerned. I specialised in hydro-geology, focussing on ground water exploration. I guess that knowledge is okay, it has scientific basis, the technology and instruments are impressive, the theory and explanation too, but its failure and success rate don't compare all that well with the ordinary diviner's knowledge and skills. I have tried to find an explanation for it, and I realised that the knowledge comes from careful study of the drainage pattern of the land, the exposed surface of the rock, its parent rock, the kind of plants that grow in the area, and most importantly, how well the structure of the land favours water absorption and how it impounds the water, thereby creating an underground water source. These are things that an instrument will not tell you. Is there a magic beyond this which helps villagers locate a water source? I don't know, but personally speaking, I think it is also little bit about a feeling. It has been my experience; you concentrate while walking over a pocket of land, and suddenly, you have this feeling that this particular step of yours will help you find water, and in what quantity, of what quality, and at what depth.' Traditional water divining skills helped the Tilonia team lay water pipes in Ladakh, when trained engineers had given up, convinced that there was no underground water source for at least 130 metres. 'Now, they get water even in minus 30 degrees Celsius,' says Laxman Singh, 'and you cannot call it a *karishma* (miracle) just because no syllabus teaches this or because there is no apparent scientific basis, because after all, it does give you practical solutions.' Like most conversations, differences in intensity and context notwithstanding, this too is a near-Bunker echo, with the same test-fired conviction. 'Life here is good,' muses Laxman Singh, 'I need not take permission from a "*Sahab*" (superior), it is very *khulla* (open) here. We can try everything. Bunker once suggested we try rainwater harvesting in the mountains. I thought, "*Chalo, Bunker aap Bangali dimaag se soch rahe hai*" (Come on, Bunker, you are thinking with your Bengali mind). Everyone thought *paagal ho gaya hai* (he has gone mad), how can this work in Sikkim? But he went ahead and made a tank at the top of a mountain to store water up to 1.5 *lakh* litres. Nothing happened in the first year, and everyone started criticising. But, the next winter, there was water in the tank. Tank full! All the villages in the south district of Sikkim have now adopted this technology.'

Bunker's '*bangali dimaag*' (Bengali mind) is the subject of many a smiling reverie ('How do I know what Laxman Singh means by that?' retorts Bunker), also cause for many a confident Barefooter, for the affection he inspires in Tilonia, for many avoided interviews (!) and an exploration of a side by Ram Niwas. 'I will show you how he behaves with us,' and we get a quirky, impromptu puppet spoof via the Bunker puppet, as he clears his throat, the prelude to a peremptory, school principal-ish inquisition (amusingly familiar). 'Hmmm. How did you like it here? What did you see? Did you meet people? *Kaam karne waalon se baat cheet hui?* (Did you talk to the working people?)' But Ram Niwas is quick with a context to his puppet caricature. 'There were questions in our mind that if Bunker works so hard for the village, then why doesn't he stay here for long periods of time? It is only now that I've realised the enormous responsibilities he has, how he needs to travel for funds, etcetera. When we first staged this, we were worried, but he just laughed! That was great,' grins Ram Niwas respectfully. And 'Oh God! That Ram Niwas,' groans Bunker when we let him on the Bunker puppet surprise that followed our introduction to *Jokhim Chacha* (Jokhim Uncle) and *Bua* (Aunty) with (brilliant, we may add) masks and other puppets (Aruna Roy and Vasu, for example) for company. 'It shows that the organisation is healthy. To be able to laugh at and crack jokes on me show at least they think I am human!' Try separating the gruff principal act from the man, and you get 'BR is a bit of a recluse and has managed to avoid publicity of any kind that brings him into the public eye. Notice how I have managed to avoid you', followed by a surprisingly candid, 'I distance myself from people, because I do not want people to get close to me. Aruna is one of the few people who is allowed to get close but if you ask her, she will tell you she still does not know me.'

And to our badgering him about the legend behind Bunker Roy, he says, 'There is no aura. I feel a sense of mission and there is nothing great about that. On the contrary, it makes you feel humble and awed by the task ahead. I feel an urge and an urgency to do something tangible and lasting and use (misuse) all my influence to reach the rural poor and see them live and develop with dignity and self- respect.' He concedes, 'In this day and age, that is really too much to ask, so it is an eternal struggle.' And not surprising that he says, 'No, never felt like giving up. The thought never crossed my mind since 1967. The struggle and the challenge make it worthwhile. And the thought that I have managed to help so many people has kept me going.

I do not expect gratitude or thanks. I am doing it for myself. It is a personal exclusive journey, (this) finding out more about yourself. Dealing with simple life and death situations every day, and knowing that I could make a tangible difference, keeps me going. Tilonia, which he describes variously as 'great job satisfaction', 'a challenge every day', 'not one lifetime's work but many in one!' At multiple levels, it is also 'watching many babies grow up all over India - from a distance. So many BFCs started all over India now have their own identity, their own legal status, their own independence, all on their own. And some, even larger than Tilonia. Does it unsettle him that Tilonia (and the other 'babies') can carry on without him? 'That you are indispensable?' He checks, 'The best feeling in the world is to be dispensable in your lifetime!'

© Reprinted with kind permission of First City
First City was a Delhi city magazine that published its
final issue in October 2013

The UN and Poverty II
Why the Millennium Goals Won't Work

Bunker Roy

Originally published in *International Herald Tribune*,
14 September 2005

In 1978, when Robert McNamara, then president of the World Bank, and McGeorge Bundy, president of the Ford Foundation, spent a night at the Barefoot College here in Tilonia, McNamara asked a man whose family lived on much less than a dollar a day what he looked forward to in life. He smiled and said very quietly, 'Two square meals a day.'

I remember the stunned silence even today and think back to that meeting when I read the United Nations' report on its Millennium Development Goals (MDGs) for 2005. For all the high-powered officials who put the report together and for all the 25 UN agencies and international donor groups it depends on, it reflects a naive and gullible attitude towards poverty.

The virtual reality in which its authors live, full of action plans, road maps and fact sheets, is frightening. They should listen to someone who has lived and worked for the last 34 years with the rural poor. Eradicating extreme poverty and hunger (MDG No. 1) does not need indicators and databases. Only intellectual activists who have no idea how to reach the poor need those.

So long as governments in the Global South are powerless to break the hold of corrupt private contractors and larcenous village-level politicians, the poor will never be free from want or free from fear, whatever the UN report envisions. The possible solution? Get every government in the Global South to work towards a Right to Information Act like India's. Ensure transparency and accountability, with rural communities putting pressure on Government from below to disclose how much money has been spent. Ask Transparency International. They will help.

If we want to achieve universal primary education (MDG No. 2), UNESCO's approach has not worked. With 60 per cent of the poorest rural children not going to school in the morning because they have to help with domestic chores, far from a solution the development report offers only a demonstration of an inability to think out of the box. But there's a common-sense people's solution – have school at night.

Few government teachers sleep in the villages. So train literate but unemployed rural youth as part-time 'barefoot' teachers by the thousands, all over the world, to run the night schools.

Are the development report's authors aware that the tremendous work that community-based groups are doing in primary education is not reflected in the official statistics either of UNESCO or of governments? This is because their work is still not valued or recognised and never will be, because it is a threat to village officials who represent Government and who do not believe in changing the status quo.

There are many innovative ways of empowering women (MDG No. 3) used by community-based groups the world over. In my experience, to the disbelief of urban paper-qualified experts, semi-literate rural women have become solar and water engineers and have begun repairing hand pumps, building rainwater tanks in schools, solar electrifying villages and feeding data into computers without any technical help from outside.

Speaking of rainwater, it falls on the roofs of schools everywhere. It should be collected, by the billions of gallons, for drinking and flushing toilets. Expensive centralised technology solutions with hand pumps or piping systems must be phased out. This simple solution to meet a basic minimum need will advance not only MDG No. 7, which specifically calls for greater access to safe drinking water, but almost every other MDG as well, either directly or indirectly.

We do not need the World Health Organisation in the villages: it's so simple and inexpensive to upgrade the skills of traditional midwives, improve their confidence and build on their knowledge. Where these small community-managed steps have been taken to involve the traditional medicinal systems, child mortality has fallen sharply, maternal health has improved and waterborne diseases have been tackled more effectively (MDG Nos 3–6).

If the primary focus is really on ending poverty, the partnerships we need to strengthen are of a sort other than trade (MDG No. 8): partnerships between poor communities so that they learn from one another and share traditional, practical knowledge and skills. Importing expensive, unworkable ideas, equipment and consultants from the Global North simply destroys the capacity of communities to help themselves.

Any goal that is driven from the top by international donors and governments not accountable to the communities and without financial transparency is doomed to fail. That model encourages colossal falsification of figures, the excessive hiring of private consultants and contractors, conflicts of interest and a massive patronage system.

When poor communities think at the human level, all their goals are interconnected. But under the present top-down model, in the absence of a global grassroots movement with the communities as equal partners, the goals have been broken up compartmentally into project mode to suit donors and governments.

That's the ultimate recipe for disaster, and that's why the MDGs will be achieved only on paper.

Bunker Roy is the founder of the Barefoot College and chairman of the Global Rainwater Harvesting Collective. A complete list of the Millennium Development Goals and the related UN report can be found at www.un.org/millenniumgoals.

7: The Experience of Tilonia

Heather MC Malcolm and Aruna Roy

A good friend once said that coming to Tilonia was like coming into an oasis of peace and caring. It was a place where knowledge, both traditional and 'modern', was shared and ideas were welcomed. It was a place where the visitor quickly became a member of the family, sitting companionably to drink tea and share thoughts about anything and everything that bothered or intrigued them.

Such openness and acceptance is the gift of a culture where most people live on less than US$4 a day. In this culture, there's a curiosity and interest in people, which has permeated the Barefoot College. In Tilonia, people share what they know: there are no copyrights, no hierarchies and no hegemony. The sharing leads to the strengthening of real knowledge and skills, and stands in quiet but strong opposition to the greed and competition of the acquisitive world.

Indeed, in a sense, Barefoot is its own world – rich in ideas. It's a world where Gandhi's 'last man' is comfortable squatting on the floor and exchanging thoughts – a stark contrast to the rich person's universe in which, for many years, we have struggled for access to internet data.

Bunker saw the divide between the rural and the urban. But he also saw the two as compatible and complimentary. Barefoot College has crafted the sense of equality and camaraderie that comes from learning by doing, and learning for all, with grace and dignity.

Both Gandhi's dream of rural India and Nehru's determination to bring scientific thought and industrial growth were necessary for the building of a new India. A major aspect of the Barefoot way was, and is, to work with demystifying technology, and to couch rural knowledge in a terminology acceptable to the marginally literate. Another is to challenge traditional misinformation through explaining, demonstrating and adopting scientific reasoning and those modern techniques that address needs. As Bunker has often said, technology must work for the people, and to make this happen is the task of those of us who understand that knowledge must not be in the control of the few.

Barefoot College redefined education, literacy and schooling. To Barefoot, education was knowledge in which literacy helped but was not of critical importance, while literacy had to shed its arrogance and stop claiming superiority in the face of knowledge gleaned over centuries. The Barefoot view was that, while school trained children formally in the skills of how to learn, every single day the community taught many things casually and informally. The community educates us about life.

Tilonia saw development through the eyes of the people for whom it was planned. They did not prioritize their needs. To the people of rural India, education, health, water, women's issues, poverty and work, livelihood and crafts all stood equally important on the shelf of necessity. Understanding this, Barefoot saw that the answer must be to integrate development. This is a concept that stands in opposition to the 'target' approach, where isolated development issues remain unrelated to a whole and rounded lifestyle and vision.

Pivotal ideas such as these, as well as techniques for putting them into practice, were seeded as Bunker and his colleagues travelled widely through India and abroad, communicating their conviction that people had to be at the centre of any plans for their development. Through stories drawn from their experience, they were able to show how much more successful implementation is when it is rooted in the reality of the people for whom plans are made. Having heard them, scholars, volunteers and researchers have spread the spirit of the Barefoot approach, not only all over India but also through much of the global south.

Barefoot managed to connect and build a community of people who shared a vision. SAMPDA[7] is a network of Barefooters with separate identities, and is present in 19 Indian states. In addition,

---

[7] Society for Activating, Motivating, and Promoting Development Alternatives

similar affiliations beyond India's shores came into being as international volunteers, scholars, researchers, doctors, and writers came to Tilonia, to live and work for a while in 'the Tilonia way'. One result of this is that books appeared, such as the one that Italian author Maria Pace Ottieri wrote about Bunker. Maria Ottieri's book was published in Italian, and she called it '*Raggiungere l'Ultimo Uomo*' ("Reaching the Last Man"), a title which evokes one of Gandhi's most celebrated sayings: 'I will give you a Talisman. Whenever you are in doubt, or when the self becomes too much with you, apply the following test: Recall the face of the poorest and the weakest man whom you may have seen, and ask yourself if the step you contemplate is going to be of any use to him.'

Six Good Reasons to Go the Tilonia Way

Bunker Roy

Originally published in *Yojana*, April 1-15 1983

I LIKE TO THINK OF TILONIA not so much as a project but more as a Movement. People like to think of us more by the name of the village – Tilonia - than by the name of the project – Social Work and Research Centre (SWRC) – which I feel is a good start because it identifies us with people, the very people we have been working with the last 10 years.

It is time we asked ourselves, have we done well? Let others judge. We started with four professionals – a geologist, a geophysicist, a cartographer and an odd job person in late 1972. Now, there are more than 400 of us professionals and para-professionals spread over the states of Rajasthan, Haryana, Himachal Pradesh, Gujarat, Orissa, Union Territory of Delhi, Tamil Nadu, Madhya Pradesh. The professionals include geologists, doctors, geophysicists, teachers, engineers, agricultural graduates, nurses, soil chemists, economists, chartered accountants, sociologists, anthropologists and village-level, village-trained para-professionals who are being trained constantly with a view to taking over the management of Tilonia in the foreseeable future.

Each one of these sub-centres of Tilonia is autonomous, some more fiercely independent than others, all obliged to procure their own funds, recruit people and chalk out their own method of working. The time has come for them to register separately and the process has begun. The time has come for them to branch out on their own and establish their own identify in the State.

The Different Options

Tilonia provides young professionals with different options offering opportunities to find out what they want to do, to decide which field they would like to work in and which they would like to adopt: Tilonia gives them the time to make up their minds, provides them with the institutional support to choose the area (state, district, block, village) to train identified village people, preferably Scheduled Castes, in health, education, supplementary skills and communication with a view to taking over the responsibilities of the professional in the future and hopefully the leadership of his own community from the village he comes from. It has started yielding encouraging results. Is this doing well?

I wonder. Giving an opportunity for professionals and Scheduled Castes, rural artisans, rural women to grow into responsible vocal and confident human beings is, perhaps, not what many so-called experts would call doing well. It is, after all, intangible and we have no yardstick to judge this process. But if we have put 500 hand pumps in Scheduled Caste areas, trained over 50 *dais* and trained more than 400 women under TRYSEM, that is more easily understood as doing well. If, since Tilonia started more than 3,000 children, all first-generation learners, have been through our evening schools and nearly 1,000 women have attended our family planning camps and more than 2,000 impoverished agricultural labourers turned farmers have been assisted to improve their land and increase their income, then people would of course like to know *how*. More important is, even if we explain the process of how we have managed to achieve these modest accomplishments, can it be followed by others? Are others in a position to learn from this example we have set or will they say: 'We can only admire, we cannot copy!'? In which case, the purpose is defeated because Tilonia has shown by setting an example of how it can be copied not by extraordinary people with an extremely high degree of motivation but by average plus human beings. Let us for the moment discuss HOW.

The Six Good Reasons

One

Tilonia's appeal to the young professional is different. We do not expect him to be dedicated, but committed; we do not expect sacrifice but consistency and perseverance. We expect him to look on rural development as a professional challenge rather than a social service. We respect him for his skill and knowledge and treat him as such by paying him. This makes him accountable and answerable to Tilonia and the community. Tilonia has never had problems finding young people who want to live and work in the villages, in spite of the fact that we do not have the expected physical comforts like electricity and running water.

Two

We are not influenced or guided by ideological considerations. Tilonia feels every approach is relevant, is important, and needs to be tried out by any person who believes in it. So, there is room for a *Sarvodaya*, a *Ramakrishna*, a Marxist, a social service, a professional and a charity approach and Tilonia provides this umbrella to young men and women who want to try out these approaches within the law of the land. To each his own. We provide the atmosphere and the area for people to test their beliefs, to try their strengths and weaknesses, and learn from their experiences.

Three

There is unity in diversity here: unity of purpose and diversity in methods and approaches. The purpose is to integrate services and lifestyles at the village level. It is to learn from the rural people and go through a process of unlearning ourselves. It is to train people, the poorer people, and provide them with the tools and the skills to help them become better leaders in their own community and more responsible citizens in the area. It is to build up the confidence of the people and make them demand funds and programmes earmarked for their own welfare; in other words, make them more aware. It is to de-mystify technology to the extent desirable and possible and use rural technology – what we have discarded as useless and primitive – for development purposes and make it respectable.

Four

Tilonia believes in organisations not institutions. To do rural development work and bring about fundamental change, the existence of an organisation is essential. It should be accountable to Government (registration, audit statements, etc.) as well as to the people, the beneficiaries, and there should be flexibility and freedom enough for a change in thinking, in strategies, in emphasis and in shifting responsibility (from the professional to the trained, village-based para-professional). For instance, at the end of the year, all the members of SWRC staff give each other points to evaluate each other's performance. This self-evaluation could decide the rise and fall of salaries and everyone, regardless, has to go through this scrutiny. We do not believe in salary scales or that educational qualification is more important than experience.

Organisations tend to become institutes, and in due course, cease to be either effective or in close touch with the people. To avoid such complications, Tilonia has deliberately spawned smaller groups spread far apart so that each does not influence the other if their approaches are different.

Five

Tilonia's definition of community assets in a village differs substantially from the accepted conventional version. To my mind, it is wrong to identify 'community assets' with inanimate things like buildings and roads, quite apart from the fact that the whole community does not use them. In any case, 'community assets' really means the human assets that the village uses that are accessible to all: live human beings like shop-keepers (tea shop, provisions) priests, moneylenders, *dhobis* and *lambardars* (village headmen). Their community skills in communication, in education, in medicine and in disseminating the right sort of knowledge are grossly un-utilised and, in fact, are not even recognised by Government as community assets: we are so cut off from reality.

Six

The need to replicate non-governmental organisations (NGOs), the need to come together on one platform, the need to learn from each other has been long overdue. The feeling that Government alone cannot respond to the demands and need of the people, the suspicion that alternatives have to be found and bold experiments tried out, the conviction that voluntary agencies need to be supported more and more in growing with the Establishment and encouraging moves of bringing NGOs and Government together on one platform is gaining sympathy in many states. The Rajasthan Government has set a fine example in forming a Consultative Group and there are signs that Himachal Pradesh will follow along with Orissa, Tamil Nadu and Bihar.

Involving the Have-Nots

In the ultimate analysis, the issue is people's participation. Not the whole community, not the rural rich, not the people who control public opinion, not the upper and the more influential castes who have abused their positions in rural society, but the 40 per cent of those who live below the poverty line who have never seen or heard of (let alone read) the Constitution of India, who are never free from hunger and want. The key factor of HOW we can do well depends to what extent we can mobilise, involve, the people who are more non-persons than citizens. To a considerable extent, Tilonia and its satellite centres have managed to bring these people around to participate, to ask questions and seek answers – and it has not been without problems.

Who is stopping us from doing well? What is preventing us from doing better? We, ourselves: we educated people can be the most narrow-minded, inflexible and ignorant, and what is worse, we blame the rural poor for not responding to alien, outlandish and ludicrous ideas.

Look at the Sixth Plan document: it is the most radical, most daring and indeed the most challenging of documents ever to come out of the Planning Commission. If only we got down to practising what we are preaching! The Planning Commission has called for the 'mobilisation of people', has committed itself on record and said that unless the participation of people in development programmes is achieved, no lasting change is possible. It has pleaded for reducing inequalities, for social justice, for removing poverty and suggested that one way would be to organise the poor and demand their share. Brave new words.

It is suggesting, in fact, the politicisation of development. It is implying that when the Government forms a cooperative of sorts it is development, but when the poor get together on their own initiative, it is politics, which is the sort of development we need at the moment. This is what self-help is all about.

People's participation is a movement that must necessarily be anti-establishment. To think that those representing the Establishment will sincerely work towards undermining their own hold and influence on the poor at their own expense is like chasing a crooked shadow. To break this hold, the threat must come from outside the Establishment and it is one of the vital functions of NGOs to see this potential threat exists.

Community Accountability

The other meaning of people's participation is community accountability. The NGO must prepare the poor, must educate the poor, must be there to guide them but finally, when it comes to testing the system, it is the people's organisation that must do it. Obviously, no village-level bureaucrat would welcome a system where he has to account for his deeds and performance to someone he has always considered inferior. The fact that they are already having to face a threat from MLAs and *pradhans* which makes them work a trifle harder is a source of much resentment. If such power percolates down to the *gram panchayat* level to the s*arpanch* to the village community leaders from the *patwari's* point of view it will be disastrous. From the people's point of view, this should be our goal. It will make the system move, it will ensure that funds reach the right people and it is well spent. Isn't this what we want?

The question of duplicating services at the village level is obviously the first step. We have a private and public sector at the national level, at the state level and at the district level, so why not at the village level? When bureaucrats ask me: why duplicate services? my answer is: where is this not being done? There are private practitioners in villages duplicating health services, water diviners virtually taking the place of geologists, *bal mandir*s (schools for small children) and evening schools taking the place of government schools or competing where schools are running. Government cooperative societies are being run by *banias* (merchants), who have made a mockery of the Cooperative Movement, and no one says a thing. Shopkeepers are actually sponsored by Government to sabotage the consumer societies and everyone keeps mum. The answer is to have a supplementary service that offers the rural poor an option to pick and choose, to offer a healthy competition so that people start asking questions, like how is it that Tilonia can install a hand pump in one week and it takes the Government four months? How is it that it takes the Government six months to repair a pump while Tilonia can respond within 10 days? The process of questioning is the beginning of awareness.

The Mythical System

The next step is to de-link literacy from education, and qualification from experience. This whole edifice, built on a mythical system and expectation of competence, has proven to be a colossal failure and alternatives not only need to be found but tried out in the field and given every encouragement. Of course, the people who are dead against the very idea are the so-called educated who have a vested interest in keeping this system going. In the village, however, there is an entirely different way of looking at things. Why must we impose these strange ideas on the poor and expect them to toe the line? If you look at what is being taught in primary schools, the teachers who are supposedly teaching in primary schools and the subjects being taught, I submit that what the poor families are doing by keeping their children away from morning schools is about the wisest move that sensible families could make. If 70 per cent of the primary school age going children are not going to school, it is not a reflection on the poor, it is a severe indictment of us. But we refuse to look at it that way. We are literate – how can we be uneducated? Paper degrees give us protection, they safely hide incompetence and generate unemployables. So what?

As it Goes at Tilonia

At Tilonia, we have set an example by de-linking qualification from experience. Our health programme is run by a village-level health worker who has a degree in some arts subject from Kishengarh, but he knows more about health and medicine than most MBBS doctors. When the Deputy Director General of Health Services, Government of India, saw the quality of the slides he made, he could not believe it. Doctors with MBBS degrees and ANMs as their qualification have to work under him or we do not consider their appointment in Tilonia. Our education programme which involves the running of 30 night schools for 1,500 dropout children in 30 villages is run by a priest who has no degree, and he has B.Ed trained teachers working under him.

The agricultural extension programme is looked after by a youth from the village who has no qualification in agriculture but has produced tremendous results. The traditional media section where puppetry is the most prominent means of communicating messages is run by a one-time sheep farmer who has received no training in this art: he has just picked it up. Our soil chemist was trained by ICAR scientists under their Rural Orientation programme.

Our geologists are expert trainers in the repairs and maintenance of hand pumps: they have already conducted 3-4 courses with UNICEF assistance, thus proving that mechanical engineers are not really required, just common sense. The women's programme, the training of traditional midwives, the establishment of *balwadi*s (village child daycare centres) and their training are looked after by a widow whose only paper qualification is a diploma in *Ayurvedic* medicine. A social anthropologist with a degree from Chandigarh and a sociologist with a degree from Jawaharlal Nehru University have to work under her and listen to her when it comes to her experience with women in the area. When the Government came to discuss the ICDS training of *anganwadi* (village child daycare centre workers) with us and we insisted on the importance of de-linking qualification and experience, the point was immediately rejected even though on many occasions Government have said ICDS is a flexible programme, that there is room for experimentation and voluntary agencies must be involved.

Many interesting issues emerge: does this approach produce results? Do the rural poor think the way Tilonia does on this particular point? The sort of integration that is evident in the village, the overlapping of responsibilities that lead to many functions being performed by the same man – hardly qualified to do the job – is this really the answer, or is this bifurcation and compartmentalisation so typical of governments the only way?

If we want to do a job well in the rural areas, is it not important that we learn from the likes of Tilonia? Why should the HOW that we suggest, so eminently simple, scandalise experts? To do the job really well, one has to take risks, one has to try something out of the ordinary. Tilonia is doing that and will continue to do that. The effort is all.

© *Yojana/Kurukshetra, Publications Division, Ministry of I&B, Government of India.*

Why Not Now Demystify This Technology!

Bunker Roy

Originally published in *Yojana*, January 26 1985

Good understanding of the existing conditions in rural India and psyche of its poor is the pre-requisite to achieving breakthrough in the sphere of technology transfer, argues the author, and narrates in detail all that happens when the so-called experts plan their strategies living away from the scene. He examines here the UNICEF designed 3-tier system, 'adopted without much thought' by all state governments, for providing drinking water to problem villages. The real answer to the problem, he asserts, is his Hand Pump Mistri and not what is being tried to be sold.

I WISH WE WERE a bit more balanced and open over this issue of technology transfer for the rural poor. This word 'technology' has come to mean many things to many people. What we associate with this word today is either irrelevant or unrelated to solving the problems of the rural poor. With our extremely limited exposure to the actual real-life, immediate and urgent problems of the poor, if we are not pontificating on what technological options are available for the rural poor, we are doing the next worst thing of thrusting it down their throats, thus impoverishing them more in the process.

Technology, as we know it now, is modern, vague, frightfully expensive and exploitative, and to nearly 300 million people in this country, the benefits are indirect, intangible and by and large invisible. This has happened because we have had to take someone else's word for it. We are told to think our technologist is better educated, more widely read, ostensibly more knowledgeable, more exposed to scientific advances so he should know what is good for the poor, what practices the poor should adopt, how and why they should keep silent and take what's coming; and any voice raised against it smacks of ingratitude. If and when the people should come up with a counter-idea that exposes the faults and limitations of a system thought of by so called experts and UN-types sitting in air-conditioned offices, this is not playing cricket.

As It Goes in Rajasthan!

The State of Rajasthan has 33,305 populated villages, out of which 24,037 were identified as problem villages as far back as 1981. A problem village is defined as (i) which does not have an assured source of drinking water within 1.6 kms or within a depth of 15 metres; in the cases of hilly regions, within a vertical height of 100 metres (ii) where the source of water is susceptible to water borne diseases like cholera and guinea worms and (iii) where water has excessive salinity, iron or fluorides. In 1981, more than 20,000 hand pumps had been installed and more than 50 per cent were out of action for want of proper maintenance. By 1984, more than 40,000 hand pumps were expected to be installed. What arrangements had the Government made to repair and maintain these pumps?

What was in operation at that time was a UNICEF-designed three-tier system, adopted without much thought by all state governments in a conference in Madurai (Tamil Nadu) in 1979. What made it far easier was the fact that UNICEF agreed to provide equipment, jeeps, trucks, training materials and cover the costs of training everyone from the top to the bottom. The system they agreed to was as follows:

This 'Three-tier' system!

1. Tier One: A district mobile maintenance team (one team for every 500/600 hand pumps) consisting of 5 men (driver, mechanic, two helpers, mason) who work under the supervision of a Junior Engineer. This team is supposed to do minor and major repairs.

2. Tier Two: The Block-level mechanic from the Public Health Engineering Department (PHED). His duty is to regularly check 50 hand pumps and carry out minor repairs above the ground. If and when the hand pump assembly has to be taken out, he has to summon the district maintenance unit. He has no transport provided to him.

3. Tier Three: The village-level hand pump caretaker. The buck stops here. He is selected by the Government. He works free of charge. The other name for it is *shramdan*. He is trained for 2 days. He is given some spanners to keep the nuts and bolts tight. He is supposed to keep the foundation clean and give some health education. No more, no less. If anything more happens to the pump, he is supposed to send a postcard.

And Its Pitfalls!

It is immediately evident that the Three-Tier System has been designed by 'experts' who have never lived and worked in a village. They have, to be sure, never experienced what it is like to live without water for months just because the hand pump is out of order for want of a simple leather washer. Since Tier One and Tier Two workers are not answerable to the community because they are permanent government employees, the fact that pumps have remained out of order for months has not bothered them the least. To add insult to injury, the community was told that the Government owned the pump. The community had no stake in the hand pump and the Government made it clear that the pump was government property. This is reflected in the Three-Tier System where neither the Block Mechanic nor the District Maintenance team will allow the community to take their own initiative and get the pump repaired by someone in the village. Why? Because the person is not trained.

The HPM is Born!

These were some of the issues that were responsible for the birth of the Hand Pump Mistri (HPM). The idea grew out of a discussion in a village tea shop. A villager saw the district maintenance team driving past in a fancy truck donated by UNICEF and said, 'All for a washer in a hand pump. Isn't it too stupid for words? We have wayside machine shops in villages repairing tractors, diesel and electric pumps, bullock carts and agricultural machinery. Most of them do not have degrees, diplomas or are even literate. And the Government thinks we are incapable of changing a washer 100 feet below the ground. It's just another way of wasting money.' He could not have put across the point better. There is a vested interest in making simple issues look complicated, easy solutions look expensive, and practical ideas look as if it has taken a great deal of research and field testing to think out.

We realised it was too vast a problem to be left to the engineers and experts alone. By far the most serious flaw in the Three-Tier System is the marginal and cosmetic involvement of the community which actually uses the pump. The 'experts' have come up with a caretaker who is normally an unpaid youth doing something else for a living. For major repairs, he corresponds with the district maintenance unit by a system of post cards where even the postage stamp is supplied by the Government/UNICEF because he is supposed to be so poor.

And The Job He Did!

In 1981, Tilonia trained semi-literate rural youths under TRYSEM to repair and maintain the 200 hand pumps installed for Scheduled Castes with assistance from the Ministry of Home Affairs. After three months' training, they were placed on the field with startling results:

1. They were in a position to carry out 90 percent of the minor and major jobs on the hand pump above and below ground.
2. The community was willing to pay between Rs.40-100 to get their pumps repaired and offer manual labour when needed.
3. A trained mechanic or degree holder in mechanical engineering was not required to repair hand pumps. A semi-literate village youth could do the same job, perform the same function as the caretaker, the block mechanic, and the District Maintenance team *without leaving the village* given the proper training and the right set of tools.
4. Jeeps and trucks were not necessary for repair and maintenance. The same job could be done on a cycle.
5. The HPM was answerable to the community. He was identifiable in flesh and blood. He was not a government servant and was only working part-time in repairing and

maintaining hand pumps – for which, as a professional, he deserved to be paid.

6. It was cheaper to maintain.

Once this experiment had been conducted, we went to the State Government of Rajasthan with the results, with the hope that they would study it and possibly replicate it elsewhere.

To the credit of the State Government, where the political will of the Chief Minister played a significant part, the following decisions were taken:

a) The repair and maintenance of the hand pump will be the responsibility of the community and not the PHED.

b) A rural youth with some mechanical background will be selected by the community and sent for training for three months under TRYSEM. After training, he will be appointed as a Hand Pump Mistri (HPM).

c) The HPM will not be a government employee. He will be answerable to the community that selects him. The employment will be part time.

d) The HPM will look after 36-40 hand pumps within a radius of 5 kms from his village.

e) The State Government will pay Rs.150/hand pump per year with Rs. 50/hand pump per year included for spare parts. After training, the HPM will get a grant of Rs. 250/for tools from the Government as per TRYSEM rules. For a set of the special tools he will need for below-ground repairs, which costs Rs. 2,500, he will get a subsidy (50 per cent) if he is a Scheduled Caste/Scheduled Tribe when he gets a bank loan.

As of May 1984, a total of 37,151 hand pumps have been installed all over Rajasthan. The State Government estimated that a total of 1,175 HPMs needed to be trained through Industrial Training Institutes and voluntary agencies like Tilonia. In varying degrees of competence, 886 HPMs have been trained and placed in various districts. In many areas, the system has not been working smoothly because of poor or no understanding of the whole idea of the HPM.

It does not help when we go into the background of most of the HPMs. What is so extraordinary about them is that they are so ordinary. The profile of HPMs placed in Ajmer District, for instance, should give some idea how easy it is to find such people all over India:

Table showing profile of HPMs placed in Ajmer District

Occupational status:	Blacksmith (2 HPMs); agricultural labourer (51); cycle repair shop (2); electrician (1); pan shop (1); barber (2); grocery shop (1); vegetable shop (1); sweet shop; (1) mason (1); famine work (8); general labourer (10)		
Age group	18-25 years 26-30 31-35 Over 35	59 HPMs 14 6 2	
Income from other than repair and maintenance	Rs.50-100 101-150 151-200 Over 200	30 HPMs 41 10 Nil	
Educational qualifications	Up to 5th Standard 6th-8th 8th-10th 10th plus	*Scheduled Caste* 15 16 2 1	*Scheduled Tribes* 14 19 4 -
Land holding	Landless Marginal (0-5) Small (5-12.5) Over 12.5 *bighas*	*Scheduled Caste* 9 16 8 1	*Others* 10 18 8 1

And The Demystification!

The demystification that has taken place by making technology simple, accessible and understandable can be inferred from the following chart:

Comparison of various socio-economic factors for the 3-tier and 1-tier systems

Socio-economic factors	3-Tier System	1-Tier System
1. Cost hand-pump by year	Rs.400-500	Rs.150; Rs. 50 for spare parts included
2. Tools and equipment	Trucks, jeeps, trailers, heavy repair equipment	cycle, special tools
3. Educational qualifications	Mechanical degree holder, Diploma ITIs	4th-10th Standard pass; primary school
4. Personnel	Addl. Chief Engineer, Supd. Engineer, Executive Engineer, Asst. Engineer, Block mechanics, caretakers, lower staff	HPM at the village level
5. Training	No long term training at any level. Short term orientation courses for engineers, two days for caretaker	3 months' training under TRYSEM: one month theoretical, 2 months practical
6. Community participation	Marginal, at the caretaker level only; not answerable to the community	HPM identified by the community. Priority given to SCs/STs living below the poverty line
7. Community accountability	None. Answerable only to Government (Tiers 1 and 2)	Users have the right to recall the HPM and send someone else if his work is poor. *Sarpanch* signs work done then only HPM can get amount from BDO

8. Community resources	None	Use of village resources, knowledge and skills is total
9. Institutional finance	No provision	HPM takes a loan from nearest bank for special tools worth Rs.2,500. 50% subsidy for SC/ST

And the Problems!

1. The One-Tier System is not without problems. By far the biggest threat to the idea not working on the ground is the breed we call the Educated Man. In spite of all the work that has been done, the international experts in UNICEF call it an 'experiment'. The Three-Tier System has by and large failed and they are looking for alternatives, but these people have not got intelligence nor grace enough to accept the One-Tier System – because they themselves could not think of it. The One-Tier System has been adopted all over the State, but UNICEF in public statements have said it is still 'unproven'. I have written a number of articles on the One-Tier System; in their eyes it is premature. Because it sounds too good to be true in its simplicity and effectiveness, I am accused of misrepresentation and distortion of facts. These experts cut sorry figures.

2. Funds for maintenance that should have been transferred from the PHED to the Development Department is taking time. Many BDOs do not know what the money is for and how it is to be paid to the HPMs.

3. The training institutions need support. Vehicles to take the trainees out to the damaged hand pumps which are presently lying with the PHED.

4. The selection of HPMs have been faulty in many cases. Instead of one HPM per 5-km radius many DRDAs have

sent five trainees per village for TRYSEM training. This makes the appointment of the HPM very difficult.

5. Bank managers are reluctant to given loans for special tools because they think the HPMs will not pay it back. If they look after their hand pumps properly, there is no reason why the amount cannot be paid back.

6. There is confusion over the right type of tools. Project Officers, DRDAs turn to the local PHED engineer for guidance on the type of tools to be bought and because HPMs are looked on as caretakers in many areas, the wrong set of tools are given. Naturally, they cannot carry out the major and minor repairs, so the feedback 'See, we told you. They are just not competent enough to repair a hand pump' is given.

7. The *sarpanches* in many villages are not prepared to take the responsibility of monitoring HPMs. They have to countersign that the pumps are in working order and with that receipt the HPM gets the money from the BDO. In many cases, *sarpanches* are not prepared to get their hand pumps repaired by Scheduled Caste HPMs.

These are all problems that could be sorted out in time. None is very serious. For once, the community has responded spontaneously and even the BDOs are quite excited over the idea of the HPM. It solves the major problems we are all grappling with:

a) technology transfer takes place;

b) community participation in this case is total;

c) community accountability is assured;

d) village knowledge and village skills are being used;

e) employment in the rural areas is being generated;

f) village-based institutions (*panchayats*, banks) are being used (TRYSEM, SC/ST subsidies) to the fullest extent;

g) it is a system which is totally dependent on the HPM and not inter-dependent like the Three-Tier System where one cannot do without the other. This promotes self-reliance.

And Why This Prejudice?

The tragedy with too many experts spending too much time on a simple problem is that they can never come to a decision acceptable to all. This has happened with the One-Tier System. The people who use the pump want it: it's the best, most acceptable and definitely by far the most effective system because it is located closest to the village. The only trouble is that our high-powered experts do not want the system to work. It has damaged their pride, it has exposed their limitations and they are desperately looking for a way of saving face. The top engineers are all for it but the middle and low rungs within the Department look on this process of demystification as a distinct threat. UNICEF's narrow vision does not help.

Now different versions are coming out: two-tier systems, three and a half tier systems – just so long as it is not the one tier, because that identifies it with Tilonia and the State Government of Rajasthan. The Ministry of Works and Housing have not even acknowledged it in their Working Group Paper on the 7th Plan. Not to allow the demystification to take place on a large scale just shows the lobby that is at work (or is it lack of understanding?). But that, I am afraid, is the only answer if we want technology to reach the poor.

© Yojana/Kurukshetra, Publications Division,
Ministry of I&B, Government of India.

Barefoot Pioneers

Peter Coles

Originally published in *New Scientist*, May 10 2002

THE NARROW ROAD OUT OF TILONIA is so full of potholes that Bhanwar Jat prefers to drive our jeep on the desert earth beside it whenever he can. If you didn't know who he was, you'd think this quiet, scruffily handsome man with the gold flower ear stud was 'just' the driver. Earlier that morning, as I sat cross-legged on the floor, Jat had silently served tea. But a stay at Tilonia's 30-year-old Barefoot College soon teaches you not to judge by appearances.

An illiterate farmer, Jat and a team of other 'barefoot' architects designed and built the new campus using traditional materials, techniques and local labour, yet with no formal plans. Entirely solar-powered and with hundreds of structures to harvest rainwater, the building earned last year's Aga Khan Award for Architecture.

Tilonia is a large village down a dirt track off the Delhi to Ahmedabad trunk road, west of Jaipur. Sandwiched between a railway line and a barren red hill, this is where, back in 1972, a handful of university graduates from all over India decided to set up the Barefoot College – more properly called the Social Work & Research Centre (SWRC). Their goal was to improve the lot of the poorest of rural poor, while themselves living with the bare minimum, following the example of Mahatma Gandhi. Today, even the most illustrious visitors must help themselves to the simple vegetarian dinner and sit cross-legged on a thin carpet in the communal dining room washing their plates afterwards. In class-ridden India, these conditions can be humbling – if not humiliating – for those who take their power or paper qualifications too seriously.

This is no ordinary college. There are no classrooms or lecture theatres. It is impossible to tell teachers from students, and 'experts' are anathema. As the training is entirely practical, it takes place either in small workshops, offices or outdoors. Today, the college's 200 full time and 287 part-time staff are nearly all local people. There are Barefoot solar engineers, pathologists, teachers, midwives, architects, mechanics, accountants and computer data processors. Most have just a few years' primary education, or secondary schooling at best. No one is paid less than the national minimum wage of 60 rupees a day (about 85 pence) or more than 90 rupees a day, including the college's founder and director, Sanjit 'Bunker' Roy. But most of SWRC's activities take place in the 100 or so surrounding villages, in the shape of night schools for goatherds, water committees, women's groups and specific projects involving education, hygiene, rainwater harvesting and solar energy – whatever the villagers need.

As we drive from one dusty village to another, my uninitiated eyes cannot, at first, see the fruits of the college's efforts. Brightly clothed women still wield pickaxes, doing hard manual labour; other women and girls carry 20 litres or more of water on their heads from distant wells. But the men perch like birds by the roadside, drinking spiced tea and playing cards. Ingrained in the fabric of every village are near-feudal conditions of bonded labour, illiteracy, untouchability and exclusion, with women at the bottom of every list. Added to this are the effects of poor hygiene and seasonal migration of the landless in search of work.

But, as my Barefoot guides slowly reveal, the changes triggered by SWRC are there – and they are profound.

After an hour's spine-jolting drive with Jat, we arrive at the village of Panwa, about 100 kilometres west of Jaipur. The road curves round by the village *nadi,* a large pond to collect rainwater – a tradition over a thousand years old. The level is low, as only 10 centimetres of rain fell in last year's monsoon. A stone's throw from the pond is the village well, with a raised mud ring sculpted on its rim, where, as all over rural Rajasthan, women set down their round-bottomed urns before filling them. At least, they used to. A bank of blue solar-energy panels now stands next to the well, alongside a towering concrete water tank. Installed by villagers in 1995, under Jat's supervision, the panels pump underground water into the tank during the hours of sunlight. For an hour in the morning and evening nearly 60 houses have piped drinking water, direct to their courtyards.

But this project, still the only one in Rajasthan, isn't just using modern technology to relieve the drudgery of carrying water. The solar panels have also short-circuited one of the most pernicious effects of India's caste system. The well belongs to the better-off, higher-caste community. Until the pipeline was installed, a 'scheduled' or low-caste woman could not take water from the well. Instead, she had to beg a higher caste woman to pour water into her pot. The Indian constitution outlaws untouchability, but in remote villages like Panwa it is still part of everyday life. Even today, Scheduled Castes cannot enter some shops or drink from ordinary cups at tea stalls. They have to live on the outskirts of the village and can expect rough treatment if they overstep the time-honoured limits.

Slowly, the Barefoot College has become a kind of social equaliser, chipping away at the feudal systems that keep the landless poor and ignorant. 'We have looked at the problems that the poor face from their point of view and not from the point of view of so-called experts looking from outside,' says Roy. 'We have come to the conclusion that, using their own knowledge, skills and practical wisdom, it is possible for them to solve their problems themselves.'

Gulab Devi, 35 years old and already a grandmother, is a typical Barefoot graduate. Born into the low, leather-worker caste in neighbouring Harmara village, she came to SWRC looking for work when her husband fell ill. Like most women of her generation in Rajasthan, she had a mere two years of primary education and could not read or write. After a month's training at SWRC, she could repair the hand pumps previously maintained by an engineer from a distant town at great cost. 'It was hard work,' she says, 'not least carrying a 20-kilogram tool kit to surrounding villages, up to 6 kilometres away.' But she stuck at the job for nine years, going on to train dozens of other engineers. Gulab also helped to install the piped water system in Panwa, before retraining as a solar engineer, making, assembling and repairing solar lanterns.

As with all SWRC projects, the idea of piped water for Panwa came from the villagers. And it was a 12-year-old girl, Koshalya, who brought the problem to the college's attention through the world's first Children's Parliament, started at SWRC to promote children's rights and teach about democracy. At the time, she was Prime Minister, elected with her cabinet from 3,000 children attending the Barefoot College's 110 night schools, lit by the solar lanterns. SWRC opened these schools, run by local Barefoot teachers, to give primary education to children who look after animals by day.

When, a few years later, Koshalya married a boy from Panwa, she single-handedly persuaded the village's 56 families to pay an initial 1,000 rupees (£14 sterling) and a monthly subscription of 20 rupees, to make sure the water supply was sustainable. As a precondition for providing help and the solar panels, SWRC insisted that the community elect a village water committee to manage the system and share experiences with other village committees at the Tilonia campus.

For Bunker Roy, the Panwa project is a vindication of SWRC's principles. 'The pipes were laid by the villagers, the planning was done by the villagers, with community contributions. It's a myth when people say they are so poor they can't pay.' In another village, Chota Narena, 200 families pay for piped water collected from a rooftop rainwater harvesting system.

The relative comfort of today's campus and the steady stream of foreign visitors hide SWRC's tough history, which included a siege by local landowners. It also survived a merciless audit by the State Government, retaliating after the SWRC helped uncover a corruption scandal in which poor women were not paid for road construction work. For Roy, 'the biggest problem is convincing our own kind – educated Indians.'

But some are already converted. Some 24 affiliated grassroots centres have started in 14 states of India. Barefoot engineers from Tilonia have helped local villagers in Ladakh install hand pumps and solar power for 1,000 homes in the area. SWRC has also advised villagers in Mali and Morocco on traditional rainwater harvesting techniques.

Roy is clear about the wide-scale application of Barefoot College methods. 'If we want to focus on solutions that improve the quality of life for the rural poor then we can address problems that exist all over the world – drinking water, health, education, energy, housing, legal issues are also a problem because of the high percentage of illiteracy.' Roy doesn't believe development programmes need urban-based professionals. The skills usually exist locally, he says, but are not valued simply because the local experts are poor and illiterate.

The best place to start such programmes, he says, are inaccessible (to keep out the urban experts), with a high rate of illiteracy, a strong oral tradition and where 'families depend on each other and not on outside help.' Prerequisites for those starting such a project in a new area are patience, humility and perseverance, according to campus veteran Vasu, who was with Roy in the 1970s.

Like Gandhi before them, Roy, his colleagues and the local villagers have created a very Indian solution to their problems. By carefully choosing which technologies they introduce, they create change without adopting Western values wholesale. Yet they are still challenging the injustices that are a part of their own culture. 'The process of social change is slow,' says Vasu. 'It will take another 20 to 30 years before what we have started here achieves its goals.'

© 2002 New Scientist Ltd. All rights reserved.
Distributed by Tribune Content Agency

The Barefoot Approach: Diversity and Inclusion - The Path to Innovation

Bunker Roy

Originally published in *Racing Towards Diversity*, Winter 2013

Innovation

WE HEAR A GREAT DEAL ABOUT INNOVATION and the need for more of it in business and enterprise. I continually turn my thoughts towards what I have witnessed in my life, which is that nothing and no one is more innovative than a poor man or woman. Necessity and desperation often breed innovation. A woman who has seven children but one kilo of rice for the week ahead will somehow manage to keep her family going. There is little that separates the concepts of resourcefulness and innovation. When one has more than enough to eat, one ceases to think as hard of how to make one's meagre food stuffs go farther, of how to waste less.

So, managing this concept in the framework of a thriving economy and business is certainly a point of dialogue in today's world. Caring for others' assets and resources is something that requires a constant and tenacious need for innovation and resourcefulness.

Promoting a Different Vision of Enterprise

In its purist form, enterprise is productivity. All human beings strive to be productive and valued in a collective society. The rural village model is the perfect place to witness the power of the individual to drive a common Quality of Life augmentation: thinking for the community but acting individually. In this context, I use the word 'community' to describe our larger human community.

The idea of communal thinking is merely mindfulness about the other beings to whom we are connected in our human experience. It is critical to imbuing enterprise with a 'right thinking' that focuses on the betterment of MORE, versus LESS people. Ideas that this is a communist or social model are incorrect. It is simply the ability to turn one's resourcefulness of thinking to a higher level of excellence. It is about unleashing 'goodness'. A drive to achieve one's personal best intellectually but carrying the collective good up the wave, instead of making that journey alone.

Daunting. One must be stronger, better to carry a heavy weight on the back, remaining buoyant. Should we not demand so much more of our decision-making, that it becomes unconsciously conscious and mindful of others? This is the lesson that diversity and inclusion teach us.

Dealing with Success

In any endeavour, the challenge has always been dealing with success. More things fail in the face of success than in the face of difficulty. Barefoot College has demonstrated that semi-literate rural women can solar-electrify remote villages and look after solar units more competently than paper-qualified solar engineers. In so doing, it has turned established perceptions upside down, and debunked the basic assumption that formal education is required for development work. Those most hostile to the Barefoot approach are people who have invested a great deal in acquiring an education through the official system and then applied that misguided 'expertise' to drive dependency. The very idea of semi-literate women being able to manage and control initiatives at the village level undermines those hard-earned credentials and credibility, and even threatens the existence of their jobs. Indeed, one result of the Barefoot approach in India, where it is most widely replicated, has been the replacement of cost-intensive initiatives and jobs by low-cost and low-intensity initiatives providing gainful employment within the villages.

Captains of industry must look within their organisations to nurture and grow a more pervasive culture of innovation, where ideas that profit not only the company but also profit the consumer and employee begin to take hold. They must move in a direction of betterment for the larger community, and not simply the individual. Those most hostile to this type of demand for excellence that is both economic but also human will no doubt threaten those least likely to change and grow.

Learning from Failure

A further major idea is being equipped to learn from failures. Taking risks, trying new ideas, failing and trying again is a process that is respected in the Barefoot College because we recognise that we should learn as much from failure as from success. But the formal education system has no room for failure. In that system, failure is considered a matter for shame and regret. We are living through one of the greatest opportunities to learn from economic failure in the last 100 years.

You Do Your Best Work When You Are Insecure

When your back is against the wall and you have nowhere to run and no one to turn to, you have no choice but to face the consequences. When a crisis arises and could possibly lead to violence, urban professionals normally do not have the staying power. Because they have somewhere to run to, they are not prepared to see the crisis through.

If we think of every enterprise as a community instead of a disconnected place where people come to perform a function yet have no emotional or vested connection, an altruistic culture will develop naturally. This will infuse the organisation with far greater skills, abilities and productivity than it previously possessed. This will lead not only to better financial success but also a sense of shared impact and common good. If it is then able to leverage outside itself this spirit of 'giving' and commitment to community, it follows that it can become an important player and catalyst for real change and impact.

This exact revolution and inward thinking within the world of business and commercial corporations is necessary. Ideas about self-reliance, listening to ideas of those below and beside in the corporate structure, valuing each individual's contribution and reinforcing a sense of 'community' give confidence that positive solutions are within our grasp to craft. This spirit of thinking could free the commercial sector from years of malaise and stagnancy. It will inspire innovation and begin to reinstall hope and action.

© *Courtesy Racing Toward Diversity*

Kulhad chai – tea in an earthenware cup

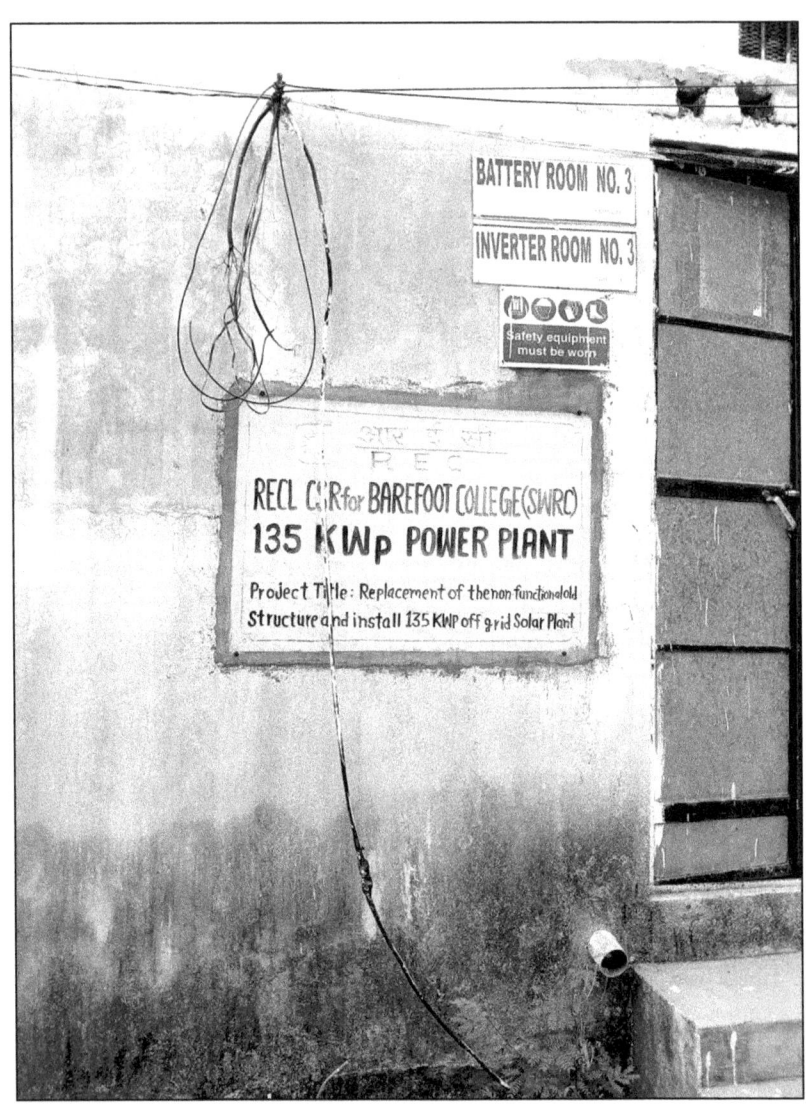

Barefoot Power Plant

Traditionally a taboo subject

Reverse osmosis drinking water station new campus

8: A Place in the Sun

Heather MC Malcolm and Aruna Roy

*'Traveller, there is no path.
Paths are made by walking.'*
Popular saying

The struggle to secure the natural resources necessary for life goes hand in hand with a constant worry about the environment. The two cannot be separated, and this is particularly true in arid Rajasthan, where water has always been in short supply while the sun is generous to a fault. Except for a few rainy months, it shines down brightly and often relentlessly on its people. Water comes during temperamental monsoons. Sometimes, there is too much to harness, and sometimes there is none at all. Extreme conditions such as these make daily life a constant battle for the rural people who must find a way to live with them. In recent years, however, an alliance between rural knowledge and modern technology has put new hope on the horizon.

Water sustains life. From the time of India's monarchies and through the times of colonial administration, the communities of Rajasthan have used traditional knowledge and skill to harness water by building *bawadies* (step wells) and *tankas* (for underground water storage). At Barefoot College, Barefoot technologists worked with those communities, drawing on their knowledge to design, and with them build, *tankas* capable of storing enough water to see the area through the long months of drought.

The knowledge and skills that produced the *tankas* was traditional, but in addition, modern technology contributed the idea of the hand pump, which the Barefooters borrowed. According to rural tradition, members of the *Dalit* caste were not allowed to touch water pots or use common water sources. But since Barefoot College lives by its principles, and these include equality and inclusion, the people chosen to train as hand pump *mistris* (mechanics) to install and maintain the pumps were drawn from the *Dalit* community. In this way, taboos of untouchability were addressed, and an important point was made.

The idea of using *tankas* to collect and store the community's water spread, and they were installed in the grounds of schools and public areas. This provided drinking water to satisfy thirst, but other benefits soon became evident. Because there was enough water, school toilets functioned. School was a better place to be, and attendance – especially girls' attendance – grew.

The Rajasthanis, like other dwellers in deserts and semi-deserts, know that protection from the scorching sun is vital to life, but they also know that along with the danger comes good. For example, for many generations the sun has been used to dry vegetables that could be stored for use when the earth turned dry and hard. In India, the January solstice on the 14th is a religious festival, welcoming the return of the sun to the northern hemisphere.

So, it was well within the tradition of seeing the sun as benefactor that the Barefoot College harnessed its energy in a way that would help address environmental concerns. Barefoot's involvement in this began when, as founder and head of the organisation ASVIN (Solar Applications in Villages in India and Nepal), Pierre Amado,[8] holder of the Légion d'honneur, brought a set of solar panels to Tilonia. A generous grant from ASVIN provided sufficient funds to start Barefoot on the road to its tryst with the sun, sowing the seeds of what was to become a great journey.

By the mid-1980s, Tilonia was already beginning to train women as technologists: they were taking responsibility for repairing hand pumps (which, up until then, had been an exclusively male domain). But when women with no schooling began assembling

---

[8] Pierre Amado was French Cultural Attaché to India during the 1950s. Holding the Chair of History of the Civilization of the Ganges Valley at Paris's *École Pratique des Hautes Études*, he directed the ASVIN organization until 1984. He is also one of the founding members of the *Aide et Action* association in India, the first French association to have set up sponsorship with foreign children.

voltage charge controllers, inverters, and making solar lamps, it was clear that a mini-revolution had begun. The programme to train women solar engineers, now known as 'Solar Mamas', has become a global phenomenon, and Barefoot College Tilonia has trained women from 96 countries, as well as from several Indian states.

The training to become solar engineers has empowered the women and made them independent. A good illustration of this comes from the solar woman engineer from Afghanistan who, when she returned home, chose to sit with the men in her village assembly. The men were shocked. 'Sit with the women!' they ordered her. Her reply was, 'I will sit here. I am not merely a woman; I am a solar engineer. I have electrified your entire village.'

The idea of the Solar Mamas has fascinated the world. Robert Redford's *Sundance Films* made *Rafea Solar Mama,* and Bunker's *Ted Talk* has had five million views in 45 languages. But the importance of such publicity pales against the most valuable thing of all: that the people living at the margins now have light by which to cook, sew, and read.

The Barefoot Mama-engineer's dream is to use modern technology so that people can adapt to and control the conditions in which they live, and are able to assemble, maintain and repair all the equipment needed for this, for themselves. It is a vision that has electrified remote villages the world over, and charged the designers of this extraordinary programme – those at the Barefoot College, Tilonia – with renewable energy!

Read on for stories of encouragement and hope.

Preventing the Deserts from Growing: The Barefoot Approach

Bunker Roy

Originally published in *Circular on Desertification*,
16 December 1996

TILONIA IS A VERY SMALL VILLAGE located in the deserts of Rajasthan, 400 km south-west of India's capital city, New Delhi. Temperatures rise to 44 Celsius in the summer and drinking water has to be pumped by hand from 200 feet below the ground. It is in this village 25 years ago that a voluntary agency, Social Work and Research Centre (SWRC), started operations. The Barefoot College in Tilonia has found the mental and physical space to try new ideas, make mistakes, learn from the failures of others, and try again, mainly due to its unusual and unconventional approach to identifying problems and implementing solutions, depending entirely on the knowledge, wisdom, skills and technology of the rural people themselves; healthy disrespect for urban, paper-qualified professionals whose awareness and feelings for the problems of the desert is almost counter-productive and threatening to the lifestyle and environment of the people in the deserts; and indifference to inviting 'experts' who only write papers and attend conferences but cannot dirty their hands in the soil planting trees or making water channels or installing hand pumps or spending hours in a village talking and listening to people in a village who have their own way of solving problems that we do not have the patience to listen to. As Oscar Wilde said, 'Experience is the name men give to their mistakes.'

Located as I am in the middle of a desert and having lived through two spells of severe drought and famine lasting four to five years without a drop of rain, I find the tangible achievements of the Barefoot College a source of satisfaction.

It is also the reason why I am totally sceptical of the present desertification process and, ultimately, what it is going to achieve. If the people who drew up the Focal Points have a grassroots base and personal experience of living and working in the deserts, they have something to contribute at the global level, other than communicating second and third-hand information each time they speak out.

The Urgency is Missing

While conferences, workshops and meetings are being organised and tons of paper are wasted, deserts are growing, water levels are dropping and fuel and fodder getting harder to obtain from the immediate environment. Pressure from grassroots groups in several countries has forced national governments to allocate funds from national budgets to combat desertification. And now, two years down the road, the International NGO Network on Desertification and Drought (RIOD) is suggesting National Desertification Funds (small grants), yet thousands of dollars are spent on meetings. Is that all we have to show as NGOs in action?

Have any of those who identified Focal Points spent days and nights in any village? Have any of those groups being called to these global conferences ever seen a desert? Has any of the money reached what Mahatma Gandhi called 'the last man' in the village?

What grassroots groups have painfully realised (I suspect all over the world) is that policies formulated at international and national levels do not mean a thing: they are not worth the paper they are printed on. It is a futile and pointless exercise pointing out that national governments are signatories to Conventions on Biodiversity, Children's Rights, the Law of the Sea, Desertification and Climate Change. At the village level, when it is a matter of life and death, when there is not enough food to eat in the house and there is only contaminated drinking water and the money lender is harassing the individual to pay back a loan or send one's child to become a bonded labourer doing menial work in the house, what protection can these useless conventions provide?

Focal Points Must Be Made More Accountable

For the air tickets they receive, thus damaging the ozone layer, participants should plant 100 saplings, as Miguel Sotto in Costa

Rica made us do (and many of us were too unfit to finish the task). Sending irrelevant information through electronic mail is just not enough. Since when was that classified as action?

Have we no conscience, that public money is spent while the situation on the ground remains the same? I want to start a debate within all global networks, including the ELCI. If we are supposed to be facilitating the voice of the grassroots, and many are located in deserts, what tangible benefits are reaching them that are improving their quality of life?

The effectiveness of the Barefoot approach is its replicability all over the world. Before the urban-trained expert arrived on the scene, what did the villagers do? They constructed rainwater harvesting structures without blueprints, which are still used today, hundreds of years later. They planted trees that were indigenous, and did not need to go to college for that. They knew how to respect the deserts, not fight them artificially. They knew how to use the sun, the air and the wind and the plants and animals; an ecosystem that is pulsating with vitality that no one has the eyes to see because all they see is sand and waste.

Environmental Conservation Measures

The Barefoot project utilises two approaches to address environment problems: Protection and Rehabilitation.

Protection of the Environment

With regard to the provision of water:

- Installation of 1,300 hand pumps to save precious ground water pumped from 150-200 feet below the ground. Over 300,000 people use these hand pumps to access clean and safe drinking water. For the first time since the hand pump technology was invented, safe drinking water is now available at 15,000 feet up in Ladakh in the Himalayas (Kashmir region) where the pumps operate at temperatures of -40 Celsius, which government engineers had said was technically impossible to accomplish.

- Piped water supply schemes now exist in six villages, benefiting 14,000 people. These were planned and implemented by Barefoot engineers from the villages, who have barely passed primary school.

- In 103 rural primary schools located in brackish water areas, 5 million litres of rainwater have been collected through traditional rainwater harvesting techniques, increasing the attendance of girls in schools.

- To improve the quality of drinking water and protect communities from waterborne diseases, a total of 1,374 samples were tested by Barefoot water chemists, in 78 villages in eight states.

In respect of energy:

- The only totally solar operated (11kW) Barefoot College in India was started in Tilonia in 1986.

- Solar electricity was installed in 300 Adult Education Centres in eight states in India, thereby saving 35,000 litres of fuel, increasing literacy and improving environmental conditions. In Ladakh (Kashmir), 930 houses located at 11-15,000 feet up in the Himalayas have solar electricity. This is the first time ever basic lighting has been provided on such a large scale so high up in the mountains.

There are also activities aimed at combating desertification:

- Within an area of 500 square miles, 600 acres of waste land have been rehabilitated using traditional fuel and fodder species.

- Where scarce wood is used for building, 50 Buckminster Fuller's geodesic domes have been fabricated out of scrap metal to encourage the use of alternative materials.

Environmental education is also carried out through various means, in particular formal and informal, and through women's groups. So far:

- 84 night schools for drop out children attended by 1,634 boys and 1,110 girls are being run. The children tend sheep, goats and cattle during the day.

- In order to discuss environment and development issues, 120 teachers' meetings, 60 rural parent meetings and 89 village education meetings are called every year.

- Using traditional media, including glove puppets, nearly 940 performances are staged every year; highlighting environmental issues in villages. These reach up to nearly 300,000 people.

- The first environmental walk in the history of the State of Rajasthan was organised through street plays, puppet shows and village theatre. 30,000 people in 64 villages were exposed to messages on the need to conserve the environment.

- 45 active women's groups with a membership of nearly 2,000 women have been established in the villages around the Barefoot College.

Rehabilitation of the Environment

At the moment, 573 unemployable rural youth who have barely passed primary school have been trained in the repair and maintenance of hand pumps and providing safe drinking water. These Barefoot mechanics maintain 15,000 hand pumps serving 3.7 million people in the deserts.

Another 115 rural youth from eight states have been trained as Barefoot solar engineers to install, repair and maintain 75.5 kW solar panels. Most of them have not reached the 10th standard and have never received any formal training in electronics or solar technology.

Another important activity is recycling of waste, which also generates employment.

- Waste paper from the library in the form of government reports, UN studies, etc. are re-used in making glove puppets for the village theatre.
- Waste from leaves and the kitchen is used in the biogas plants to generate fuel for lighting and in the laboratory to test blood and urine samples.
- During the monsoons, waste waters are collected in open wells and collected in a 400,000-litre tank located in the College.
- Agricultural waste is used for handicrafts made by women, which earns them $15 per month each.
- Waste tyres from vehicles and trucks are used to make swings for children for use at school.
- Waste scrap metal is used to fabricate geodesic domes for housing in desert areas and also provides employment to village blacksmiths.
- Waste cotton from weaving is made into rugs and sold as handcrafts, providing employment to women. Waste, such as unused pens, rubber from tyres, bus and railway tickets, are used to make educational toys for night schools.

The Barefoot approach has produced: 15 rural youth who are drillers; 573 Barefoot mechanics; 35 chemists and 20 traditional communicators; 10 civil engineers who plan the drinking water schemes and 115 solar engineers drawn from previously employable youth; and 137 teachers running night schools for drop out school children. The Barefoot approach also has 150 traditional midwives, 80 night school teachers and 41 pre-primary school teachers who are trained as Barefoot doctors.

Where Water is More Precious Than Milk

Bunker Roy

Originally published in *The Indian Express*, 23 February 1989

(This article is reproduced entirely in its original form.)

IN NOVEMBER-DECEMBER 1988 a small village-based voluntary agency called Preyatna organised a walk through 45 villages of Dudu Panchayat Samiti barely 60 miles from Jaipur, capital of Rajasthan. It was a walk to make people aware of their drinking water problems.

You ask the so-called responsible people in Rajasthan if Jaipur district has problems of drinking water and the response you get borders on disbelief. Either I am being funny (which, in other words, means I need to get my head examined) or I just do not know Rajasthan.

The answer invariably is that Jaipur has no problem; it is there in Barmer and places like that where villagers have to walk several kilometres for sweet water, where the government services have virtually collapsed. Well, by sheer coincidence, some village sarpanches from Barmer were visiting the area and what they saw of the state of drinking water horrified them. Barmer is never so bad, they say.

Who will believe that 60 miles from Jaipur there are villages where women scoop out water by hand from puddles in drying ponds? Villages within 10 km radius of the largest salt lake in India, the Sambhar Lake, are forced to live in the 19th century because we, you and I, have neglected them. We have taken it for granted that just because they live close to Jaipur they must have basic amenities. This is not true.

Ask for something to drink and they offer you milk, not water because that is more precious. Milk is available at their doorstep: for water they have to walk three kilometres or more. Marriages are decided on the basis of whether there is a perennial source of sweet water. More children attend a primary school if that school has a sweet water source. No primary or middle school in all villages we walked through had a safe sweet water source!

We saw many sights that defy explanation. In Korsina village, there is a sweet water source, but the villagers have been denied that water; the Government is pumping it to Nagaur in the adjoining district. Hand pumps have been installed but the water is unfit for drinking. Villagers ask, why waste so much money when everyone knows the water will be brackish? But this year contracts have been given by executive engineers PHED for more hand pumps!

In Sartala village an old man told us that out of 100 children born in the village only around 20 just survive: the rest die because of brackish water. In Nangal, Ringee and Dobri villages we heard the same sad story of neglect and callousness.

The Walk for Water resulted in 70 men from 11 villages going for the first time collectively to the Sub Divisional Magistrate demanding water fit for drinking. Twenty-six women from five villages got together and agreed to form Paani Panchayats of women members only. Ten women's groups in different villages have met several times to chalk out a long-term plan of action.

A small beginning but in the right direction.

Traveller, there is no path.

Paths are made by walking.

Reprinted from THE INDIAN EXPRESS, with permission of The Indian Express (P) Limited © 1978-1996. All rights reserved through the world.

Not a Drop to Drink

Bunker Roy

Originally published in *India Today* ('Grass Without Roots'),
31 May 1990

ACCORDING TO THE BABUS, BUREAUCRATS AND SUPER TECHNOCRATS, there's supposed to be water, water everywhere in rural India. Or at least in about half of India's 583,000-odd villages by 1990.

Yet for millions of the country's villagers, there's not a drop to drink. And this is tragic fact, notwithstanding the Technology Mission's fatuous claim that in 1989 only 132,560 villages remained to be provided with a safe drinking water source. Any thorough investigation will reveal that these claims are but one more example of the Big Lie with which the Government periodically dupes its citizens.

To secure a supply of clean drinking water is not impossible. But it is made to remain an impossibility by local bureaucrats and engineers who want to protect their turf and thereby prevent the people most capable of finding the solutions – the villagers themselves – from taking charge of the problem and in the process, their own lives. Big Brother Engineer knows best. Distrustful of devolution of more responsibilities to village *panchayats*, he insists that the provision of drinking water is a technical problem that cannot – and must not – be demystified.

However, the problem is not technical. It is social. The purely technical approach has resulted in colossal waste running into thousands of *crores* of rupees. For example, the generation of information through costly scientific source-finding methods of satellites by different departments (Central Ground Water Board, State Water Boards, ISRO, NRSA) is never really used by the on-the-spot well driller. The driller, in most cases, selects the site after a casual talk in a village tea-shop.

The waste of money and inefficiency is constantly compounded: poor ground water surveys lead to boring where there's no water, and often overstaffed water boards and public health engineering departments exhaust the resources meant for the rural poor. Also, hand pumps, open wells and piped water are provided to villages through such a plethora of departmental schemes with different rules and regulations that while some villages get water, thousands of others remain dry or receive only brackish, contaminated water with high content of fluorides, iron and salinity. And yet even this poisonous brew and the pipes and pumps that propel it into rural buckets are included in government statistics as "drinking water" success stories.

Like war is too complicated an issue to be decided by generals alone, the problems of drinking water cannot be tackled by engineers and urban-based experts alone. The community, the real beneficiaries, must be consulted at every stage. Not because of some utopian ideal but because, in village India, *the community knows best*. But the Government has been consistently reluctant to look at the community point of view. The only problem, the *governmentwallahs* insist – after they have wasted precious money – is a lack of adequate financial resources! And yet, tackling the social issues – community control – is essential to introduce overall efficiency and success. Some examples:

Government documents state that the hand pump or the piped water supply system is a community asset. Yet, when either breaks down, the community must get permission to repair it and remain without water until the bureaucratic hassles are resolved.

It does not make sense that a junior engineer or overseer should decide whether a village has adequate potable drinking water. This should be the decision of the users of the water.

In the site selection for the location of hand pumps, it is essential that the women are also consulted as a rule. The excuse for not consulting women is that they will not understand technical surveys. But, in point of fact, these expensive surveys are never used.

The choice of technology is also a social issue crying out for community involvement. In shallow water-table regions like the Indo-Gangetic plains, the Uttar Pradesh *Jal Nigam* is wasting *crores* of rupees by installing deep-well India Mark II hand pumps when they are technically not required. The users prefer locally-made shallow hand pumps but they are ignored.

The battle lines have already been drawn on the maintenance of hand pumps. While the government maintenance cost of hand pumps is Rs.1,000, it has been proven that community maintenance reduces the cost to Rs.300 a year. Slowly, Rajasthan has adopted the local maintenance scheme under which 40,000 hand pumps in nine districts are covered. This has generated employment among village youth, instilled a feeling of self-respect in them, and freed villages of at least one suffocating tentacle of the Government.

Elsewhere, there is still resistance because this idea has come from the community. But the idea is one whose time has come. A small beginning, perhaps, in the war for water. But at least one right step in the direction of self-reliance. And dignity.

© *Courtesy India Today magazine*

Water on the School Roof

Bunker Roy and Bernd Niedermann

Originally published in *The World Economic Forum*, 2003

Georg Fischer supports a drinking water project in the Himalayan State of Sikkim.

The Indian social entrepreneur Bunker Roy has gained worldwide acclaim for founding India's so-called 'Barefoot College.' The basic idea behind this college, which was founded in 1972, was to teach urgently needed skills to as many poor people as possible – hence the name 'Barefoot' – with the aim of enabling them to get down to work as architects, engineers or IT specialists as fast as possible. 'Barefoot' graduates in power engineering and water supply engineering, for example, have already installed thousands of solar power plants and pump stations in eight Indian states.

THIS IS A PLAN OF ACTION designed to make the practice of collecting rainwater on rooftops a Global Movement.

The present mindset among planners and engineers prefers the exploitation of ground water for the installation of hand pumps. Where this is not possible, the second preference is for piped water supply schemes, sometimes from sources hundreds of miles away. Many companies and businesses provide back-up support to make it possible to implement these technologies – from gathering and interpreting information from satellites to manufacturing pipes, diesel and electric pumps, hand pumps, desalination plants and accessories at costs running into billions of dollars.

The practice of collecting rainwater where it falls needs to be revived if the ultimate purpose is to provide inexpensive drinking water to everyone. This was what people did for generations and it could be found in many remote villages all over the world from Colombia in South America to the Atlas Mountains in West Africa, to the Himalayas in Asia and in the deserts of Rajasthan in India.

Rural communities have the technical competence to collect rainwater where it falls. This is an urgency that only communities facing acute drinking water shortages can understand. They cannot wait for the Government to act. The ultimate and final solution is that they have to get together to contribute labour and materials to construct the rainwater harvesting structures themselves. In the process, they collectively decide on how much they are prepared to pay for water that will be under their control and management.

The Plan of Action will involve community-based organisations (CBOs) who are working at the grassroots and are in constant touch with the communities who face acute water shortages. The idea is to concentrate and focus on providing drinking water in schools and places where services are being provided to whole communities like dispensaries, family planning clinics, training centres and women's hostels where there is very little water available for drinking water and sanitation. Where resources permit, this is already being done on a small scale.

The Global Rain Water Harvesting Collective Plan of Action (GRWHC) will be to increase the size and volume of the tanks so that rainwater is not wasted and more water is collected. Where 200 litres are already being collected it should be possible to collect 20,000 litres since they are already aware of the importance of rainwater. It has been calculated that to collect 100,000 litres of rainwater should not cost more than $5,000 to $7,000 depending on the location of the tank.

At the recent Johannesburg World Summit on Sustainable Development (August/September 2002) 144 CBOs from 44 countries mandated the GRWHC to start implementing the idea of collecting rainwater on an urgent and priority basis. The idea was to set up a legal body. They also endorsed the idea of developing a new long-term partnership with as many stakeholders as possible interested in promoting the initiative on a global scale.

Objectives

The Objectives need to be simple and focused. The Objectives of the Global Rain Water Harvesting Collective Plan of Action (GRWHC) are twofold:

- to collect rainwater from roof tops in community places like schools, dispensaries, family planning clinics, training centres and women's hostels in desert and mountain rural and semi-urban areas;

- to collect as much surface water in unused open wells in villages as possible so that the dry hand pumps in the thousands can be revitalised and these assets can be productive again.

Methodology

The first step will be to collect as much information as possible on communities already collecting rainwater to meet their water and sanitation needs. A *pro forma* has already been prepared by the Collective to be sent to all CBOs who have already expressed an interest in the Johannesburg Summit and are looking forward to being involved.

The second step will be to collect and analyse the information relating to cost of labour, materials, traditional knowledge available and location. The idea is to establish the competence of the CBO and the preparation of the community to implement the project as soon as possible. The third step will be to call a meeting of the CBOs who have responded to the GRWHC initiative with a sole purpose of finalising a Joint Plan of Action. This will contain:

- the name and location of CBO;
- the name and location of the school/community place where the RWH structure is to be constructed;
- the cost of digging, raw materials, water proofing, supervision, monitoring and documentation;
- the work plan and time plan;
- the time it will take to complete the work.

What Has Been Accomplished So Far

The registration of the collective in India is now in its final phase. Leading politicians, donors, practitioners and opinion-makers from all over the world have been invited to become members of the first International Board. A body legally empowered to receive payments is being set up in the Netherlands.

At the January 2003 World Economic Forum in Davos, Switzerland, the Water and Mountain Initiative (WAMI) lent its support to the action plan of the collective – the first genuinely private-public partnership to be founded in the United Nations International Year of Freshwater. There, in the presence of UNEP President Klaus Töpfer, Georg Fischer signed an undertaking to support the collective to the tune of USD 50,000.

The concept of rainwater harvesting on the roofs of schools and other public buildings was also high up on the agenda of the World Water Forum in Japan in March 2003, where it was the subject of several sessions.

Thanks to what India's 'Barefoot College' has already accomplished in the field of rainwater harvesting, it was among the 150 grassroots organisations which the Japanese Government selected from over 800 applicants to attend this year's World Water Forum.

© *World Economic Forum*

An Uphill Struggle

Bunker Roy

Originally published in 'Water Stories' (book) by *IRC International Water and Sanitation Centre*, 2003

THE PEOPLE WHO LIVE NEAR THE MOUNTAINS CLOSE TO KANCHENJUNGA in India see plenty of water. It rains regularly but the water is allowed to cascade down to the rivers, thousands of feet below. Then what the engineers do is put big pumps in the valley where the rivers flow and pump the water all the way back up the mountain, costing thousands of dollars. In the mountain State of Sikkim, engineers think that this costly system is the only solution.

Five years ago, the people from the Barefoot College said that they would like to try a rooftop rainwater harvesting system on the top of the mountain. The engineers and politicians thought we were crazy. They thought it was technically impossible. The Chief Minister of Sikkim shrugged and said: 'My engineers say it cannot be done, but if you build the first system that works, I promise I will come and open it.'

We managed to get some money from the Central Government of India. With this we built the first rainwater harvesting system in the State of Sikkim. We did it without any help from the paper qualified engineers. The system was built by the people themselves with their knowledge and skills, and the raw materials they collected themselves.

After we completed our work and the system was full of rainwater (160,000 litres), I went to the Chief Minister of Sikkim. 'Remember what you told me?' I asked him. 'You said you would officially come and see the rainwater system once it was completed.' The Chief Minister was quite surprised, but he also looked very pleased. 'Can I bring my chief engineer along?' he asked.

When the Chief Minister came and saw the rainwater that had been collected, he said to his chief engineer: 'Now tell me, what is wrong with this?' The engineer could not find an answer.

After this visit, the Chief Minister changed the policy of the Government of Sikkim. He immediately agreed to spend more money on constructing this kind of rainwater harvesting system in the drought-prone regions of the State. He sanctioned the development of 40 more systems like the one he had personally seen. They were to be built by the people themselves and the Government only had to provide the raw materials.

Today, all 40 structures are fully operational. The total cost is only a quarter of the cost of the piped water systems built in the past by the engineers. Sikkim has decided to allocate extra money for more systems like this every year.

© IRC Publications

India's Self-help Solar Villages

Bunker Roy

Originally published in *UNESCO Courier*, January 1995, 'The Sun – Ancient Myths, New Technologies'

India is full of contrasts and contradictions. On the one hand, there is 'Bharat' or traditional India with its 600,000 villages, where life moves slowly, where centuries-old social structures remain unchanged, and where 70 per cent of the country's 940 million people live and die. And then there is 'India', a young country struggling to overcome the usual problems of underdevelopment. 'India', argues Bunker Roy, has often opted for large dams or electrification projects that sometimes fail to respond to the needs of the humbler inhabitants of 'Bharat'. Here, he talks about two successful community-based projects which, with the use of solar energy, have transformed the lives of poor farmers in the depressed regions of Bihar and Orissa and of people living in remote Himalayan villages.

IT TAKES 29-YEAR-OLD TSEWANG NARBO two days to walk across the 6,000-metre high Khardungla pass, the highest in the Ladakh area of India's Northern State of Jammu and Kashmir. A further 60 kilometres by bus and army truck bring him to the district headquarters in Leh. Here, he picks up distilled water, fuses and other equipment before beginning the long trek back home to his wife and five children.

But Tsewang Narbo does not mind the hardship or the strain. Since 1993, this barely literate man has become one of the most important persons in the remote Himalayan villages of Diger where he is responsible for the upkeep and maintenance of 59 solar photovoltaic units (SPVs) which provide lighting for his and surrounding villages and which have transformed life during the long snow-bound winters when temperatures can reach -30°C.

Until 1989, the energy needs of these far-flung villages had been most inadequately met by Diesel Generating (DG) sets, which are costly, centralised and unreliable, as well as using fossil fuel that pollutes the environment.

Since it takes 25 days to haul up as many litres of fuel to these villages, located at a height of 5,000 metres, the inhabitants used it extremely sparingly to make it last the six months of winter. At night, entire families huddled around a single light no stronger than a candle flame. Solar lighting therefore seemed nothing short of a miracle.

When the idea of training semi-literate, unemployed rural youth to install, maintain and repair solar units was first put forward by an organisation called the Social Welfare and Research Centre in Tilonia, Rajasthan, engineers and government officials felt it would never work. They were convinced the rural poor were too backward and illiterate to be given so much responsibility. There was also resistance from contractors and transporters who supplied DG sets, transmission wires, poles and diesel, and who stood to lose their business.

But the response from the villagers was so enthusiastic that it ground out all opposition. They were even willing to pay one dollar per unit per month for solar lighting; paying for such services, however heavily subsidised, is unheard-of in Ladakh. So far, nearly $3,000 has been collected from the 28-village community.

Tsewang Narbo, who was selected for the job by the village community in June 1993, is now capable of fabricating inverters – devices that convert direct current into alternating current – and other apparatus, repairing fuses, changing tube lights, filling batteries with distilled water, and installing solar units in villages which can only be reached on foot. (When the SPVs were installed in 1993, the batteries and panels were brought up by yaks and then airlifted by helicopters of the India Air Force). His job has so far brought him a total of $260, a welcome addition to his meagre earnings from goat farming.

Tilonia's efforts have also brought about a change in the energy policy of the State Government of Jammu and Kashmir. There are now about a dozen trained persons like Tsewang Narbo who look after solar units installed in 500 individual houses in over twenty villages.

Solar Pumps Bring Life to Dying Villages

The large-scale use of solar energy in India was first promoted by Pierre Amado, often described as 'a Frenchman with an Indian heart'. Amado, who served as French Cultural Attaché in India between 1953 and 1960, was so fascinated by Indian culture that he specialised in the Ganges Valley civilisation and now teaches post-graduate courses on the subject in Paris.

'As I became older,' he explained, 'I began to ask myself: "I have taken so much from India, but what have I given back?" I thought the time had come to pay my debts to India. Since I knew the villages in the Ganges valley particularly well, I decided to launch a project there. I talked to several researchers and came to the conclusion that the use of solar energy for pumping irrigation water would be most appropriate.'

India has over 90 million farmers with small land holdings. Most of them remain without water during the summer months. There is water but no power to pump it and so many farmers are being forced to migrate to the cities. 'I realised that unless something was done to help these very tiny hamlets inhabited by very poor people, they would be condemned to underdevelopment for centuries to come. The villages I am talking about are not connected to roads and have not been electrified,' says Amado.

In 1979, Pierre Amado launched an association called ASVIN (Application of Solar Voltaics in Villages in India and Nepal), which in Indian mythology signifies the twin sons of the sun, symbolising agriculture and animal husbandry. Working with local voluntary organisations in the villages of Sarwar (Bihar) and Gobalpur (Orissa), ASVIN has been able to demonstrate that if the community is taken into confidence during the planning process, and if local skills are mobilised, barely literate villagers are capable of installing, maintaining and repairing solar pumps for irrigation on their own.

'I remember the ceremony to inaugurate the solar pumps in the village of Sarwar in Bihar in 1982,' says Amado. 'The Development Commissioner gave wheat and vegetable seeds to each family. Since in this region wheat has not traditionally been cultivated, I thought the villagers would either sell the seed or grind it for flour. But not one of them sold the seed. They told me "We want to eat the wheat grown with our solar water." I call it harvesting the sun.'

SANJIT (BUNKER) ROY is director of the Social Work and Research Centre at Tilonia, Rajasthan State, in northern India. He is also chairman of the Environmental Liaison Centre International (ELCI), a non-governmental organization based in Nairobi.

From India's Self-help Solar Villages, by Bunker Roy, © 1995, United Nations. Used with the permission of the United Nations.

Lighting Up Ladakh

Bunker Roy

Originally published in *Resurgence*, No. 187, March-April 1998

TSEWANG NORBU lives in the village of Digger across the 4,500-metre high Khardungla pass in Leh District. He is 28 years old, has five children and keeps goats. He was selected by his community to be trained in the installation, repair and maintenance of solar photovoltaics units. All the solar units he installed were brought to the village by yaks and on the backs of people from the village. He was trained on the job: he installed 59 units himself, taking three months to complete the work. The units were installed in 1992. They are still working.

Abbas Ali is 31 years old. After training, he installed solar power in the village of Chunlangha.

Thondup Dorze is 35 years old. He grazes 10 head of sheep when he is not looking after the 50 solar units he installed in 1992.

Sonam Stobdan is 39 years old. He installed 67 units after training and has the competence to repair inverters and charge controllers for the solar units he looks after.

Today, there are 19 Barefoot engineers living in the remote villages of Ladakh. They are providing light to 25 villages.

Ladakh is one of the most inhospitable regions of the world. For six months of the year, it is cut off from the outside world by snow, and temperatures reach -50°C. In some places, the only way out of the house is through the roof. In winter, goats, animals and people are all huddled together in one room – the kitchen – where a single kerosene lamp with an open wick is all that they have. To get 20 litres of kerosene, they have to walk for two days to the nearest governmental depot, pay black market rates (though kerosene is supposed to be subsidised) and that kerosene has to last one month!

To provide three hours of light, the Government has resorted to diesel generating (DG) sets supposedly providing light to villages within a five-kilometre radius from the station. In actual fact, in winter these DG sets very rarely function. They belch out fumes and are prohibitively expensive to maintain. When the solar option was suggested, the government engineers said, 'Impossible, too expensive, and solar technology is not proven.' We argued that the answer in Ladakh was not centralised but decentralised, individual household systems where the involvement of the people was a must. We challenged them, 'Choose anyone from the remotest village, illiterate or literate, and we will train them to be a Barefoot solar engineer in three months.' Our conditions were that the trainees must be selected by the community, which must pay for the service.

'Absolutely out of the question,' the engineers said. 'No rural community has ever paid for electricity in Ladakh.' We said, 'If they maintain it themselves, they will pay for it.'

The project started in the village of Gurgurdo on the Indo-Pakistan border in 1989. Abdul Karim, an illiterate rural youth, whose job it was to supply the Army border posts with essential goods by mule, was trained to be the first Barefoot solar engineer. Since then, he has become a trainer and assisted in the installation of over 600 units in Ladakh. There was a phenomenal response from the remote village communities, and each family paid for the service. Every year nearly US$3,000 has been collected and that is enough to pay a small salary to the local Barefoot engineer to carry out repair and maintenance, purchase spares and even change batteries in solar panels.

In 1989, it was supposed to be an experiment. The government engineers reluctantly agreed because they were convinced that we Rajasthanis would run away from the severe cold conditions of Ladakh. In fact, in four months from the time the money was received from the State Government, the job was completed. It totally baffled government officials that rural youths who had never been out of their villages could handle 21st century technology with such ease and confidence, when people who had been through five years of university had proved incompetent when it came to working with their hands.

A study of the provision of conventional power through DG sets indicates that electrifying 532 houses would involve a capital outlay of Rs.15 million (US$470,000) and annual recurring costs of Rs.2 million (US$62,000). This includes maintenance, salaries, diesel, transportation and accessories.

To install 532 solar units in individual houses would cost Rs.10.6 million. The annual recurring costs for the maintenance, replacement of spares, salaries and solar panels would be Rs.100,000 (US$3,125) which would be completely covered by contributions from the community. So, in effect, there would be no maintenance cost to the Government at all.

By installing 532 units in 25 villages, the Barefoot College has saved the community and the Government a huge expenditure on kerosene. Every family has saved Rs.720 (US$22) annually on kerosene, and by not having to supply subsidised kerosene to these 25 villages the Government has saved nearly Rs.200,000 (US$6,312) annually. 100,000 litres of diesel have been saved because trucks no longer need to carry kerosene from Srinagar, 400 km away.

Usually, when a new technology is introduced, it is the petty officials and the local politicians who get access to it first. The Barefoot College insisted that the solar project should start in the remotest, the furthest, the most inaccessible villages in Leh District.

Now village after village is sending petitions to the District Development Commissioner demanding solar units. What's more, the villages are willing to pay for them.

So, what are the lessons we have learned in the last eight years in Ladakh?

- People with formal qualifications are not needed. Any villager, literate or illiterate, can be trained to do the job.
- Any remote village can easily be made self-sufficient in solar power, however poor the community may be.
- The community must be involved in the selection of the Barefoot solar engineer, in the transportation of the panels

to the village and in the installation in their own houses – only then will they pay willingly.

- The rural community must accept only that technology that does not deprive them of jobs and does not increase dependency.

- The demystification of technology is a process that cannot be rushed. It must move with the pace at which the community moves, slowly carrying everyone along.

Bunker Roy is the director of the Barefoot College in Rajasthan. A 25-minute video, *Reach for the Sun*, is available from the Social Work and Research Centre, Tilonia, Madanganj, Ajmer 305816 Rajasthan.

This article was first published in Resurgence *Issue 187, March/April 1998. All rights to this article are reserved to The Resurgence Trust. To buy a copy of the magazine, read further articles or find out about the Trust, visit www.resurgence.org*

Barefoot in Afghanistan: Solar Electrification of Villages in Afghanistan

Bunker Roy and Gry Synevvag

Originally published in *Renewable Energy World*, May-June 2006

In the mountains of Afghanistan, villagers must walk long distances and pay high prices to buy fuel to survive. Here Bunker Roy and Gry Synevvag report on an innovative solar electrification scheme which has enabled villagers to be self-reliant installers.

SINCE THE FALL OF THE TALIBAN four years ago, international donor agencies have spent billions of dollars on foreign consultants, urban infrastructure and on training people from governments and universities. But despite this huge influx of money, the quality of life for the very poor in rural Afghanistan remains as grim and desperate as ever.

Much of the development aid has been ineffective — largely because it has been donor-driven and has come from the top-down, with little attempt to look for rural community-based initiatives. Instead of developing the capacity and competence of the people from within, the aid regime has encouraged dependency on human, technical and financial resources from outside. Furthermore, for a variety of reasons, the focus has been on the development of urban areas at the expense of rural ones.

Afghanistan is one of the poorest countries in the world. Sparsely populated, with soaring mountains, there is a harsh, almost mystical beauty to the land. During the winter, temperatures drop to well below zero. The literacy rate is the lowest among developing countries, and life expectancy is alarmingly low – infant and maternal mortality rates are among the world's highest. One out of five children dies before the age of five. The situation of women is difficult and it will take a great many years for them to find an equal place in Afghan society. It is only by giving them an opportunity to show what they are capable of doing that their reality of being insecure, marginalised, sometimes abused and forgotten will change.

Most of Afghanistan's 25 million people have no access to electricity, gas, or liquid fuels for lighting, cooking or heating. The remoteness of the rural locations and the topography of the country have made the expansion of a centralised grid system impossible. To survive, the rural population depends on diesel, fuel wood and crop residues for cooking and water heating, and on kerosene for lighting. These fuels are polluting or inefficient, damaging the environment and creating an unhealthy indoor atmosphere.

Neither a conventional grid system nor diesel generating-sets is a long-term answer to providing electricity for remote villages in

Afghanistan. A grid is simply too expensive, too centralised and too dependent on engineers, personnel and fossil fuels from 'outside', while diesel is polluting and difficult to transport. Since it is estimated that Afghanistan has sunny skies for over 300 days a year, the obvious answer is to use solar energy, and for the community to own, manage and control their solar systems. The ultimate goal should be to have technically and financially self-sufficient, solar-electrified villages.

In 2004, in a fundamental departure from the way development assistance is often 'handed down' to the poor of Afghanistan, Norwegian Church Aid (NCA) – along with their local Afghan partners – initiated an approach with a difference. The key to the success of this project was that rural communities were taken into confidence and made an essential part of the decision-making process.

The idea was to get the whole community to agree on how much they would pay for the use of solar units and then select local men and women (who were only semi-literate) to be trained as 'Barefoot' solar engineers. Once the community had decided on these issues and the engineers were trained, the technology could be introduced.

Afghan NGOs selected five remote rural communities from the Provinces of Badakshan (where there are the Rajik Communities), Daikundi, Bamyan (Hazaras), Faryab (Uzbeks) and Urozgan (Pashtuns). *Shuras* or Councils from these communities then agreed (in writing) to pay around 40 Afs/month (Euro 0.70) per light when their houses were solar electrified. They then each agreed to identify two people from their villages to be trained as engineers.

The villages picked were deliberately chosen to be inaccessible and challenging. If it could work in these villages, it could work anywhere. Families in these communities spent hours fetching firewood or purchasing kerosene and diesel for lighting and cooking, spending 200 Afs (Euro 3.50) per month on an average, so it was hoped that the new solar scheme would save them a lot of money.

In a quiet way, three of the five communities created history by choosing two couples (husband and wife) and one mother and son, thus enabling two women to be trained as solar engineers. Never before in the history of Afghanistan have semi-literate women from remote villages been selected by the *shuras* for training – let alone to be solar engineers!

In the National Solidarity programme of the Afghan Government, the choice of technology is left to the *shuras*. Engineers come from outside the village to install the diesel generating sets and repair solar units. But the Barefoot approach is radically different. Its aim is to train the poor to carry out all repairs themselves.

The secret is to demystify and decentralise. It is possible for a rural man and woman who can barely read and write, with absolutely no technical background, to assemble and install the most complicated of solar lighting systems and repair and maintain them at the village level.

For six months, from January to July 2005, seven men and three women lived together as one community in the Barefoot College in Tilonia, Rajasthan, India. More than just being trained as Barefoot solar engineers they learnt about how to cooperate – in spite of their different ethnic backgrounds. They ate together, lived together and trained together. Despite not knowing any Indian language, they were still able to participate in the activities of the college, and learn about charge controllers, solar energy and electrification. But they said they now knew what hell was like because summer in Rajasthan (45°C) was too much for them!

Solar electrification of five villages in Afghanistan

Implementing partner organisation	Solar engineers	Village	District	Province	Number of households solar electrified
Future Generation (FG)	Mohammad Ishaq / Mohammad Esa	Habashi	Shibarto	Bamyan	3
Ghazni Rural Support Program (GRSP)	Mohammad Jan Gulzaman	Katasang	Shahristan	Daikundi	17
Cooperation Center for Afghanistan (CGA)	Doast Mohammad Gul Ghotai	Gumbaz	Kisham	Badakhshan	21
Afghan Development Association (ADA)	Shair Muhammad Abdul Hamid	Yaklinga	Tarinkot	Uruzgan	20
Coordination of Humanitarian Assistance (CHA)	Alaoudin Gul Bahar	Gulqudogh	Shirin Taqab	Faryab	30

Solar electrification of health clinic

Implementing partner organisation	Solar engineers	Village	District	Province	Solar panels for health clinic
Afghan Development Association (ADA)	Shair Muhammad Abdul Hamid	Yaklinga	Tarinkot	Uruzgan	17

In addition to solar electrification, they learnt about the importance of collecting rainwater from the roofs of schools into underground tanks so that no water or snow was wasted. They also teamed up with rural women from other locations to learn how to fabricate solar cookers.

The participants agreed that their time in the Barefoot College gave them confidence in their own capacity to manage, control and own the most sophisticated of technologies. Two weeks after the panels arrived in the villages, within one week all the houses were electrified.

Solar Light

So, what has been the impact? How has electric light changed the lives of the people? First of all, it has increased income-generating activities like the weaving of carpets and *kilims* and other traditional handicraft skills – especially among the women, who are bound to remain in their houses because of cultural restrictions. Secondly, it has improved the quality of life, creating space for a whole new world of opportunities. Children who work during the day in the field can now study at night.

But there have been other consequences. Never before in known memory in Afghanistan have the men and the women sat together in public meetings. In Daikundi, when Gul Zaman went and sat with the men at the *shura* meeting, she demonstrated her courage to change a custom and tradition as old as time. She said to the *shura* she was first an engineer and then a woman. But unlike a man, a female solar engineer could now gain access to households where only women were present to carry out the repair and maintenance of the solar lighting. It was agreed in writing in front of the whole village that the contribution from the community would pay for the salaries of the Barefoot solar engineers.

Cost-effective

The life of the 70W solar panels is 25 years (although the 75Ah batteries have to be changed every 5 years). Each of the solar units can power four lights, each of which is ten times stronger than a kerosene lamp. As mentioned, families used to spend about 200

Afs/per kerosene lamp per month (Euro 3.50) and walk about 10km to buy fuel. With solar light, they have agreed to pay 40 Afs per light/month, reducing their expenditure substantially. As a result of this project, 183 families in five remote villages now have five hours of environmentally sound and secure light every night for five years.

But what did it cost and was it cost effective? It has been calculated that the whole process, including the selection and identification of the Barefoot solar engineers, the cost of their travel and training, and purchasing insuring and transporting all the solar panels and batteries to the villages cost roughly $120,000 – about the same as the UN or World Bank would probably spend on one consultant for a year.

Conclusion

Despite the billions at their disposal, these organisations did not solar electrify even one village in Afghanistan in these last 4 years. What prevented them? It is a sad commentary on their lack of vision, courage and capacity to act.

A centralised power system is not the answer for Afghanistan. The distances, landscape and nature of the culture make it unlikely to succeed. Projects such as the Barefoot College succeed because they involve the local community, allow them to set the rules and train them to be self-sufficient. This scheme has shown that poor, badly educated villagers can operate and maintain sophisticated electrical systems, and has had a positive impact on the lives of five villages. In response to the success of this project, the Indian Government has indicated that it will fund the electrification of a further 100 villages in Afghanistan.

© Reprinted Courtesy of Renewable Energy World

Rwanda's Semi-literate Grandmothers Aspire for Solar Engineering

Clemence Bideri, Christine Muhongerwa
and Bunker Roy

Originally published in *The New Times*, September 12 2008

RWANDA IS SET TO MAKE HISTORY when four semi-literate rural women from the village of Batima in the Rweru Sector of Bugesera District leave for India on the 13th of September – for six months' training that will convert them into 'Barefoot' solar engineers.

Since 1998, the Norwegian Church Aid (NCA), an international NGO, has been operating here in Rwanda, with the main objective of achieving sustainable development through addressing reconciliation, at community levels.

NCA implements its programmes through their capable local partners. A 'practical reconciliation' village consisting of 110 houses has been constructed by the NCA approximately four kilometres from the Burundi border. Those settled in the village include released prisoners and genocide survivors.

Batima is a village of some 1,380 families with two schools and a dispensary. The nearest electrified village is Nyamata 35 kilometres away. Batima is 10 kilometres away from the recent tarmacked Kicuiro-Nemba road.

At present, all the houses use very small improvised kerosene lamps about half the size of condensed milk tins. These poor families spend about 1,000 Rwandan Francs a month on lighting. The basic design of the houses is four rooms with a kitchen and a toilet outside.

What they need – which will tangibly improve their quality of life – is only one 18-watt solar unit with one bright light inside the house and one solar lantern that is mobile and that will help in the kitchen and when visiting the toilet at night, to make life for the women more comfortable.

The four rural women – all grandmothers – will not need proficiency in any language but they will learn through sign language; they will be required to identify parts only by their colours.

They will also learn how to fabricate sophisticated charge controllers and inverters at the village level; how to install solar panels and link them to the deep cycle batteries; and how to establish a Rural Electronic workshop.

A building to be used as a workshop has already been donated by the community. At this workshop, they will be able to carry out all major and minor repairs at the village level instantly without depending on any paper-qualified urban-based solar engineers from the city. It is all about capacity strengthening and confidence building.

This is the first time the Barefoot approach is being tried in Rwanda, but not the first time in Africa. Rural grandmothers turned solar engineers have solar electrified their own villages in Cameroon, The Gambia, Mali, Sierra Leone and Ethiopia. Grandmothers from Benin, Mauritania and Malawi will soon be trained as solar engineers. If they can show the impossible is possible, why not rural women from Rwanda?

At a public meeting held on the 3rd July 2008, attended by all the village members in the presence of the Executive Secretary of Rweru Sector, the people endorsed the approach as well as agreeing to meet soon to decide on how much they are prepared to pay towards repair and maintenance; this amount will be used to pay a monthly salary to the solar engineers.

The community members would pay for solar what they would otherwise pay for firewood, kerosene, candles and torch batteries. There could not be a more effective way of showing how the rural poor in Rwanda are tackling the serious issues of climate change.

This is a partnership model (as against a 'business' model) where the community makes the important decisions in a transparent and collective manner, thus controlling, managing and owning the project from the very beginning. The other partners – Norwegian Church Aid, Government of India, Safer-Rwanda and possibly SGP/UNDP – are only facilitators. The project is an example of a genuine bottom-up approach that is replicable all over the country. The total cost of solar electrifying the whole village of Batima and benefiting nearly 6,400 men, women and children will be close to $100,000.

Bunker Roy has been invited to the world Economic Forum in Davos since 2002: identified as an Outstanding Global Social Entrepreneur by Schwab (2002) and Skoll (2005). In January 2008, The Guardian, London, identified him as one of the 50 environmentalists in the world who could save the planet.

Clemence Bideri is the Programme Coordinator for Norwegian Church Aid in Rwanda. Her contact Email is: clemence@ncagl.org.rw

Christine Muhongerwa is the Director of SaferRwanda. SaferRwanda is a national NGO and is the implementing partner for this project. Contact address: saferrwanda@yahoo.co.uk

Reprinted with kind permission of The New Times, Rwanda

Barefoot engineers doing a soil test

Bunker at the controls of a drill

Pure drinking water draws children

Open air stage showing water collection area

Women making solar panels

Trainees, Bunker and Janjibar President Nikon

Solar Women's Training Centre, Barefoot College Tilonia

Dalai Lama with trainee team against solar panel

Bunker Roy with Barefoot solar engineer from Senegal

9: The Greatest Wealth of All

Heather MC Malcolm and Aruna Roy

'It is health that is real wealth, and not pieces of gold and silver.'
Saying attributed to Mahatma Gandhi

In Barefoot's early years, social workers on the campus were worried by the lack of medical attention in the villages around Tilonia, and by the strength of villagers' belief in traditional cures. At that time, there were many public warnings about the dangers of the killer disease tuberculosis, which was rife, and village men seemed to be more concerned about the welfare of their animals than their families' health. Child mortality was common and usually attributed to a witch's evil eye, while home births took no account of dirt and unhygienic conditions.

All these factors made it inevitable that the young group in Tilonia should focus on health care provision. The village people mistrusted modern doctors, and were afraid of injections and having to go to hospital. Because of this, to begin with, the Barefoot College deliberately (and wisely) chose people who were not themselves doctors to set up its health care programme and let people know about it. As had been hoped, this approach put fears to rest.

Two women, a social worker trained in community health care and partnering with a woman doctor, laid the foundations of the Barefoot College health care programme. The work began when the social worker made friends with young men from the villages who were as concerned as she was about the scarcity of medical care and the many misunderstandings about the reasons for illness. Superstition was rampant – never more so than in the people's attribution of illness to supernatural causes, and traditional practices varied. Some of these, like that of the bone-setter and the chiropractor, were excellent and the naturopathy they practised had a scientific underpinning. In any discussions about health practices, it was important to distinguish work like this from traditional attitudes to mental health (in which people were seen as possessed), traditional remedies for snake bites (which it was believed could be cured with prayers to the snake god) and other illnesses, for which patients were taken to a religious shrine which never seemed to work.

The health care offered at Tilonia was participatory from the start. Local midwives worked with nurses who had come from Kerala, and were instrumental in helping the curative part of the health programme to take off. A crucially important incident was a very difficult but eventually successful breach delivery of a boy, who is now a middle-aged man living in Tilonia. The story, recounted in 'Rural Doctor', is an important one because successes like these caused people's confidence in Barefoot College's health programme to grow.

Gradually, Barefoot's health services and village health workers added to the types of care they offered, expanding to include education about disease and what it is, the value of natural cures and how to use them, and the role played by hygiene and disinfectants. David Werner's book *'Where There is No Doctor: a Village Health Care Handbook'*[9] was extremely helpful and used extensively for reference, and when David came to Tilonia, the visit gave a little back to him, as it helped deepen his understanding of the efficacy of local medical practices.

As it developed, the health programme focused increasingly on helping people to understand the body, its functions and the reasons for illness. This understanding became an essential part of the College's larger education programme and was built into the school curriculum, into training sessions, and into meetings with the village community and women's groups.

As time passed, it became possible to venture into newer areas, focussing on specialised issues. This was not always straightforward, however. The first major argument with the authorities came when Barefoot College offered birth control but not family planning. The distinction was subtle but important: birth control was the exercise of one's rights over one's body,

---

[9] Macmillan Education, 1980

while family planning was the Government's working plan for population control. The College's sensitive approach to this difference encouraged innumerable women to attend the sterilisation clinic – and, ironically, Barefoot College won accolades for educating people about population control. Interestingly, in rural Rajasthan, men stayed away from these camps, worried about their virility, and were progressive only to the extent of allowing their women to undergo the operation!

Barefoot's outreach health programme had sub-dispensaries and clinics dotted throughout the districts it covered, which included 100 villages. Midwives met regularly for discussions and mutual support. In this area, over time, the infant mortality rate visibly decreased, and deliveries ceased to be a dreaded nightmare for the women and their families: almost all survived without succumbing to sepsis.

Dentistry was another new venture. It was made possible when an Italian dentist, Dr. Giuseppe Petretta, spent six months in Tilonia during which, in memory of his wife Cristina Gobbi, who had died very young, he trained Barefooters – all women – in basic dental care. The attention these dentists were then able to give villagers' teeth was greatly appreciated and had a huge impact.

There is a nice story associated with the women dentists. At Barefoot College, people are glad to give their time and effort without expecting rewards, but one day, the dentists had an unexpected treat. Not far out of the campus is a helipad that many people (including foreigners) use. To show his appreciation of their work, one day, one of the foreign pilots took the women dentists for a free 'copter ride. They were jubilant for days!

Now that Government has passed progressive legislation for free healthcare, the health situation in Rajasthan has improved somewhat. This has left Barefoot College more free to concentrate on preventive health, nutrition, and women's menstrual needs, as well as continuing its work with midwives. However, the Covid-19 pandemic brought a situation far out of the ordinary. During the dire times of lockdown, in partnership with others from the community Tilonia's health workers were brave and tireless, distributing food packets and RAT (rapid antigen testing) kits to a million people. By setting up and maintaining isolation facilities at the campus's small health clinic, they helped with the task of keeping infected patients separate. This was a huge problem in rural India, where houses are small and it was impossible to put patients in different rooms.

Tilonia's health programme continues to hold camps for various medical issues, on the one hand coordinating with hospitals, and on the other organising and mobilising people. The latest challenges Tilonia faces are how to fight against the commercialisation of medical care, and how to promote the government's progressive schemes for health care that is free and comprehensive. Bunker's article from 1986, 'Adding Insult to Injury', illustrates that the role played by industry in health care is nothing new, however, and suggests that we should be wary of it. Commercial healthcare takes on the garb of efficiency and it may indeed be so; but compassion has been lost. Tilonia and its medical team continue to bridge the gap between the patient and medical care with kindness, understanding and empathy.

Rural Doctor

Dr Arti Sawhney & Dr Shyam Mathur

Originally published in *Youth Times*, 19 September 1975

THE PROCESS STARTS WITH the entrance into a medical college – entrance examinations, competitions, applications (the numbers increasing every year and medical colleges mushrooming everywhere). Then comes the selection. How many of those selected have an aim at this stage? The majority do, ruling out a few who enter because of family pressure. The question is, what aim?

Five years of exposure to a medical college and an urban-based hospital reinforced the dream and increased our determination to the point of conviction. It was almost always the urban patients who got preference, either because they belonged to the upper class, or being literate were able to follow the treatment.

The rural patients – the few who did reach the hospital – after having spent a couple of hours in a rickety bus would inevitably get lost in the hospital corridors and arrive after OPD (Out-Patient Department) hours. Those who managed to reach a doctor in time will be rewarded with a quick prescription (who has the patience to explain?) or handed a number of investigation forms which mean repeated bus journeys. The desperate cases who manage to reach a hospital bed (a major achievement) will be subjected to indifferent scrutiny or at the most be discussed at a clinical meeting. How could one be blind to all this?

The question now was how to reach a village and make oneself useful. The compulsory rural posting was quite different from setting off to live by oneself and starting a practice. A government dispensary seemed the only answer till I heard about the Social Work and Research Centre in Tilonia.

Finally, after reaching the rural area, we were almost frightened at first by the tremendous responsibility, the complete change of environment and the enormous social barriers – the customs and the traditions we had to break through.

Initial acceptance by the villagers was of vital importance. As expected, there was a lot of suspicion and hesitation. But a *vaid*, like a *vakil*, is a respected individual. It was only a matter of getting used to a different version of a *vaid*. Since the organisation had already reached out to the people and the medical social workers had overcome the initial obstacles, we did not face too many problems.

Dealing with patients in a village is very different from working in a hospital. One has to be much more thorough and cautious because villagers often would not hesitate to pick up a *dunda* at the slightest provocation or think twice before spreading damaging rumours about the medical facilities and the personnel.

Besides, one has to almost solely rely on clinical diagnosis, facilities for investigation being negligible. Apart from just diagnosing the disease, winning the confidence of the patient requires a knowledge of local customs and remedies and their adaptation.

For example, feeling the pulse is of extreme significance to a villager and one had to make it a point never to forget this even if it may be for a little blister on the toe!

It really does help to respect the local remedies, even though at times this becomes extremely difficult. For instance, a boil in the armpit is treated by tying a live frog there because its urine is supposed to have a healing effect. A foreign body in the eye is extracted with a tongue. (There are special experts for this in the village.) A tumour is supposed to be cured by catching a live snake and rubbing it on the spot seven times.

Curative medicine is the easiest way of gaining acceptance. Once a sick individual is treated, he or she is bound to develop a certain amount of faith and confidence. Hence, we found it imperative to fully equip two of our existing dispensaries.

Involvement of the community and their active participation was extremely important. We did not think it sensible to impose any of our programmes. We tried to make the community aware of the facilities and services we had to offer but at no stage did we offer the services till the community came forward and asked for them and also fulfilled our conditions, like free space, accommodation, etc. We faced some difficulty in the beginning but now the response to the programme is so good that we are running two dispensaries on these lines.

We found that the attempt of the Barefoot doctor scheme attracted the rural people in ten villages around the two dispensaries. Their job was to draw patients to the dispensaries, make them aware of the facilities and educate them. Our job was to give them in-service training in basic illness care and health education. Since these ten village-level health workers were selected by the villagers, they agreed to supervise their work and also to contribute a portion of their salary. This was a way of involving the whole community.

A doctor is meant for curing illnesses and hence the focus is generally on the disease rather than the diseased. Dealing with rural people, the focus is the other way round. Very often we have had to go to the patient rather than the patient coming to us because he is suspicious, afraid and lacks faith.

Yet the curiosity to learn more does exist and very often the patients demand an explanation and continue treatment only when they are convinced. A large majority, however, have blind faith. These are the ones who stand back and watch. A few cases treated successfully draw them out. Honesty and kindness are two things a villager respects but these are not easy to come by these days. An old woman with a scorpion bite once came to the dispensary during working hours and said that she had actually been bitten at night, but thought that if she disturbed us at night, she would not be treated.

They also forgive mistakes, provided one admits them. An honest explanation of one's capabilities is a must for the villagers for, though they are simple, they are also intelligent and not easily fooled. In every village, we found ourselves carefully studied and our responses and reactions judged at every step. A common feature everywhere was the initial challenge to treat a few chronic cases – this is their test. With the women it is almost always a case of sterility. They demand a cure or else refuse treatment. This is invariably the first stage. For cases that require delicate and sensitive handling, it is the first principle to invoke the help of God for a speedy and complete cure.

The first delivery conducted in our maternity centre was a big test. I was all alone because Dr Shyam was not allowed to assist me. We are three of us – Manya, our social worker, Sugandi and Maniamma. The future of the programme depended on this delivery. As luck would have it, it turned out to be a complicated case. The expectant mother had had a previous Caesarean, two still-borns, and now she was bleeding.

However, I decided to go ahead. A number of women collected to wait and watch the result. The baby finally arrived with a cord around its neck, blue and had aspirated fluid. It was almost five minutes before he breathed. We did not have any suction apparatus. In sheer desperation, I cut off the drip and made do with the tube. Luckily both mother and child lived. The local *dai*, who was watching, had given up hope. Seeing the child survive won her over to our side and in her we now have the best communicator in the village.

Another time, one of the villagers came and asked me for an injection for his cow. Since our drugs were in short supply I refused and the cow died. The entire village was furious and wanted to stop all our programmes. It was a tricky situation. Luckily, the local vet came to our help.

One had to face these tests at every stage – from having to spend nights out in the wilderness because the jeep has broken down and there is no way of avoiding discomfort, hunger and cold, to having to fight mothers-in-law or forcefully take a five-month case of pregnancy and severe bleeding to the dispensary.

Very often, we have been asked why so few doctors work in the villages. Now, with our experience, we feel we can answer that. It is partly because of lack of confidence, courage and facilities. A large part of the blame must be shared by the faulty medical education system. It inculcates wrong values, putting stress mainly on the disease and modes of treatment, ignoring the diseased and also increasing the need for sophisticated methods of investigation and confirmation of diagnosis.

The day a graduate leaves the college with an MBBS degree secure in his hand, he is confused, nervous, lacks confidence and is desperate for a job. That doctors are human must never be forgotten. But a hospital is the last place to develop human feelings which are so essential in the medical profession.

The village environment would provide excitement and experience for an up-and-coming doctor. But, on the other hand, there is fear of stagnation, the fear of intense sacrifice and lack of courage. This is the real dilemma.

© Reproduced with kind permission of author Dr Arti Sawhney

Barefoot in Tilonia

Trevor Drieberg

Originally published in *India Today*, 1-15 November 1976

LIKE THEIR COUNTERPARTS IN CHINA, the Barefoot doctors of the Social Work and Research Centre (SWRC), based in a village in Rajasthan, a night's run by train from Delhi, do not really go unshod. They wear country-made sandals or *chappals*. And they perform very much the same function – to provide a grassroot medical service for the villager – which lays stress on public health programmes to keep disease at bay.

Housed in the buildings of an abandoned missionary-run tuberculosis hospital near the Tilonia railway station in Ajmer district, SWRC's medicare programme, started in 1973, now covers 11 villages with a total population of 9,300.

Headed by a doctor who graduated from Maulana Azad Medical College, New Delhi, its infrastructure comprises educated village youths who have had a practical training for a few weeks in the basics of preventing and curing common diseases. In February 1973, SWRC opened its dispensary at Tilonia to treat the sick. By early 1975, it had treated 70,000 persons from 60 villages. Out of this emerged a community health programme for which OXFAM has provided the finances. The programme aims at covering 25 villages and more than 20,000 people.

Each village included in the project has one health worker selected by the *panchayat*. He has been trained in Tilonia for 15 days in simple anatomy, surgery, identification of communicable diseases, preservation of medical records, family planning, first-aid, and personal hygiene and environmental sanitation. The village-level health workers (VLHWs) are between 16- and 25- years old, residents of the village they work in, and have studied up to at least eighth class in school. They carry out house-to-house surveys to get to know their fellow-villagers better, and when there is sickness they visit sufferers in their homes. The SWRC's doctor, stationed in Tilonia, goes to each village once a fortnight; the health workers in turn come to Tilonia regularly for in-service training.

A new dispensary building is now coming up in the nearby village of Chhota Naraina. SWRC is meeting part of the cost and the villagers the rest by providing building materials, free labour and small contributions.

Dr Arti Sawhny heads the medical service. She had planned to specialise after graduation, but two months at Tilonia made her decide to continue working there. She joined the Centre in March 1975. The work is heavy and exacting but 'challenging and exciting'. There are no fixed hours, and health workers often have to answer midnight calls from a distant village where a woman might be in labour or a suffering child in need of instant relief.

Most of the villagers cannot afford treatment by western methods, and at the same time they accept willingly what is familiar. On her visits to villages, she collects facts about local cures. She thinks the present system of medical education should be changed. The average young medical graduate is a 'complete misfit in a rural set-up. He must make so many adjustments to make himself acceptable to the village community, but very few of them are able to do so.'

Before the health programme was launched in June 1975, a medical social worker from Tilonia spent two years just meeting villagers and talking about their problems to win their confidence. In that initial period, there was much suspicion and even open hostility.

'At first we visit a village and find out whether it has some form of health service already,' Sawhny explained. 'If it does not have one, we organise meetings in which all the major castes are represented. We explain the programme and list all the services we offer and leave them to decide whether they want the programme. If they do, they are asked to send us a written application. Then there is a second meeting at which the villagers select one of their number for training as a VLHW.'

The villagers undertake to pay part of the worker's salary in cash or in kind. They set up a committee to collect this amount, which may range from 10 to 25 *paise* a month. Very poor households are exempted.

Supervising the activities of the health workers presents no problem, because the villagers keep a sharp watch on them and report dereliction of duty to the Centre at Tilonia.

Because the villagers now have faith in the health workers and seek their help not only in overcoming their ailments but also in matters relating to farming, SWRC has decided to convert the VLHWs into multi-purpose operators.

When SWRC proposed building a new dispensary building at Chhota Naraina, the matter was referred to the village elders for approval. There was a heated discussion over whether facilities to treat expectant mothers or sick cattle was more useful. One speaker said he considered his buffaloes more valuable than his womenfolk, and it looked as if he would take the majority with him. At this point, a village notable stood up and said he had been born of a woman unlike the previous speaker, who seemed to have sprung from a buffalo, and a clinic for humans should get priority. The argument carried the day.

The VLHW programme has shown such impressive results that it is being introduced in *Khol* community development block of Mohindergarh district of Haryana with help from the State Government and the United Nations Children's Fund. The second SWRC project was started in this block in August 1975.

The most striking thing about Tilonia is that a score or so of professional people, including the doctors, connected with the project are under 30. All of them could get well-paid jobs in the cities or towns from which they come.

They are dedicated people, working for a cause – rural uplift. In the words of Sanjit Roy, SWRC's founder-director, this project was conceived as 'an integrated rural development agency providing technical and socio-economic services from a rural base.'

© *Courtesy India Today magazine*

Adding Insult to Injury

Bunker Roy

Originally published in *Express Magazine*, 23 March 1986

(This article is reproduced entirely in its original form.)

The proposed national drug policy caters to the demands of the pharmaceutical lobby and not to the country's health needs, says SANJIT ROY

The national drug policy, if it is accepted in its present form and content, is going to open India to ridicule and shame in the western world. Quite apart from the fact that the first sufferers will be the rural poor, our so-called socialist image will have received a grievous blow. It will have violated in spirit and principle our assurances that we will implement an integrated national drug policy in order to ensure access to essential drugs at reasonable prices. (This assurance was given at the Fifth Non-Aligned Summit Conference in August 1976 which endorsed the recommendations of the Expert Group in Resolution No 25 on pharmaceuticals). It will have made a mockery of the recommendations of the Joint Task Force on pharmaceuticals of four UN agencies – UNAPEC, UNCTAD, UNIDO and WHO – set up in 1978. It will reveal the scant respect we have for WHO recommendations and criteria for a rational drug policy.

The best collective brains in the country that brought out the ICMR-CSSR report, *Health for all by 2000 A.D.* has had little or no effect on the preparation of the national drug policy. To add insult to injury, we hear the national drug policy is based on a National Council of Applied Economic Research (NCAER) Report sponsored by the Organisation of Pharmaceutical Producers of India (OPPI) in 1984, largely represented by multinational drug companies.

In socialist India, the drug policy for the poor has been outlined by the drug industry. In the National Drugs and Pharmaceutical Development Council (NDPDC), there is a heavy representation from the drug industry, the very multinationals who were forced to discontinue their unethical practices in Bangladesh. This is one reason why this country is still producing 60,000 formulations of all drugs in the market. According to WHO, India needs 250 drugs to take care of 95 per cent of its health needs.

Yet we have shortages. The lobby is so strong that the drug companies can reduce the production of essential and life saving drugs while the government looks on helplessly. Today, shortages of anti-TB, anti-leprosy drugs and vaccines and even iodised salt exist. Production of Vitamin A is steadily declining and, as a result, over 40,000 children are becoming blind each year but this does not seem to be the cause of any concern. Why is the government allowing this to happen? Why is the government so callous and criminal in its attitude to providing essential and life saving drugs? The answer is simple: because there is no profit in it for the drug companies, so let the rural poor suffer.

It is the government's job – and not the drug industry's – to formulate a drug policy. Whereas the Hathi Committee had looked into the entire drug scenario, the NDPDC's national drug policy recommendations are limited to "drug pricing and drug production" from the industry's point of view. One-third of the total primary health care services are provided by the voluntary sector but representatives from this sector, from consumer bodies involved in the drug issue and women's organisations, have been deliberately excluded from being members of the NDPDC. So the policy is bound to be lopsided and tilted towards satisfying the needs and interests of the drug sector, at the expense of the people and the actual users in the rural areas.

Significantly, the drug policy has virtually nothing to say on the following issues which are of great concern: priority production and distribution of essential life saving drugs; the identification and withdrawal of irrational and hazardous drugs (WHO recommendation flouted by Government of India); and the establishment of a National Drug Authority handling production and distribution and information dissemination of drugs and vaccines (Hathi Committee recommendation of 1975 not being implemented).

In an effort to perform pressure group functions on the drug industry and the government, 11 groups from the voluntary sector got together to form the All India Drug Action Network. They comprise Arogya Dakshata Mandal, Pune; Catholic Hospital Association, Delhi; Consumer Education and Research Centre, Ahmedabad; Consumer Guidance Society of India, Bombay; Drug Action Forum, West Bengal, Calcutta; Delhi Science Forum, Delhi; Kerala Sashtra Sahitya Parishad, Trivandrum; Locost, Baroda; Lok Vigyan Sangathana, Bombay; Medico Friends Circle, Pune; and Voluntary Health Association of India, Delhi. The All India Drug Action Network has been responsible for extensive documentation on a vastly professional scale with frightening data on incalculable damage to come should the national drug policy be accepted in its present form.

But no one is prepared to listen. Members of Parliament sitting on consultative committees of the ministry of chemicals have no time and are not prepared to speak out. MPs who have raised awkward questions have been gently eased out for whatever reason. Without even looking at the data and studying its contents, bureaucrats dismiss the data on grounds that this is too specialised an area for voluntary agencies.

Producing low cost sub-standard drugs to dump on people in the third world is big business; appropriately it is handled by the ministry of chemicals, department of industry. The ministry of health and family welfare, the implementing agency, are out of the picture and have no say. Voluntary agencies and consumer groups, the actual eyes and ears of the people in villages, have also been kept out of the process of formulating a drug policy.

If the government has the interests of the poor in mind and it is serious about a rational drug policy, voluntary and consumer groups, in the All India Drug Action Network, demand a policy which ensures:

• Availability of essential and life saving drugs: This means, at whatever cost, the government should ensure there is no shortage of drugs and vaccines for tuberculosis, leprosy, iodine deficiency (goitre), measles and polio.

Reprinted from THE INDIAN EXPRESS, *with permission of*
The Indian Express (P) Limited © 1978-1996.
All rights reserved through the world.

10: When Learning is Fun

Heather MC Malcolm and Aruna Roy

Knowledge transfer lies at the heart of everything that Barefoot College is about – knowledge about education, about skills, and about gaining an understanding of the different ways in which people define learning, and think about varied learning practices. This understanding facilitates the use of different learning methods. It makes learning at Barefoot College an option open to anyone, but especially to 'drop-outs, cop-outs and wash-outs', as Bunker affectionately puts it. The College does not recognise failure in conventional terms. There is no certification, and there are certainly no degrees!

In the initial years, when a handful of people came to Tilonia to begin working for the community, schooling was a major concern. Very early on, the Barefoot College added to the dictionary of development understanding by defining literacy, education and schooling as three different concepts. (Bunker often introduced himself as 'literate, but uneducated'.) This distinction was a huge breakthrough, an important contribution to the argument that different ways of obtaining knowledge and skills have equal merit. It helped all those who worked 'the Tilonia Way' to understand that there are different ways to learn, that different modes of learning are suited to different people, and that each is as effective as the others.

In every society, the school system remains a self-contained separate unit where a certain set curriculum is transferred through lessons to children. In remote Rajasthan, schools set up by Government with the best intention of reaching far-flung areas simply did not work. Not wanting to live in remote villages, teachers had to travel long distances. They often depended on public transport, arriving and returning home by bus or train. Naturally enough, they were unwilling to do it for long. It was a predicament.

Government-run evening literacy classes for the 20-40 age group also encountered problems. It was not surprising that these late-night sessions were ill-attended by both women and men, and as time passed, they morphed into elementary schools that attracted young children (with more energy than their parents!) who were eager to learn their alphabets.

Tilonia, always honest in assessing situations, faced up to reality and argued for the setting up of schools that would be able to cater not just to children who could attend during the day, but also to those who – working with their parents for the family livelihood – could only come after they had eaten their evening meal.

This pragmatic re-thinking of what a rural village school could be and do included plans for training teachers from within the village – people who would therefore not be dependent on transport – and who had basic literacy skills. This visionary idea was supported and promoted by the Centre for Educational Technology in Delhi. As an experiment, the district administration handed three government schools over to Tilonia for the three years between 1975 and 1978. A period of phenomenal learning began, not only for Tilonia but also for the community and the Government. Enrolment increased, and levels of scholastic achievement rose to above the average.

However, in 1978, a change of government and new politics stopped the programme. Government withdrew support. The day schools closed down, and the night schools became a separate programme which the Barefoot College continued to run. The night schools influenced Government thinking, however, and encouraged it to begin what is called 'the *shiksha karmi* programme': the training of young people from far-flung villages as teachers so that they could take the day schools over from teachers who lived far away.

It was always important to Barefoot College to make sure that the night schools would be happy places for learners to be. Children would come after a day's often tiring work, but they saw their school as somewhere that gave them the freedom to behave as the young children they were. School was a place where games helped them to learn alphabets and numbers. A place to discover how the local village council – the *Panchayat* – worked. The mock parliament helped them learn about elections, how to vote in them, and why it was important to do it. The teacher was a familiar figure, one of them, so the children were not afraid to ask questions or be honest. Fear disappeared. The night schools alone managed to attract 90,000 children, who over the last 50 years have transferred into mainstream schools.

In later years, Tilonia also ran a formal school called *Shiksha Niketan,* as well as a 'bridge school', which made it easier for children from nomadic communities to join the mainstream. These joined with the night schools to make sure that formal schooling was what Barefoot College believed it should always be: meaningful and fun.

Together *Shiksha Niketan*, the bridge school and the night schools formed part of what became known as the Children's Parliament, which features in all the articles in this chapter. It was a huge success and was so different that it captivated the world. When one of its Prime Ministers went to Sweden to receive an award from the Queen, the Queen asked her, 'How do you manage to do all this?' Devaki simply answered, 'I am the Prime Minister.'

Perhaps because the Children's Parliament was such an unusual feature of learning, it fascinated both educationists and journalists, and many articles were written about it. But there's a lot more to know about Barefoot's approach to learning, and we urge readers to visit the website, where they will find videos and many other articles about the Barefoot College learning process. It's easy to sum up the Barefoot view of this, though. When asked about methodology, all those involved simply say: 'It's easy. It's just learning by doing.'

India: The Children's Republic

By Jean-Christophe Klotz

Originally published in *Sources*, UNESCO, October 1999

THE MAN GLARES AT THE YOUNG GIRL. He won't let her move a step forward. The 15-year-old looks him straight in the eye. She's on a surprise visit to this small carpet factory, one of hundreds in Rajasthan (north-western India). Five or six of the dozen employees are under 14, the minimum legal working age. The younger they are, the quicker they weave, young fingers being more agile.

Mehrun is the young girl's name. She is home minister of the Parliament of the Children of Tilonia. Elected for two years by children from 150 evening schools in the region, she is there to take stock of the reality of the conditions the children live and work in. 'The right to education, health, speech … It would be time to leave by the time I listed all the violations of our fundamental rights,' she says smiling, looking elegant and dignified in her bright blue *sari*.

The man mutters, 'You should have let us know you are coming. The boss isn't here. I can't allow you to enter in his absence.' It turns out later that he is the boss.

The Children's Parliament is an initiative launched by SWRC (Social Work and Research Centre), an Indian NGO also known as the 'Barefoot College', based in Tilonia, a small village in the State of Rajasthan. SWRC has been working for over 20 years with the poorest of India's rural population. The point of departure was the fact that in this part of the country, almost 70% of children are not in school. Not all of them are exploited by unscrupulous bosses for a miserable salary: most of them help their families by tending the animals or helping out at home.

Eleven-year-old Kartar is a shepherd. His whole family works in order to survive. Kartar wakes up at six, and washes his face, feet and hands. Then he takes the goats to graze in the fields and chases the birds away from the crops. When he gets back, he has to collect the dung and dry it for fuel. When does he have the time to go to school?

The SWRC set up evening schools to enable children like Kartar to obtain an education comparable to those who have access to formal education: 275 such schools exist today in nine Indian states.

With 30 students per class, Tilonia's children are made aware of their rights through songs, puppets and classroom theatre. The curriculum gives them an idea about language and reading and writing in Hindi, as well as the basics of mathematics. Then they make links between letters and words, and between words and phrases. Over the following years, they are taught about social and rural behaviour, how to be self-sufficient, and about the caste system. Then come the theories of social and political thinkers and national heroes, as well as lectures on agriculture and cattle breeding. The focus of the lessons is the environment they live in. The children are taught how to make arid land cultivable, and the destructive effect of chopping down trees for firewood. Powerful links are established between the school and everyday working life.

Food First

The NGO takes a pragmatic approach, because without child labour, most of these families wouldn't survive. This reality has to be taken into consideration while giving new generations the tools necessary for their emancipation. And the first step is education, says Ram Niwas, an SWRC volunteer.

'You in the West spend your time saying, let's ban child labour! But if we prevent these children from working, how will they eat? A child's first need is food. If he has nothing in the stomach, everything else is secondary. Children need to be taught what is good for them and what is not; to acquire the ability to make decisions in the world they live in.'

SWRC's headquarters feel like a haven tucked away in the hills of the desert. The ingenuity of its volunteers makes SWRC a self-sufficient institution. Electricity comes from solar energy. The villagers, trained on the spot by teachers from the Barefoot College, built the professional training centre set up by SWRC.

Several hundred water pumps have been installed using extremely simple technology, sparing the villagers from having to wait for hypothetical visits from government experts.

'The aim of all technology distributors is to increase the dependence of their clients,' explains Bunker Roy, the college's director and instigator of the whole adventure. He is convinced that villagers are perfectly capable of becoming solar electricity engineers, health workers or sanitary technicians if given the opportunity. A visit to Tilonia is proof enough of his convictions.

On the day of our arrival there for the production of a documentary film, a thousand children had come from all over India for the annual session of the Children's Parliament. A dozen children step up to the podium and one by one respond to questions translated from several local languages. The youngest minister is just 10, the eldest 15. It's question time and the focus is as much on child labour as it is on child marriage.

But the first task of the Parliament is the management of evening schools. It is the Parliament that hires and fires teachers and looks after school equipment. 'These children come from a very poor background,' says Bunker Roy. 'A ten or twelve-year old girl is already an adult. She has a huge economic responsibility to her family. We are merely harnessing this maturity for the better management of the evening schools.'

Mehrun, the home minister, is also on the podium. Before closing the session, she appeals to all the child workers present: 'Today I am 15 and in class five. If I could have gone to school earlier, I would have had my diploma by now!' There is a gleam in the children's eyes. No doubt that is what makes Bunker Roy smile. 'We want to transmit the essential values of democracy,' he says. A process that is not made easy by the anachronistic rigidity of the caste system, or the status of women and children in Indian society.

Mehrun was married off very young, like so many children in rural Rajasthan. But she won't go to her husband's home until after puberty. She will then have to persuade him to allow her to continue her work at the Children's Parliament.

'The people here think girls get a swollen head, and that afterwards they will never want to go their husband's house. In any case, I will never miss a single meeting. I will continue to attend them, even if they cut my head off.'

> The French production house Point du Jour has made a television documentary on the Children's Parliament which will be available through UNESCO in French and English.

From India: The Children's Republic, by Jean-Christophe Klotz, © 1995, United Nations. Used with the permission of the United Nations.

Lessons Instead of Bedtime Stories: Night Schools in India

Originally published in *UBS Optimus World*, August 2006

The UBS Optimus Foundation is supporting the Barefoot College with an annual contribution of CHF 200,000

LAURA FROM LUGANO is eight years old and is in her second year at school. Every evening at seven o'clock she has a bedtime story read to her and goes off to sleep, so that she has plenty of energy for the next day at school. Kaushalya from Tilonia in India has a very different routine. She too is eight years old, but every evening when the sun goes down, she packs her school bag and goes to school. After a hard day at work, she enthusiastically takes part in her two hours of lessons.

It is by no means a matter of course that Kaushalya is able to attend school. Generally, children from poor families have to help their parents looking after goats, sheep and taking their animals out for grazing during the daytime. If a child is permitted to attend school, then it is the boys who are chosen. It is precisely this problem that the Barefoot College addresses.

Tried, Tested and Proven

The Social Work and Research Centre (SWRC) Tilonia is also known as the Barefoot College. For over thirty years it has been committed to helping the poorest sectors of the population in rural areas, and is the only institution in India to address their concerns. As well as improving basic services such as drinking water and lighting, and tackling preventive health and environmental issues, the Barefoot College focuses on educating the people.

Five Years of Basic Education

The ongoing project is set to last for five years and will provide 5,000 children each year with a basic literacy and education skills. Two out of every three pupils are female, indicating that the schools are particularly important for educating girls. A total of 100 schools will be set up in six different areas. The children should attend school for at least five years in order to be able to achieve a good standard of reading, writing and arithmetic. They also learn many things about their own village which are useful for their daily work, such as how a post office, a bank and a police station work. They learn how to measure land, the importance of rain water harvesting for drinking water and the need for toilets so that girls can have some privacy and learn about sanitation.

Unique Children's Parliament

These 100 schools are administered and supervised by a unique Children's Parliament. Every two years, children from the night schools elect a Prime Minister and a Cabinet from among their own ranks, who are then responsible for managing, overseeing and administering the schools. For example, they can make decisions about how their schools are run and dismiss teachers who do not fulfil their obligations, thus learning to take responsibility for their own rights and interests at a very early age. For tasks which are more demanding, such as financial planning, the Barefoot College is there to assist the Children's Parliament.

Sincere Thanks

This project was made possible thanks to the commitment of UBS clients to the UBS Optimus Foundation.

© *Reprinted courtesy of UBS Optimus World, August 2006*

School for Life

Originally published in UBS *Optimus World*, August 2006

The UBS Optimus Foundation

LIFE HAS NEVER BEEN EASY FOR KAMLESH and her family, but it became even harder after her father died and her three older sisters got married. Today, she and her 52-year-old mother are left to fend for themselves. What's left of the family couldn't survive without the efforts of this girl of 13. Kamlesh lives in a small village in Rajasthan, one of the poorest parts of India.

Her day job is herding 12 goats. The dry earth is infertile, and finding feed, water and fuel means walking long distances. By the time her job is done, the state schools have long since finished for the day.

This is a fate she shares with thousands of other children. It is estimated that about two-thirds of children in India's rural areas are unable to attend school because they have to work.

Needs-based Education with a New Perspective

The innovative Barefoot College offers these children an alternative. When the sun goes down, the evening school lights up its lamps ready for class. 'Why should we gear our timetable to the teachers? We have to consider the children's needs,' says the organisation's founder and head Bunker Roy.

Poetry, theatre and song are used liberally to ensure that children learn not just the alphabet and multiplication tables, but also things that matter more to anyone living off the land, like tending and irrigating fields, health, crafts and building houses. 'This school isn't meant to heap yet more work on its pupils. It's supposed to be fun. We want to show the children that rural folk can also enjoy a good, healthy and dignified life,' stresses Roy. Giving the rural population back their dignity and faith in themselves and their abilities is very close to his heart.

He explains, 'It's the only way we can stop people migrating into the cities.' Most people moving into India's big cities end up stuck in the vast and hopelessly overcrowded slums. Here in Tilonia, Mahatma Gandhi's belief that progress should come from the abundant resources of village culture rather than forced academic learning is lived out. Gandhi also believed that humility, modesty and respect for nature are important, as is the fact that all people have the same rights, regardless of caste or gender.

Although recent years have seen a great deal of effort on the Government's part to break out of the caste mentality, members of the lower castes continue to be marginalised by society. They often have no access to drinking water, healthcare, education or work. Girls and women lose out twofold as they are discriminated against on the basis of both caste and gender.

In Tilonia, Everyone's Equal

'Here in Tilonia and in the night schools, there are no divisions,' Roy is keen to point out. 'Each and every boy and girl is treated with the same respect and given the same chances.' These children's many duties mean that they are compelled to live adult lives from a very early age, but centuries of stigmatisation are hard to undo. For the children and their parents, it is anything but self-evident that they can be accepted as fully-fledged members of society, even though this is essential if they are to participate actively in political life, become involved in the democratic process and thus help to shape their own community.

The Children's Parliament: Not Just Role-Playing

This is why the Children's Parliament was founded within the Barefoot College on the initiative of one of its students.

About 5,000 school children vote for representatives from their own ranks in democratic elections. The Cabinet comprises 15 Ministers, and there are a further 52 MPs. Kamlesh was appointed Education Minister in a landslide vote in 2002. In this role, she is responsible for the smooth running of the school system and has to inspect other night schools four times a month and report back to the other Ministers.

She tells us excitedly, 'It lets me get to know a lot of new places and people.' Her mother has to look after the goats while she's away. 'She does it because she knows I've got an important job to do for the school and for the other children,' the young girl explains proudly. The Children's Parliament goes a lot further than mere role-playing. Roy tells us more: 'The Prime Ministers – all of them girls to date – have a lot of power. They can even hire and fire teachers, provided they have a good reason. If the water supply or the solar-powered lighting breaks down, the problem is discussed seriously and fixed. Their extensive research into topics such as rainwater collection, solar energy, hand pumps for water and marketing hand-crafted products earns them a lot of respect in their local communities.'

Making Life Better on Your Own Initiative

The experience of becoming actively involved and being able to make a difference stays with the children for the rest of their lives. Kaushalya, for example, was Prime Minister in the Children's Parliament before leaving her village to get married. Tradition dictates that the young daughter-in-law has no say in household matters, but she proved very persuasive in her new village and succeeded in getting a solar-powered water pump and 100,000-litre tank installed there.

Santosh, meanwhile, lived in a village that had separate wells for each caste. Based on what she had learned at the night school, she shocked her friends by drinking the water intended for the lowest caste of all. Contrary to the whole village's expectations, she didn't fall ill. Everyone now drinks from all the wells, which is fairly revolutionary for a rural Indian community and a huge relief for those who used to have a long way to go to their caste's well.

With its Gandhi-based philosophy, the Barefoot College is so much more than a school. Respecting an alternative value system and drawing on all the skills and talents inherent in the villages regardless of people's official qualifications, caste or gender gives it the strength to enhance rural life over the long term. One thing is clear for Kamlesh and her fellow night school pupils, and that is that they don't want to leave their villages. Thanks to the broad education they receive from the Barefoot College, they know how to make the simple life in the countryside a good one.

Project Success

The complete project, comprising the schools, the Children's Parliament, drinking water, solar energy, healthcare and opportunities for selling handicrafts has already won a number of international prizes in recognition of its innovative approach.

There are now around 100 night schools in six Indian states, and demand among other communities is strong.

The organisation's founder, Bunker Roy, has been invited to attend the World Economic Forum (WEF) four times as innovative social entrepreneur. The organization also advises similar projects in Asia and Africa.

The UBS Optimus Foundation supports this project with a contribution of CHF 200,000 a year.

Thanks to this donation, some 4,000 children, two-thirds of whom are girls, can attend school, take part in the Children's Parliament and benefit.

Project Partner

The organisation Social Work and Research Centre (SWRC) Tilonia, also known as Barefoot College, has been working to help people in India's poorest rural areas for over 30 years.

© *Reprinted courtesy of UBS Optimus World, August 2006*

Tending to saplings at Tilonia nursery

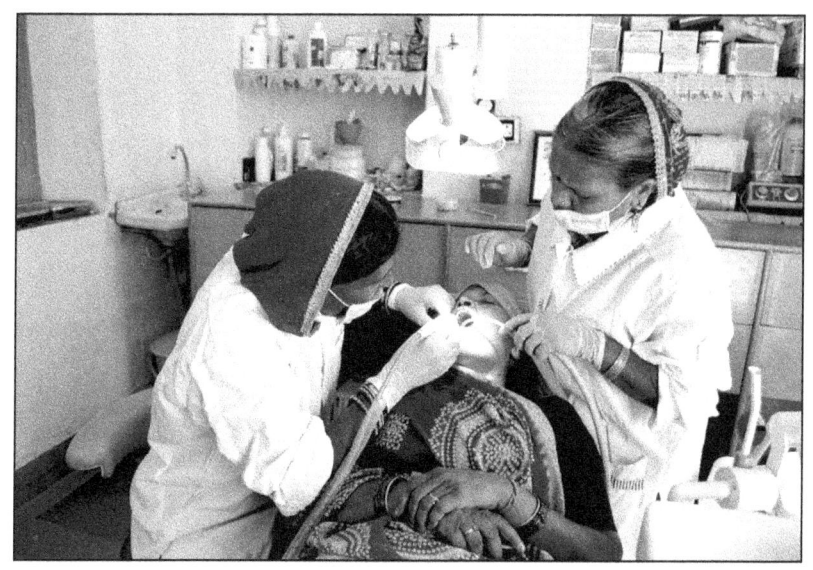

Barefoot dentists at work

Outdoor eyesight check

Small classroom but crammed with teaching aids

Children's Parliament at work

Counting votes

Learning with tablets

11: The Art of Communication: Tradition, Puppets, Street Theatre and the Digital Camera

Heather MC Malcolm and Aruna Roy

Education is communication with a purpose, and what a marvellous array of communicators awaited Barefoot College on its initial entry into village life! The College came into contact with Rajasthan's rich heritage – its drums, its songs, the string puppets and a people who danced to celebrate. The infectious and powerful sounds and rhythms called out to everybody and brought the Tilonia Communicators invitations to attend the Festival of Fools in Oslo, Norway, and later to appear at the Eden Project in Cornwall, U.K.

It all began with Shankar, who came to join the Tilonia team in 1980. Shankar is a born communicator, and earlier in his life his stories, humour and theatre skills had secured him a job as an adult literacy teacher. Interestingly, though, and unusual in India, he was a performer not born into a performing community. But he knew about the unfortunate social taboos restricting those communities, whose members were all *Dalits* and victims of discrimination.

In Tilonia, he became acquainted with Ramlal, a traditional puppeteer. They became firm friends, and their partnership blossomed as they created the now-famous 'Tilonia Communication Team'. It was an ideal coming together of creative interests and skills: Ramlal, who belonged to a caste of puppeteers and performers, and Shankar, the curious and interested young man searching for ways to share important messages with his people. Together, they created Jokhim Chacha, the venerated puppet who has become the voice of Tilonia, its chronicler and narrator, who over the 50 years of Tilonia's existence has met King Charles, the Dalai Lama, and a host of other dignitaries. And Shankar's and Ramlal's sharp observations and imaginative skills enabled them to create performances that passed comment on life at all levels, including a critique of the

Barefoot team that spared no one – not even Bunker – from irony and wry comment.

As their repertoire of skits and street theatre grew, the pair were joined by Bhanwar Gopal, Chauthu, Babulal, and a growing tribe of inventive, beguiling communicators. Their energy was catching, and not many days would ever pass without them organising events in the villages and on campus. In 2009, KT Tunstall, the Scottish singer-songwriter and musician, came to Tilonia on a casual visit and was so enchanted by the group that she stayed on to perform with them informally.

Over time, Shankar and Bhanwar Gopal made further connections. They became friends with Tripurari Sharma, who was a professor at the National School of Drama, as well as Lakshmi Krishnamurti, the actor and social activist who set up an organisation called Alaripu. These became mentors for a stream of wonderful plays that toured Rajasthan and some parts of northern India, plays that interacted with the audiences and conveyed messages with humour. As they toured, the *padyatras* (walks from village to village) drew attention to environmental concerns, people's rights and development. Shankar and Bhanwar are now well known as song and script writers for development work, and Ramniwas, Hemnath, Satyanarain, and Moti continue the tradition they began.

Tilonia's women played their part, too. Celebrated women community leaders Naurti, Billan, and Mangi worked together to create a women's anthem, *Chet sako to chet* (Women, wake up), which Naurti took to Beijing in 1985 to sing at the women's conference. The anthem was also sung by Rajasthani women to greet Bill Clinton when he came to Jaipur.

Several photographers, either well-known at the time or who later became famous, have captured life at Barefoot College. Tilonia's interaction with the visual media began with iconic photographer Raghu Rai, who came to take photos of Bunker for the *Junior Statesman* in 1972 when Desmond Doig was the editor. (Indeed, Raghu Rai gave us permission to use one of these on the cover of this book.) The camera took centre stage in the community in 1975-6, when the now well-known Pablo Bartholomew – then a young man still in his teens – came to work with Tilonia villagers. He encouraged them to shoot candid photos which later, at night, he projected onto a large screen – to the consternation of many who were caught unawares! His archives contain rare and important photographs from that period. And internationally acclaimed contemporary photographer Sunil Gupta, interning as a student at Tilonia in 1981, took photographs which document an important period in Barefoot College's history, when craftwork was beginning to 'gel'. Some of them captured moments in Tilonia's participatory decision-making process – rare photographs that have become precious.

All this influenced and led to the concept of 'Barefoot Photographers', and a collection of photographs taken by the people of the village themselves was brought together and shown at London's Brunei Gallery. The exhibition was inaugurated in April 2005 by the Prince of Wales, now King Charles III, and its photographs were published in a book of the same name, 'Barefoot Photographers'.

The legacy of communication through art continues. Tilonia made another seminal contribution through its *Lok Utsav*, a coming together of folk artists from all over the State who were mentored by Komal Kothari, Rajasthan's well-known cultural historian. The *Lok Utsav* deepened and enriched the understanding of musical and other performing traditions in Tilonia, and was the first of many further endeavours.

Against this background, the two articles that make up this chapter clearly show the centrality of the role played by traditional communication in Rajasthan's rural life. They date from the early 1980s, and some things have certainly changed since then, but traditional art forms remain among the treasures of the rural areas. The *Alliance Française* staged a traditional version of 'The Little Prince' in 2022. The performance used *Dastangoi*, an art form of oral storytelling in Urdu that dates from the 13th century. They asked that the Tilonia team use Jokhim Chacha in conversation with a specially-made 'Little Prince' puppet, to start the show.

Gadgets are Not Enough

Bunker Roy

Originally published in *Development Forum*, Vol XI No. 7, October 1983

IT IS A FALLACY TO BELIEVE, as some development experts do, that there exists an information infrastructure available at the village level, which can be tapped and developed effortlessly and at will. The question is much more complex than that.

At the village level, knowledge is both a means of power and of exploitation. In India, for example, educational television and radio are supposed to be development tools, but the people involved in broadcasting have so little idea of rural realities that in the long run the whole exercise is proving dangerously counter-productive. Radio and television are used to impose Western ideas of what is good, what is necessary and indeed, what poverty is! They are used to prescribe solutions. The rural poor themselves are never consulted about their list of priorities.

Radio and television have resulted in transmitted public opinion being concentrated in the village in the hands of two to three families who can read and write and who have an idea of the outside world. They repeat what they hear: that high-yielding varieties of seed are good, fertiliser application is correct, having electric pump sets and electricity in the village is modern, progressive and very necessary. From the rural poor's point of view, however, this is not so. But if any of them were to say, for example, that as a result of electricity the local artisans were getting less village work and their land was being forcibly taken away, no one would believe them.

Social problems cannot simply be cured by a dose of technology. Examination at grassroots level is needed. Urban experts tend to scoff at the 'simplistic' way of seeing social problems at the village level largely as problems of communication; they further aggravate them by bringing an alien, impersonal medium into a culture that is already rich in the art of interpersonal communication. One must live in a village to appreciate and understand the swiftness with which the bush telegraph works. Not only is this method of communication faster than radio or television but it also reaches the right people.

The same urban experts argue that we must look beyond the traditional media already existing in the villages, in order to reach more people with the same message in the shortest time possible. All those who think this should spend some time in a village in order to realise how outlandish and inappropriate such technology is to the needs of the poor. The only people who will have access to it and thus benefit are the rich, who will use it as yet another tool with which to strengthen their hold on the poor. There are simpler approaches likely to be much higher yielding.

In Tilonia (Ajmer District, Rajasthan, India) an attempt is being made to use puppets as a development and educational medium. The response so far is very encouraging. A team of four rural youths have got together and have given village shows in over 100 villages. This form of communication allows the villagers to contribute to their own education on critical and sensitive social issues such as untouchability, the need to establish minimum wages and the crucial place of women in rural society.

Shankar Singh, one master puppeteer, is the most sought-after man in the area and his puppet Jokhim Chacha (known as the 300-year-old Muslim to all the children in the area) is the solver of problems. If school attendance is falling, Jokhim Chacha is called and his appeal to the parents in the evening is generally successful; if a hand-pump is to be installed, he is called to settle the dispute about payment and location; if family planning camps are to be held, he is sent to appeal to the women beforehand and as a result many more come; if bureaucrats have to be trained (or retrained, as the case may be), he is called to expose them to the realities of why a poor man stays poor.

There are many more people like Shankar Singh, whose communication skills could be used to reach the rural poor. The question is: How to get to these people in the villages and train them? Or rather, persuade them to be trained? There is thus an information infrastructure existing right there in the village which can be tapped – but generally development experts refuse to recognise it.

From Gadgets Are Not Enough by Bunker Roy
© *1983 United Nations. Used with the permission of the United Nations*

Reaching the Poor Through Puppetry: A Powerful Medium for Fostering Rural Development

Bunker Roy

Originally published in *Agricultural Information Development Bulletin, Anniversary Issue,* Vol 6 No. 1, March 1984, UNESCO for Asia & Pacific

By Bunker Roy of the Social Work and Research Centre, Tilonia 305 816, Madanganj, Ajmer District, Rajasthan, India. This article is adapted from Development Communication Report, No.42 pp 5, 6.

IF THERE IS ONE RESOURCE India's planners and policy-makers have neglected for the socio-economic development of the poor in the rural areas, it is traditional communication media.

Village-level communication could change the rural poor's way of thinking and tackling problems, their attitudes to certain government schemes and programmes, and make people aware of what is happening around them for their own welfare.

Messages that would take months to absorb through radio and television – if absorbed at all – could be conveyed through a puppet show in one evening.

The people who sit in front of a television watching programmes of dance and urban drama are not the poor in the villages. They will not understand what is happening. But when puppet shows are organised, everyone attends and they laugh at each other. We have seen this happening in and around Tilonia.

Shankar Singh is an ordinary one-time shepherd boy with an extraordinary skill in puppetry. He worked as a labourer in a famine relief camp in a village in Jawaja (Ajmer District in the Indian State of Rajasthan). After obtaining an academic degree, he became involved in a marginal way in an adult education programme sponsored by the Government. His attempts at persuading his superiors to let him try his hand at puppetry failed.

One day, he strolled into Tilonia and very hesitantly suggested that he would like to work with puppets. Could he possibly get a job in Tilonia? He got together a small group of amateurs from the village and started holding modest shows in the nearby villages, improvising all the time, weaving stories out of local gossip, bringing out a moral after reshaping true incidents so that everyone in the village could recognise the characters and have a good laugh – much to the discomfort and uneasiness of a village-level government functionary sitting in the audience.

It was not only a subtle process of awareness-building, but a crucial way of developing people. Shankar Singh is firmly of the view that essentially rural development means the development of people – not things. He has been to all the celebrated places where puppetry has been developed as an art, but he has found puppetry too centralised and too divorced from the village situation. He has seen the art and the skill of the rural people taken away from them to be fossilised in buildings located in cities when all along the art should have been alive, changing, adapting, mixing and absorbing the complexities of rural life. He has managed to do just that with his puppets, giving them an educational bias. But his work is not without struggle.

He went to the annual camel fair in Pushkar, perhaps the largest and most colourful in India, requesting that he be allowed to put on a brief show. The organisers laughed at him. 'You? We have renowned artists from all over the country coming here; we have never heard of you – go home.' With a little persuasion from a sympathetic bureaucrat, he was given 15 minutes. By the time his show was over four hours later, the audience had swelled to thousands and they would not let him go. He appealed to them all with local jokes in the language and expression they knew best, at the same time getting across serious messages on equality for women, on the evils of untouchability, on the need to pay minimum wages to agricultural labourers, on national integration and on the ills of moneylending.

Largely because of his shows and their apparent impact, the Government has included puppet shows as a means for promoting national integration in the State of Rajasthan, and schools are encouraged to use the medium.

When he started getting requests from remote schools where there was no electricity and not even any roads, Shankar Singh hardly slowed down. Often, he set up an improvised stage on a bullock cart, organised non-electric lighting and got the show going. The schools paid his expenses. He started getting invitations to local village fairs, primary and middle schools and local functions to honour a local politician or bureaucrat, and he never missed an opportunity to get across forceful messages to them.

At one function where the guest of honour was a minister, Shankar Singh asked him through the puppets what sort of forestry development programme was going on in his State. Within a week, action that had been long delayed was taken quickly, proving that the puppets got through when no one else had been able to inform the minister.

Shankar Singh's legendary puppet character in this area is Jokhim Chacha, a 300-year-old Muslim who has the audacity to call the chief minister of the State 'my child,' the inspector of schools 'my grandson,' and old respected women in the village 'my daughters' and get away with it. Jokhim Chacha is in much demand. If a school building needs repair and a contribution from the community is expected, Jokhim Chacha is called and he appeals to the audience. If attendance in the evening school is dropping, Jokhim Chacha is called to persuade the parents in front of the whole village to get them to agree to start sending their children again. If family planning cases need to be motivated he is roped in; if higher castes are practising untouchability where some hand pumps have been installed, Jokhim Chacha is dispatched to settle the problem amicably; if the poor have to be shown how moneylenders are bleeding them dry and keeping them poor, only Jokhim Chacha can do it. In many villages, moneylenders have come to him quietly and tried to bribe him to stop the show. Their business, they reluctantly confess, suffers badly after people have seen his show.

Jokhim Chacha is Shankar Singh's creation. No one else, we have found, can handle these sensitive topics with so much flair and get away from the village without incident. Chacha is the pacifier, he settles disputes, and his name is enough to make children go wide-eyed with awe.

He is the carrier of messages. Radio and television are not half as powerful as this medium because puppetry invites – indeed demands – the participation of the people in their own education. There is no fixed length for performances. If the audience is alive, shows can go on for hours; if it is dead – and Shankar Singh can make that out immediately – he winds up fast. Since he has a bewildering variety of themes up his sleeve, he makes an effort to pick up local gossip, fresh disagreements between agricultural labourers and moneylenders, and then uses them, much to the delight of the villagers who are amazed that Jokhim Chacha should be so aware of the problems in their village. He weaves these real personalities around themes that have a direct bearing on their everyday lives.

The story of 'Dukkal', the landless labourer who becomes a farmer after the Government gives him land, becomes serious when villagers see the rich farmer grabbing that land and murdering him in the process. This, of course, has parallels in real life which cannot be ignored, and has the desired effect on the audience.

After a puppet show on minimum wages was put on for rural women working in famine relief camps, months later for the first time in the history of the area, 300 women refused to take the wages because they were being discriminated against and they were being asked to sign for amounts they were not receiving. We traced this rare expression of courage and unanimity to the puppet show.

Fortunately, recognition has not spoiled Shankar Singh. Though his village-made puppets have reached Australia and Switzerland, he himself has no wish to travel where he is not understood. The puppets he has made have generated income to the extent that he is now self-supporting. From the 100 villages he has visited, he has managed to collect more than US$1,000 from donations and he is training people from other states in how to use the puppets effectively. The fact that he is responsible for changing collective attitudes on sensitive issues is a source of much satisfaction for him. This skill and resource may one day be better recognised as an input for rural development.

***

The following colour videotapes (VHS–PAL) about Shankar Singh have been made by SWRC and may be obtained by contacting the author.

1. 'Pulling Strings – Puppets For Development'

2. 'Integration: A Tilonia Experience'

3. '*Shankar Singh:* The Life and Times of a Puppeteer'

© *United Nations Economic and Social Commission for Asia and the Pacific (ESCAP), Agricultural Information Development Bulletin, March 1984, Vol. 6, No. 1, pp. 25-28*

Troupe indoors with giant puppet

Barefoot College radio station – simple but it works

Hand puppets

Bunker with HH the Dalai Lama and HH Dalai Lama puppet

Jokhim Chacha is a Barefoot College Ambassador

Night-time performance

12: Tilonia Bazaar: Where Tradition Meets Contemporary India

Heather MC Malcolm and Aruna Roy

In the winter of 1975, the amphitheatre in Triveni Kala Sangam[10] in New Delhi was resplendent with the beautiful colours and textures of Rajasthan. The Tilonia Bazaar had come to India's capital to make a statement. Not only was it bringing rural craft producers to the city's market, but it was also making the point that crafts like these were part of the great Indian heritage.

Indian handicrafts, vibrant and intricate, continue the skills and legacy of thousands of years, and behind every craft stand the people who make them. However, from the beginning of the 1970s, their artistry had been threatened as synthetic cloth, plastics and footwear made inroads into rural India. By 1975, craftspeople were in great need of new sources of finance, new markets, and alternatives in design and product. The danger that both hand and handloom would lie idle, and livelihoods disappear, was very real; the cheap items produced by the mass market seemed to be making hand-produced crafts redundant.

Searching for work that would keep their families alive, men left rural areas for the towns and cities. Women hoped that they too would not have to go, but if they were to stay at home, they also needed paid work. But where was it to be found? For many, this was a time of great worry that led to physical distress. Mangi had needed to move from place to place for several years and miscarried six times, and was apprehensive about her seventh pregnancy. Conversations with rural women revealed their fears and anguish and led those working at Tilonia to begin looking

---

[10] A cultural and arts complex and education centre often known simply as 'Triveni'.

actively for ways in which women could find ways to make a living in the village.

Ideas came through discussions with master weaver Johuruddin, Sua the leather worker, and Mangi, whose organizational skills eventually mobilized women into training for handicrafts. Those already skilled in crafts joined the Tilonia group. Others gained new expertise that meant they, too, could move into handicraft production.

But skills had to cater to markets. Their products needed to sell – but where and how? Pooling their ideas, Johuruddin, Sua, and Mangi hit upon the notion of the Tilonia Bazaar, and it was this that became the Barefoot way of saving both livelihoods and a rich, precious but dying art heritage.

The statement that rural India made when it went to the capital was about the craft and its producers. It was about those who made these beautiful things and the conditions in which they worked. It was a statement to nudge those who bought ethnic and traditional wares into remembering that real people, not machines, produced them and made their livings from the trade. It was a statement to remind people that cheap, mass-produced plastic goods generated plastic waste and were the source of much other environmental damage.

And with this work, a set of beautiful craft practices was preserved: the art of the block printer, the embroidery and appliqué of western Rajasthan, and all the intricate handicrafts, designed by and with people, that provide work for young and old, including those who are disadvantaged. The handloom and spinning – so much a part of Gandhian economics! – contributed to their gentle declaration that environmentally friendly ways to make a living really do exist.

Tilonia decided to begin its 50th anniversary celebrations with a Bazaar that would evoke memories of its first appearance five decades ago, and to hold it in the same place. Pablo Bartholomew choreographed an exhibition of photographs, drawing from his own archives as well as those of Barefoot College and Sunil Gupta. Triveni Kala Sangam was able to celebrate its memories of Mrs. Sridharani, its founder. Designer and visionary Laila Tyabji wrote about Tilonia, generously allowing her thoughts to appear in the introduction to this book. It was a great coming together to acknowledge the fruition of an idea which began with a young man turning his back on comfort to walking with people, the Barefoot way.

Instead of articles, we bring you some of those memories in this short chapter. They show a little – but only a little! – of how Tilonia Bazaar keeps Rajasthan's rural crafts and its craftspeople alive. Take a look.

A Rich Craft Heritage – Tradition Meets Modernity
Some Photographs

Heather MC Malcolm

THE FIRST TILONIA BAZAAR WAS HELD IN 1975 at Delhi's Triveni Kala Sangam. Supported by well-wishers who included artists, writers and designers, it became a blueprint for many more to come. One of the first attempts to connect rural crafts with urban India and its market, Tilonia Bazaar helped to establish craft as an integral part of people's development. Today, it enables thousands and thousands of craftspeople to find alternative markets for their goods. Recent Bazaars have been held in Bengaluru (Bangalore), Delhi and Hyderabad.

Tilonia bazaar revisits Delhi, February 2023

Barefoot College's work with crafts began as far back as 1974, when leather was 'bag-tanned', *i.e.,* tanned to make it suitable for making bags, in Rajasthani villages.

Leather bags, shoes and containers…

... purses and wallets

In 1992, Barefoot College's crafts section was registered as an independent non-profit society, *Hatheli Sansthan,* (meaning 'the palms of one's hands'). Managed by workers, it has helped thousands of artisans, many of them *Dalits* and women, to a better economic life, and the numbers migrating to cities have drastically reduced. Hatheli's diverse and unique techniques have kept pace with modern demands, finding solutions to changing needs. Women feel empowered; Hatheli has helped them in their business ventures through complementary skills training in entrepreneurship, basic banking, accountancy and literacy. Far from being simply producers, *dastkars* (craftspeople) are looking at design and what buyers want, and by selling directly, including online, they keep pace with an ever-changing market.

Jaipur pottery, a regional speciality

A *sari* made of hand-loomed cloth

Hand-loomed cloth skirt

Hand-woven shirt

Rajasthan's brilliant desert colours appear in woven cloths, prints and designs inspired by Barefoot College's environment

Barefoot College promotes and teaches craft skills, including the use of the hand loom, to non-craft communities, and makes it possible for those who wish, including the differently-abled – to work from home, for example, making the popular strings of desert birds known as bell *totas* that are often hung in doorways to bring good fortune. Hatheli Sansthan's *'Kabaad Se Jugaad'* (Trash to Treasure) section uses leftover scraps of fabric, recycled paper and cardboard to make a range of desirable new objects.

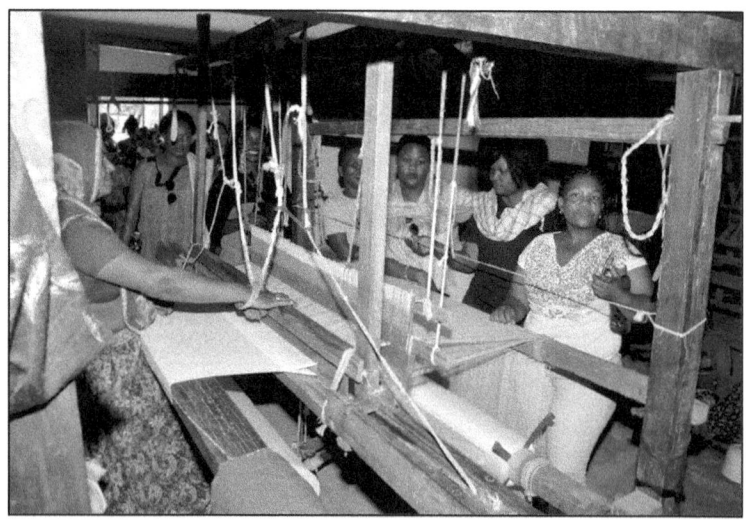

A group of visitors watching the hand loom in action

A basket of birds

A clipboard made in *Kabaad Se Jugaad* from scrap material

Rajasthan's artisans are expert at embroidery, appliqué and other fine techniques

Textiles and bell *totas* on display at Triveni Kala Sangam, Delhi

In Rajasthan, wood is rare and precious. It must be used sparingly, so working with it sets challenges. In 1999, Tilonia set up a woodcraft section to make educational toys that would help children at Barefoot's evening (night) schools to learn. New tools were introduced and new craftspeople trained – and what began as a unit set up to meet learning needs evolved to support house building, both in villages and on campus, and then expanded into crafts more widely.

Wooden trays such as these are decorated with real leaves and petals

How to write 'Ao' in Hindi – and in wood

The long and exciting journey continues. The '50th anniversary' Tilonia Bazaar in Delhi re-established the popularity of Tilonia crafts, and Hatheli maintains a growing archive of their history, in which each product has its own story and content.

A display inside Hatheli Sansthan's showroom on the Tilonia campus

How to get there: the turn-off to Barefoot College
and Hatheli Sansthan craft shop

We leave you with the URL and hyperlink to a short film, 'Tilonia Bazaar/Hatheli Sansthan: A Blend of Tradition and Modernity' in which Roop Singh, Co-ordinator/Convener and secretary of Hatheli, introduces you to the people who make Hatheli Sansthan work, and takes you behind the scenes.

https://youtu.be/-Voa3lTP0nc?si=qppbFmizRISBal7H

13: Barefoot's Online Footprint

Heather MC Malcolm

It is not the strongest species that survives, nor the most intelligent that survives. It is the one most adaptable to change. Charles Darwin

ANYONE CELEBRATING A BIRTHDAY AFTER 1990, say, was born into the age of the mobile phone and social media, and might view the pre-World Wide Web age much as they look at the Jurassic. They won't remember Internet sites carrying nothing but adverts, or pages crashing irretrievably and offering only messages like 'Broken Pipe!' and an infuriating smiley face. A friend (no ignoramus by any stretch, but whose work didn't involve computers) once asked me in great puzzlement, 'But what do you use a computer FOR?'

And indeed, there was no reason to have one of your own. In the 1980s, you had to be a bit of a geek to use a computer for anything except word processing. At the non-profit research group where I used to work, we once considered ourselves advanced because we each had our own Amstrad and prepared our own report drafts. At home, I had a BBC computer with a memory size all of 32 kilobytes. But, at that time, both were the bees' knees, huge steps up from the electronic typewriters whose days were numbered.

As we all now know, change was coming. Some time in the early 1990s, the head of information technology at my organisation had to give a talk to staff to explain what the World Wide Web was, what the Internet was, what email was and why it would be a Good Thing to have. Looking back now, it seems incredible that such a talk was necessary, and that the difference between all these things had puzzled us so much. But, daily, the Internet became more sophisticated and reliable. Improving search algorithms meant you no longer had to follow an exact formula to enter your search terms. The plethora of early-days browsers dwindled and now that 'to Google' has become a verb in its own right, who remembers 'Ask Jeeves' today?

And, of course, there were mobile phones. Some time in the 90s, they began their own transformation from huge brick-like status symbols to something altogether neater, more like the phones we know and love today.

And riding on the wave of them all came social media. In the late 1990s, Blogger emerged, and not long after that LinkedIn, the (short-lived) MySpace, Facebook, YouTube, Twitter that's now X... suddenly everyone and anyone had a public platform. As early as 1986, London's traditional hot-metal printers had seen which way the wind was blowing and went on strike, fearing for their livelihoods but – as Darwin might have said – adapt or die.

And adapt Bunker did. From the early 2000s, he wrote less and less for traditional magazines, newspapers and books and instead began to use the Internet to reach his audience. At Tilonia, he was well positioned to do this, since – from the mid-80s – he had been solar-energising the campus (as well as other places). By the time the World Wide Web and social media were ready for Bunker, Bunker was ready for them and turned to their platforms to publicise his messages. It is worth noting that solar-energising the campus also gave space for others to find and develop their full potential – people such as Nauru, a middle-aged *Dalit* working woman, who learned to use computers, then taught those skills to others before leading campaigns for work and wages and becoming the *Sarpanch*, Head of the Panchayat.

The famous TED (technology, entertainment, design) talks began in 1984, and 2006 saw them move online with great success. In 2011, Bunker delivered his own, 'Learning from a Barefoot Movement', to great acclaim. We have few traditional print media articles from him after 2013, but the Internet has made information about Bunker and Barefoot College Tilonia readily accessible to the world.

Besides covering work from a period of overlap when both print articles and online documentaries were being published, the Internet-based material carries films about new projects *such as...*

- Barefoot's waste management initiative, which empowers communities to run their own waste management systems and serves over 2,000 households in 10 villages.

- Solar digital village learning centres, where young girls and women – traditionally expected to stay at home – are offered a window onto the world and all its knowledge and, to improve their own prospects, can learn about jobs and how to seek them. (Electricity comes from Barefoot College's own solar power system, which, unlike rural India's fluctuating supply, guarantees reliable power.)

- Barefoot College's inspired decision to train bright, literate young people from the community as teachers, at one stroke hugely improving teacher quality, providing work and giving the children beloved teachers who have no interest in leaving the village to seek fame and fortune far afield.

- Barefoot College's residential school, Singla, for children whose parents, many from migrant communities, move around too often to keep them in day or night school.

So, in this short chapter, we offer online links to many things Barefoot, with a wide selection of films and links to its website and social media. It's also worth pointing out that there are recent articles for which we do not have copyright permission to include in this anthology but which are a good read: for example, there's Nicholas Kristof's opinion piece 'Can't Read? Here's a Barefoot College for You' in the *New York Times* of March 22nd 2023, or the interview with Bunker in New Delhi's *Civil Society* published on August 29th 2023 and headlined by Bunker's 'People with degrees do little to solve rural problems'.

On, then, to the links – I hope you enjoy browsing.

Lights, Camera, Action: Barefoot Films and Online Links

MOST OF THE FOLLOWING URLS LINK TO YOUTUBE, but there are many more films available on Barefoot College's website **www.barefootcollegetilonia.org** and social media platforms. These are given after the film list.

The Tilonia Experiment

The first four of these films feature Bunker speaking about the Barefoot College, its origins and its mission, while the last two tell the story from an outside perspective.

H.H. Dalai Lama and Bunker Roy in conversation, 2010

https://youtu.be/i3sUvR7TS78

Bunker Roy's TED Talk: Learning From A Barefoot Movement, 2011

https://youtu.be/6qqqVwM6bMM?si=3Vz33g5EO6mmuFtZ

H.H Dalai Lama, Matthieu Ricard and Bunker Roy, 2011

https://youtu.be/jKsZ3tyth6E?si=4aTVI7K1OzSApRrD

Innovators in Action: Bunker Roy on Village Life and Barefoot College (Skoll World Forum), 2012

https://youtu.be/rtT4m_JRcU4?si=P8KG5JNCgAA6JXs8

 **Barefoot College Story: Department of Science and Technology, Government of India film, 2023**

https://youtu.be/FhzHg62wsqk?si=NrXCh12xuM91uusu

 **United Nations' Resident Co-ordinator in India, visit to Tilonia, 2023**

https://youtu.be/s8ZwpAyuxkY?si=l857IYxNGdLez8zd

Schooling and Education

Nearly 100,000 students from 'last-mile' villages have been educated since 1975 in Barefoot night schools and initiatives like Shiksha Niketan (day school), Residential Bridge School and Solar Digital Bridge Schools. Children at the Night Schools elect a Children's Parliament and the Prime Ministers of these have become responsible democratic citizens. For women, there are Village Learning Centres that give the women and older girls the chance to educate themselves, take up vocational training or both. These foster respect, dignity, financial security and independence, as well as being places where women – who are often confined to home – can make friends and relax. An increasing number of the centres have solar power, and as Solar Digital Village Learning Centres are offering digital resources.

 **Learning With a Difference: Night School, 2008**

https://youtu.be/yiaBofDj2IE?si=p49MI1zi3FbEzcTv

 **The Solar Night Schools of Tilonia, 2021**

https://youtu.be/lvP1f51EE7w?si=un2NiwPrmE0UcRVQ

 **Children's Republic: The Night Schools of the Barefoot College, 2011**

https://youtu.be/hDYQqymdC2Y?si=Nm5X7KcKOlexynzn

 **Young Leaders of Tomorrow, 2022**

https://youtu.be/5PyL8QnCqH8?si=UrtA4kZ8izKmgDVn

 **Teacher Training: The Tilonia Digital Solar Night School Model, 2020**

https://youtu.be/1b30_tviXas?si=oN43YBl090f7W9kN

 **Beauty of Singla, 2022**

https://youtu.be/upRSnnXXo8Y?si=3UOx62ca_AcGdhfh

 **Barefoot Bridge School: A Life Changer, 2023**

https://youtu.be/fUnEYMKDOjw?si=_JsesanUhMq1Svsd

 **Celebration of Ten Years of Commitment, Residential Bridge School, Singla, 2023**

https://youtu.be/GDTmRDwxmJ0?si=zi3lJSnYvP1w61Gg

 **Digital Village Learning Centre, 2023**

https://youtu.be/ECa3Zgeftds?si=3FPaGd6bRKJ7nITl

Water

At Barefoot College, more than 70 billion litres of water have been harvested through the creation of rainwater harvesting tanks, ponds and small dams, reviving multiple traditional water sources. Often, drinking water comes from filtered school-roof run-off – it's a major attraction for children going to College schools, and makes them doubly conscious of water as a precious resource.

Every Drop Counts

https://www.youtube.com/watch?v=2jIQcKlKr_w&t=1s

Demystified, Decentralised Barefoot Water Solutions, 2009

https://youtu.be/jsKLbUhTPTQ?si=Jk59I22wYYKnAjSb

Rainwater Harvesting, India and Beyond, 2010

https://www.youtube.com/watch?v=2jIQcKlKr_w&t=1s

First Solar-Powered Desalination Plant in India, undated but post-2006

https://youtu.be/Bx3sEppnU3c?si=7QY7gO8slJBJvRyP

Rainwater Harvesting, Khatoli Pond Project, 2023

https://youtu.be/HZcVfByrWvo?si=CsgA6WVxyQ64U7pD

The Environment

Rajasthan's harsh and challenging climate and scarcity of trees and water made Bunker an environmentalist long before the need for environmental respect gained widespread recognition, but the extent to which western lifestyles were degrading the environment drove him to focus on it even more keenly. Barefoot College's gardeners identify indigenous plant species that know how to survive in the desert conditions, then make sure they're planted where they will do the most good, such as waste areas and school grounds. In its schools, Barefoot teaches children what happens when things are discarded so that they understand the value of separating waste for reclaim as compost or to save from landfill. Starting with its campus, the College also began a highly successful community-run waste reclamation and disposal programme, expanded it to nearby Chota Narena village and then to Tyod and Kakalwada panchayats. By 2022, ten villages were taking part. As well as reclaiming and recycling large quantities of wet and dry waste, the initiative provides important, dignified work.

The First Plastic and Waste Free Village in Rajasthan, 2021

https://youtu.be/Xw5iVjdpZ1c

Carbon-free campus, 2022

https://youtu.be/3GCE_SLAaRw?si=Anq2F-NcPgMY3iJP

Kamlaji, 2023

https://youtu.be/sDrQji8l0Dk?si=qHYa5Zu_axQIFV0D

Solar Energy

Bunker chose the first Solar Mama in 2000, and since then over 1,700 illiterate or semi-literate rural women from 96 countries as well as India have been trained through Barefoot's programme, leading to 1,500 villages and 75,000 houses being solar-electrified.

A Solar-Powered Campus: Wireless for Communities, Visit to Barefoot College, Tilonia, Rajasthan, 2016

https://youtu.be/HpQzU6R8Y4E?si=IRt_slFM13UOJpsk

Indian Prime Minister Narendra Modi's Speech on the Solar Mamas, 2017

https://youtu.be/0hY7o4YSVIU?si=vJDJaR8AR5E2gjFd

The Ordinary Heroes of Afghanistan, 2006

https://youtu.be/BSARbXnOhxE

The First Women Barefoot Solar Engineers of the World, 2007

https://youtu.be/8oS2iUFvdTE

Sierra Leone's First Women Barefoot Solar Engineers, 2008

https://youtu.be/v_RT8pngx1A

First Women Barefoot Solar Engineer of Andhra Pradesh, 2008

https://youtu.be/XYvQmi0F9LA

 **The First Rural Women Heroes of Tombouctou, 2008**
https://youtu.be/HHhpyS5U1KY

 **The First Women Barefoot Solar Engineers of the Gambia, 2008**
https://youtu.be/qWvwtCPnNK8

 **The Women Solar Warriors of Bhutan: Gross National Happiness in Action, 2009**
https://youtu.be/cKx7jvHocHU?si=XWdJmi8yKkPpTQmA

 **The Women Solar Heroes of Mauritania, 2010**
https://youtu.be/ktkUNvzaEOY

 **The Women Solar Heroes of Mauritania, 2010**
https://youtu.be/ktkUNvzaEOY

 **Why Poverty: Solar Grandmothers, 2012**
https://youtu.be/Hj7t5kETTfs?si=w7RWrBY4rxDxekoq

 **Solar Mamas: Why Poverty? 2013**
https://youtu.be/ON_NQ1HnRYs

 **No Problem: 6 months with the Barefoot Grandmamas, 2012**
https://youtu.be/nX3tUS-sHrc

 Bring the Sun Home, 2013

https://www.youtube.com/watch?v=DQ9ioryp-4o

 Solar Mamas – Women of Light, Madagascar, undated but post-2013

https://funny-video-online.com/watch/64g3l4l3s4s4e3i5h3p4p5.html

 Solar Mamas of the Pacific Islands, 2015

https://youtu.be/3-x1Bg4Me6M?si=Is_jVcJ_H43FHFIG

 The Solar Mamas of Asia and the Pacific, undated

https://youtu.be/6YxSB5Z7n04?si=ipbL7kOsZzA8gj8g

 Brazil – Barefoot Women Solar Engineer, undated

https://youtu.be/wKzAgPr9NpE?si=FwMMTFV3PkJoZVgB

 WBSE Africa: The Women Solar Warriors of Africa, undated but post 2013

https://youtu.be/fR2hJqx66y8

Women's Empowerment

Of course, all the videos about the 'Solar Mamas' tell a story about empowering women as well as the one about bringing light to darkness. But with its fundamental commitment to equality, Barefoot College finds more ways to put power into the hands of ordinary people – particularly women – as well as creating work.

The Making of Sanitary Napkins at the Barefoot College, 2011

https://youtu.be/0WkfTPmRdaw?si=DK2hyB4CMth6ruD1

Crèche Programme, 2023

https://youtu.be/h5-Igv94egI?si=Y_QhAAjqLjKMeFIk

Health

Ever since SWRC/Barefoot College opened its doors, it has provided basic (and sometimes not so basic) health care to marginalised village people. Existing traditional practitioners are given training to make sure that the best of their skills combine with modern practices. The result? Barefoot now has a team of Barefoot doctors, dentists, pathologists, health workers and midwives upon which communities can rely. From time to time, the College also organises medical camps featuring specific health needs – eye problems, for example, or women's health as shown in the video given here. Going out into the villages, staff raise health awareness about hygiene, nutrition, contraception and menstrual and reproductive health, as well as immunization and HIV prevention. During the worst of the Covid pandemic, Barefoot helped keep villagers alive through food distribution and vaccination.

Super Five: A Nutritional Supplement, 2020

https://youtu.be/-pstRP-e-WY?si=F2P69zFV481j1e6j

Hunger-Free Villages, 2021

https://youtu.be/DV5TH78jkfs?si=TWoFwqvwNVhcxyZ5

 Gynaecological Medical Consultation and Organ Donation Awareness Camp in Barefoot College Tilonia, 2023

https://youtu.be/ow3X6pwrSeI?si=3Djch9Yx97w97R2M

Social Media Platforms

https://www.instagram.com/barefootcollegeTILONIA

https://twitter.com/barefootTILONIA

https://www.youtube.com/barefootcollegeTilonia

https://www.facebook.com/barefootcollegeTILONIA

Website: www.barefootcollegetilonia.org

As this book goes to print, the launch of Barefoot College's new website is being planned. Both web addresses will take you to the home page but the new web address is simply **barefoot.college**

Please note: Barefoot College has no association with Barefoot College International. All impact claimed by that organisation prior to 2019 is the legacy of the original Barefoot College, which does not approve of that organisation's use of its name, logo or material. See the Delhi High Court Injunction of 01/03/2023 which restrains Barefoot College International (BCI) from using "Barefoot College" and the two-feet logo for any purpose whatsoever.

The judgement can be read at:
https://dhccaseinfo.nic.in/jupload/dhc/CHS/judgement/05-03-2023/CHS01032023SC8272022_201806.pdf

14: Foundations for the Future

Heather MC Malcolm

2022 was a glorious anniversary year for SWRC/The Barefoot College, completing half a century of experiment, audacious innovation and walking – the Gandhian way – along the path to the Last Man and Woman. They were good years, and the celebrations held for them were joyful, re-creating the magic of some of the earliest projects and bringing old friends together. They were 50 years in which marvellous things were achieved to improve people's lives in some of the most marginalised communities in the world. It is no exaggeration to say that Barefoot College brought hope and a better life to thousands.

Many philanthropists, having made their fortunes, use them for good. I don't know if there are so many who deliberately turn away from the prospect of making such fortunes in the first place to give their whole lives instead, but Bunker is certainly one. By the time he began the College, calling it the Social Work and Research Centre (SWRC), he had become very aware of how privileged his background was, and his conscience would not let him rest unless he gave something back. With him, the Barefoot choice was to help meet the basic needs of India's most deprived people in rural areas with clean water, health care and functional literacy. University friends, professionals including geologists and doctors who respected traditional knowledge and drew from it, joined the College as equals, but Bunker could also draw on his own experience from five years of digging wells in the most hands-on way possible, clambering up and down ropes and blasting holes in the living rock. He learned to do this from people whose qualifications came from sources of a very different kind.

The initial years of working vindicated this faith in the ability of ordinary people to achieve extraordinary things. Bunker attracted many young people who wanted to work with the ideas of equality and 'modern' methodology and were willing to think afresh (it was one of them, Manya, who first used the term 'barefoot' in relation to village life in India). Bunker's open-mindedness sustained this group, and his energy kept it going so that, with them, space for generating new ideas was created. And, as time passed, Barefoot College understood more and more clearly how much knowledge, how much wisdom, and how much skill was woven into the fabric of ordinary lives that were not, perhaps, quite as ordinary as one might think. That faith has borne amazing fruit. And in so many areas!

Ordinary People Doing Extraordinary Things

Water

Take water, for example. You'll have read in Chapter 7 about the hand pump *mistri* (mechanic) – how Barefoot College defied the norms of contemporary practice by choosing likely lads and lasses from the village, training them to install and maintain hand pumps, with great success and at far less expense than through the established professional engineering channels. You'll have seen from articles in Chapter 8 how rainwater harvesting came to be recognised as a more ecologically friendly approach to fresh water provision than constant reliance on ground water. Interestingly, in developing the technique, Bunker and Barefoot built on an idea sparked off by a ruined *bawdi* (traditional open well) that had been constructed by Rajasthan's feudal kings. Step wells and *tankas* (small dams) for collecting precious rainwater were studied and traditional wisdom acknowledged. Professional engineers had declared repair to be impossible, so what did Bunker and his Barefoot engineers do? They repaired the *bawdi*. With hindsight, conserving rainwater is the obvious thing to do; but after all, it took a while for humankind to discover the equally obvious wheel.

Nowadays, if you visit Barefoot College, you are never far from pure water, and thanks to Barefoot College, nearby villages enjoy equally ready access to it. No one of any caste or gender has to walk miles to find water, scoop liquid mud by hand from drying ponds, or gulp down fluid so brackish it could almost have come from the sea. Children flock to school happily knowing they can drink freely from the school's own supply of filtered rainwater harvested from the rooftop.

Health

And health. Before Barefoot College, when they were ill, villagers made use of a mix of superstition and traditional health professionals. The women working with health found that pregnant women in the villages around had faith only in the powerful local *dai* (midwife), but that with a little additional training in contemporary practice, these skilled and trusted professionals, combining the best of traditional and modern, could serve their villages superbly well. And they do: the 'Barefoot *Dai*' became a women's leader in the village, and many similar professionals work in Barefoot's health clinic where, as dentists, pathologists, health workers and midwives, they serve the surrounding area. Over the past 50 years, more than 300,000 patients have been treated.

Barefoot Teachers, Barefoot Schools

And Barefoot's schools. Bright young people from the villages, literate but not highly so, have been trained – by Barefoot – as teachers. They make excellent ones, too, who know how to make learning fun and get the best from their young charges. Because they are local, they know the children and their families, understand the challenges they face and, when necessary, make allowances. Parents and children trust them. They are so good that the State of Rajasthan has drawn many into its own system, and modelled teacher programmes of its own, such as *Shiksha Karmi* (Education Assistants), on the Barefoot College pattern.

But to start with, the Barefoot-trained teachers worked in Barefoot schools, in which – over the years – thousands and thousands of children have received an education. Many attended the experimental day school, *Shiksha Niketan*, where the College, always looking for new and better ways to educate village children, tests new curricula and teaching methods. *Shiksha Niketan*, which began by offering primary-level education, is highly valued by the community, which asked that it be upgraded to a middle school. For the children of migrant families, or parents who just can't look after their children for all sorts of reasons, there's the Residential Bridge School at Singla in Rajasthan's Jaipur district, where children are housed, educated, well-fed, cared for and happy.

And what about the many families living on the edge of survival, parents who depend on their children's input so that they themselves can keep working? Helping their parents makes it possible for the adults to work and the family to eat, but it also means the children can't go to school. Or at least they couldn't, until in 1975, in response to parents' requests, Barefoot College started to offer classes in the evenings. These soon became popularly known as 'Night Schools'. The idea took off, and over time, 580 of them opened in nine Indian states. It's in these schools that the wonderful Children's Parliament has governance. There's nothing like it anywhere else: a Parliament in which all the children come together to elect members to represent their interests. As in the wider world, the run-ups to elections are electric with tension and buzz with activity.

Breadwinning!

Barefoot's respect for tradition pointed to ways of strengthening people's capacities, so there's vocational training, too, which builds on existing traditional skills. It was always centrally important to Barefoot College to help people be independent both in mind and body. Charity was never what Barefoot was about. For the College, a large part of developing independence is strengthening people's self-belief, supporting them psychologically and when necessary through advocacy, and speaking up for the downtrodden when they are bullied by thugs or corrupt officials. And, as recorded in some of the articles in this anthology, Bunker and Barefoot did just that, pointing out weaknesses in implementation and policy, and trying to make those with the power to act understand that corruption must be tackled, even if it arises within voluntary organisations. As Consultant to the Government's Seventh Planning Commission, heading the group on voluntary organisations, Bunker galvanised Government into acknowledging these organisations' competence to act on behalf of the poor, and to set money aside to fund their work directly.

Achieving a truly independent life is much easier when financial independence supports independence of spirit. So the College encourages and, when needed, updates the skills of local craftspeople. The Barefoot approach to crafts recognised that their local markets were dwindling and, to help them understand what would sell, the College helped rural artisans to meet their buyers in city locations. The handcrafted items were then adapted to new designs.

In 1976, with the Tilonia Bazaar, the idea of an urban bazaar took shape. Here, the technologies associated with modern design, as well as the notion of credit, helped eliminate middlemen. That meant they could no longer exploit rural craftspeople, and Tilonia Bazaar is now a well-known marketplace where artisan goods are sold at fair prices that return to the makers, not to dealers hunting for profit. Barefoot College has worked with thousands of craftspeople from more than 48 of Rajasthan's villages.

And, of course, there are the 'Solar Mamas'... It would be impossible to leave the amazing women solar engineers out of any review of Barefoot College's achievements. If you haven't yet looked at any of the video links to these, this is what happens: supported through the Government of India's ITEC (Indian Technical and Economic Cooperation) programme, barely literate mature women from very remote villages travel from some of the Least Developed Countries to Tilonia, where they train for six months. They learn through colour-coding and demonstration, which makes their illiteracy unimportant and helps 'talk' across language barriers. Once back in their villages, for a small fee agreed and paid to them by their communities, they install solar power systems using Barefoot-provided equipment. Having been taught how to maintain these, they teach their skills to other women, establishing a sustainable 'cascade' model of learning and teaching.

The process transforms the women from mere 'mamas' into respected contributors to society. Mindsets are changed – men's views about women, people's views about the illiterate. At the last count, over 2,000 brave women from remote rural communities in 96 countries have trained in this way, making the long and challenging journey to India. Increasingly, however, such women can train at Barefoot vocational training centres in their home countries. To date, Barefoot has established centres in six countries: Burkina Faso, Senegal, Liberia, Zanzibar, Fiji, and Madagascar.

And oh yes – the 'Solar Mamas' also learn to make sanitary napkins and additional nutritional supplements, and how to organise and set up the Barefoot College system of rainwater harvesting. They take the techniques home. And all this is transforming remote villages across the Global South.

Greening the Desert

Solar instead of fossil fuel power helps the environment, but through Barefoot College ordinary people have been approaching that challenge in other ways, too. Although there were very few articles to include in our anthology that featured this aspect of the work, for over 50 years Barefoot gardeners have promoted plantations on wastelands, pasturelands, government school grounds, and nurseries across Rajasthan, establishing more than 60,000 native trees and plants. The College nursery raises over 500 varieties of indigenous plants and seeds, many of them grown for their medicinal properties and supporting the work of homeopathic medicines used in the clinic. Inspired by Barefoot's example, private homeowners have begun to plant trees on their own plots.

The Battle for Justice

Besides all this, from the start, Bunker and the Barefoot College team have always spoken up for those who could not speak up for themselves, marginalised people enduring thuggery, caste oppression, crooked officials, corruption and incompetence. As I mentioned above, Bunker and Barefoot fight against these with words and actions, doing all they can to draw attention to injustices. In this, they were and are supported by Barefoot's brilliant team of communicators and puppeteers, who mount plays about all kinds of social issues – the right to minimum wages, women's rights, the various ways that powerful people can dupe the poor. Such themes have featured in several of the articles included here.

Recent Work

Much of this book, being an anthology of already published pieces, has (of necessity) looked back. But something should be said about Barefoot College's work in more recent times.

Managing Waste, Creating Employment

As I said earlier, Barefoot cares for the environment through extensive plantings of indigenous trees. This has been the case for half a century. But a recent innovation has been to encourage ordinary people to achieve marvels in waste management. There's a link to a video about this in Chapter 13. India's rural villages have huge problems with plastic waste, which is not only unsightly but a death trap for animals munching on any food that might have stuck to it. Traditionally, in rural India, village streets are cleaned by people from the *Valmiki*[11] caste, who are often looked down upon in spite of the heroic work they do, but their ability to manage piles of plastic waste that are sometimes knee-deep is limited.

So, with the dual aim of better waste management and improving the *Valmikis'* lives, Barefoot College established a community-centred waste management pilot project in 2016 at nearby Chota Narena. This became Rajasthan's first plastic-free, zero-waste village. By 2017, with the involvement of volunteers, villagers, and the village council, a waste disposal site had been prepared. Family after family signed up, and by 2018, 350 households and a thousand people were benefiting from the system. Not only that, but new, dignified employment had been created for four people. By 2021, the system included Tyod district where, with the help of Kotak Mahindra Bank, all four villages and 1,500 households took part, and also Kakalwada, where five villages and 850 families were drawn in. By 2022, the system had spread to ten villages and was benefiting over 2,200 households. The expectation is that the scheme will continue to expand. There's gardening and economic value in it, too: Barefoot's gardeners create a rich organic manure

---

[11] *Valmikis* used to be called *Mehtars*, but in recent years the people of this caste have opted for a more dignified name.

from wet waste collected on the campus, and have taught those who operate the waste collection system how to do the same. So far, the system has converted over 110 tonnes of wet waste into organic compost. Where possible, dry waste – 7.6 tonnes so far – is sold to local recyclers.

Fighting Covid

One of the defining events of recent years has been the Covid-19 pandemic. During India's two main outbreaks, the College and its clinic were, literally, life-savers.

As everywhere, Covid's first wave caught everyone unawares as it killed in ways that were poorly understood. As bad as the situation was in towns and cities, it was far worse in villages where day labourers, living hand-to-mouth in any case and with no savings of any kind, also had to contend with hunger. The terrible logic of lockdown in rural areas meant that people in over 550 villages could not buy food as they were not earning. Without Barefoot's distribution of nearly 14,000 ready-to-eat food packets and well over 12,000 survival kits which contained food[12], among other things, they would have starved. The kits included 'Super 5', a nutritious and delicious mix of local chickpeas, groundnuts, sesame seeds, jaggery (palm sugar) and wheat, made at the College's own production centre. Barefoot distributed an additional 325,000-plus packets of this to nearly 3,000 children. The College supported Grain Banks, too, supplying 20 villages in Rajasthan and Madhya Pradesh. An additional benefit for poor families was that the job of putting all these together and distributing them generated paid work for 650 women.

But as we all know, Covid-19 required help with more than hunger. The survival kits also included face masks, soap, sanitiser and sanitary napkins. And by the time a second major outbreak hit, Barefoot's clinic had expanded its 10-bed medical wing into a 40-bed Covid isolation centre. Working with a network of civil

---

[12] 20 kg wheat flour, 2.5 kg dal, 1 litre cooking oil, 1 kg of salt, 250 grams chilli powder, 100 grams ground turmeric, 2 kg onions, 2 kg potatoes, 1.25 kg Super 5.

society organisations, it set up 12 further isolation centres across rural areas in Rajasthan. For the particular needs of this new disease – as far as they were understood – Barefoot's health professionals collaborated with a group of doctors who trained them in how to manage Covid-19.

Power to the Women – Opening up the World

In the early 1980s, the first of Rajasthan's women's rights groups was organised in Silora, not far from Tilonia village. That gave rise to Tilonia's founding of the Women's Development Programme, and – in 1985 – to the celebrated 'Women's *Mela*' (Fair), which drew a thousand rural women from all over India to celebrate ten years of their struggle for equality. Later that year, one of the first protests in India against rape was a powerful outcome from this *mela*. And it was women from Tilonia's villages who created the anthem celebrating women's development, an anthem that is now sung all over the state. It was sung when President Clinton met solar mamas from all over the world in Jaipur, and sung in China when Naurti Bai, mentioned below, took it to Beijing.

It would be fair to say that women's work in Tilonia shaped collective work in Rajasthan for many decades, and fair to suggest that along with the concept of the barefoot *dai*, such work contributed in no small part to the origin of the women solar engineers.

It would also be fair to say that Barefoot College has had considerable influence on rural girls, who are increasingly moving away from traditional country ways and into modern life. Running every morning in tracksuits, riding motorbikes, going to beauty parlours and following fashion – in short, being very much a part of the modern world, today's young village women are very different from their mothers; but then, they have grown up seeing what Barefoot College has encouraged and enabled rural women – including their mothers – to do.

A Level Playing Field

Dignity and self-respect are close companions to equality. Barefoot College strives to bring about equality for all but sees women as a special case. Worldwide, women are fighting for the same rights that men enjoy, but the struggle is especially tough in rural India, where negative traditional beliefs and practices hold women back.

Barefoot recognises that women have different needs from men, and that when these are met, women are strengthened. Sometimes, solutions are very practical, such as the College's manufacturing of good quality, affordable sanitary napkins. This makes sure women and girls can keep going to work or school during their periods, putting them on a more level playing field with male workers or students. Women can be empowered by apparently simple things, such as knowing how to open their own bank accounts, being given the confidence to do it, and and having their own money to put into them. Through literacy and taking their basic education further at the Solar Digital Village Learning Centres, described above, women are empowered. By becoming teachers, respected health workers, and dentists, women are empowered. In becoming solar engineers, women are empowered…

As early as in their schooldays, women's strengths shine out, as the Children's Parliament initiative shows. And in adulthood, strength of character needs only support to blossom, as proved by the case of Naurti Bai who, with the help of Barefoot College, took on the State of Rajasthan, and won.[13] And we should not forget that, as Bunker maintained in his TED talk of 2011, 'Men are untrainable…'

Gandhian Principles in Every Project

All Barefoot College's projects yield enormous benefits in themselves, and the results are readily seen. But the College has other achievements where success is harder to measure because it is of a different order: more subtle, involving altered mindsets and changes deep inside people. Changes like these lie at the heart of Barefoot College and contain the secret of its future.

---

[13] https://www.cec-india.org/cec-library-resource.php?opt=libsearch&id=41&rid=27 Accessed 24th March 2024

The College's driving aims are to build confidence, competence, belief, and aspirations for self-sufficiency, if necessary disrupting unequal systems in order to do that. Throughout, it is guided by the Gandhian principles of learning by doing, equality, inclusion, simplicity, and austerity. Through practical action that embodies these, for over 50 years it has striven to improve the lives of Gandhi's Last Man – and Woman – in Last Mile villages. It is still doing that; those principles are woven into every project. Men and women from all castes are welcomed and participate. Projects are community-run, with everyone who wants to be, involved. Barefoot may well take the lead to start with, but steps back as community confidence and ownership grows. This is true no matter what the project is: a school, a village learning centre, a waste disposal system, a young local person trained as a teacher, a hand-pump *mistri*, a solar engineer.

What is central to all of it is that Bunker and Barefoot College care deeply about human dignity. There may be times – for example, after unforeseen disasters such as Covid-19 – when charity (or service, as Gandhiji called it) is necessary, but as a way of life, with people permanently dependent on it, to the College charity is anathema. Many of Bunker's articles have made this clear. We humans are built in such a way that we need to respect ourselves, and for most of us, that means being able to pay our way. To work. Understanding this, Barefoot College works hard to find ways of bringing dignified employment to as many rural people as possible.

And the Future?

The articles gathered together here illustrate that Bunker and The Barefoot College have made an immensely important contribution to the well-being of the rural people the College serves. These contributions will continue, and the work will go on. It was always the intention that Tilonia would experiment and innovate to find ways that worked, simple solutions to problems that could apply anywhere. Barefoot College was set up to create a model that other organisations could adopt and adapt to suit their circumstances. And that is what has happened. One of the journalists who interviewed Bunker way back in 2005 for the article 'Affirmation'

(Chapter 6) reported that in reflecting on what had given him pleasure about Tilonia, Bunker said, 'So many BFCs started all over India now have their own identity, their own legal status, their own independence, all on their own. And some, even larger than Tilonia.' In response, the journalist asked if he felt unsettled that Tilonia and its 'babies' could carry on without him. Bunker's response was: 'That you are indispensable? The best feeling in the world is to be dispensable in your lifetime!'

So it's not the bricks and mortar of the lovely campus, though they will remain for many years, that are important for its future, nor even the leadership. In fact, in 2023, Bunker handed the Directorship baton for Barefoot College to a younger colleague – Ms Sowmya Kidambi, who is taking it forward brilliantly – whilst remaining on the Board as Founder and Adviser. No. The future of Barefoot College lies in the idea, the model, and the values.

The idea has taken root in the hearts and minds of thousands of Barefooters across the world. The model can be seen in the field centres of the SAMPDA network, for example.[14]

The values are alive in the 94,000 children who have lived the idea through their education and who are passing those values to their children and their children's children. Barefoot College is embodied in the hundreds of thousands of people who have been helped by its clinic, drink its water every day, earn their livings because of its training; in the 2,200-plus households that are living the Barefoot way through the waste collection system; in the more than 75,000 households that enjoy solar light because of Barefoot-trained solar engineers – in short, everyone in the global Barefoot

---

[14] Society for Activating, Motivating, and Promoting Development Alternatives. Currently 22 organisations, including the Barefoot College, are members. Founders of each of the member organisations spent their initial years of training at the College. They subsequently chose to start working in their native states using some of the most remote, inaccessible and rural villages as their base. SAMPDA members are spread across 14 states in India, including Rajasthan, Jammu and Kashmir, Himachal Pradesh, Uttarakhand, Bihar, Sikkim, West Bengal, Assam, Arunachal Pradesh, Orissa, Gujrat, Madhya Pradesh, Kerela and Tamil Nadu.

family who has been touched by its work. They will all pass their understanding of the Tilonia way on to their children, and it will continue to spread.

Lessons for Us All?

Since opening its doors in 1972, Barefoot College has faced and dealt with many challenges. But as one is overcome, another arises to take its place. As we all know, 'Life is just one damned thing after another.' Sadly, prejudice, greed, corruption, and incompetence are unlikely to disappear any time soon. That's how it is, and will continue to be. But knowing what Barefoot College has achieved, we are better equipped to deal with challenges because we have been shown a way to go forward with simple solutions to major problems – solutions that work by simplifying, demystifying, and decentralising. And that is a huge gift.

Not that it's easy to persuade everyone that simplifying, demystifying, and decentralising are the way forward. Today, the vast enterprises of multi-national companies and big business dominate, and as a development worker at one of the Barefoot College anniversary celebrations stood up to say in November 2022, that makes life difficult for those who want simplicity. 'We try to decentralise,' he said, 'but we are not getting anywhere because nobody is wanting to understand … Everything is Big Is Beautiful – big factories, big airports, big seaports, big, big companies.'

But big isn't necessarily beautiful. Barefoot's Gandhian methods are restrained, since Mahatma Gandhi believed that small can be beautiful, safe, sustainable, and highly effective. In 2022, addressing an audience as part of the College's 50th-anniversary celebrations, UN Resident Coordinator in India, Shombi Sharp, drew attention to the need for everyone to understand and act on the principles of empowerment and decentralisation, human dignity, local wisdom, and leadership, and singled out the vital importance of sustainability because '… we are of course now, sadly, in the midst of a triple planetary crisis and … it really takes an initiative like this [Barefoot College] to save our future on the planet for ourselves and for future generations.'

The question might well be asked: to what extent are lessons learned in one context capable of being transferred to others? Bunker is firm on the point that what he does, whether in India or (in the case of the Solar Mamas) in 96 other countries, is focused on rural contexts. He says he is not interested in what happens in urban settings. But does that mean that other settings have nothing to learn from his work? Recently, Nicholas Kristof of *The New York Times* suggested that even in the United States of America, there might be room for an approach modelled on the Tilonia way:

> We in America could learn from this approach in rural India. The United States as well must do better in providing training in technical skills to people who have been left behind so that they can earn a living – as electricians, wind turbine installers, carpenters and more. And there's a belated recognition that we worry too much about formal educational qualifications.
>
> *Can't Read? Here's a 'Barefoot College' For You.* Nicholas Kristof, *The New York Times,* March 22nd 2023

Kristof's thinking could apply to much of the developed Western world. Barefoot College's programmes have always been designed for flexibility and tailoring to local differences: why would they not be relevant to 'developed' countries? SAMPDA'S many members follow Bunker's Gandhian model, but all maintain their own separate identities and have devised programmes suited to their situations. Given this flexibility, perhaps one of the lessons from the 50-year Tilonia experiment is that its solutions do not, need not, and should not apply only to the Least Developed Nations. Everyone all over the world must learn to live using fewer of the Earth's resources.

To take just one global challenge: climate change. The statistics are dire. This is not the place to recapitulate them but there have been countless films, studies, reports and essays showing how plastic is invading our oceans, fossil fuels changing our atmosphere, water sources drying up, and discarded products overwhelming our ability to dispose of them. Something has to change – but what?

Bunker might say the answer is simple: follow the path Gandhiji laid out for us. But simplicity is never all that easy, as Bunker's own writing over the years suggests. We are human, and too many things get in the way: self-regard, self-interest, greed, fear of speaking out and going against the majority. Understandably enough, perhaps, we want to find a way for things to carry on as usual, with little given up.

But humanity cannot continue along the same path for much longer. Mindsets, says Bunker, have to change. His own unique contribution has been to provide fellow seekers with the space to experiment and create practical solutions, with the ideas coming out of this being absorbed and brought into the Barefoot stream of work and commitment. It's the creation of this bonding to ideas for which Bunker was spokesperson and amplifier, rather than to any one individual, that has shaped the Tilonia way – a genuine participatory method.

And SWRC, the Barefoot College, Tilonia – whatever we choose to call it – will keep on doing its best to facilitate change. Bunker himself is confident that the College's future lies in the capable hands of the people already embedded in the organisation. They are well placed to continue what he began. With their help, and the help of the thousands of other members of The Barefoot Family across the entire world, The Barefoot College will continue, until Gandhi's Last Man and Woman have been reached.

Some Thoughts

As I mentioned earlier, 2022 marked Barefoot College's 50th anniversary, and several times in that year, large numbers of supporters and well-wishers came together in India to celebrate and share memories and ideas. It seems appropriate to end this book by capturing some of them.

I know [Barefoot College and Tilonia] is not one person; it's a revolution. Not one person that supports it, but a community. It's a family of thousands of people across the world. [Shombi Sharp, UN Resident Coordinator in India]

We in the field of professional development need to continually learn from the examples of Barefoot College and Tilonia, which are – very much like Gandhi – ahead of the field. And it's taken the field quite a long time to catch up, to understand the principles of empowerment, the principles of dignity and of village wisdom and leadership. [Shombi Sharp]

[Bunker is fostering] a kind of life-related pedagogy that comes from a different ink … life-centred. [Gopalkrishna Gandhi]

I don't know how we do it, but the perception of what we call education has to change. [Bunker]

When you give a woman who has got no hope because she thinks she is just there to produce kids and look after the kitchen, when you take her out of that habitat and you give her a skill which the men think she cannot have and cannot even get … when you see her with that skill and showing it, I think that is empowerment. [Bunker]

Simplify, decentralise, demystify. [Bunker]

Listen to the ordinary people. They have all the solutions in the world. [Bunker]

Sanitary napkin manufacture

Stereotypes are challenged

Two women repairing a hand pump

Women working with metal

House to house, waste collectors and cart

Support for Barefoot's waste management system

Taking Covid advice on the road

Night school during Covid

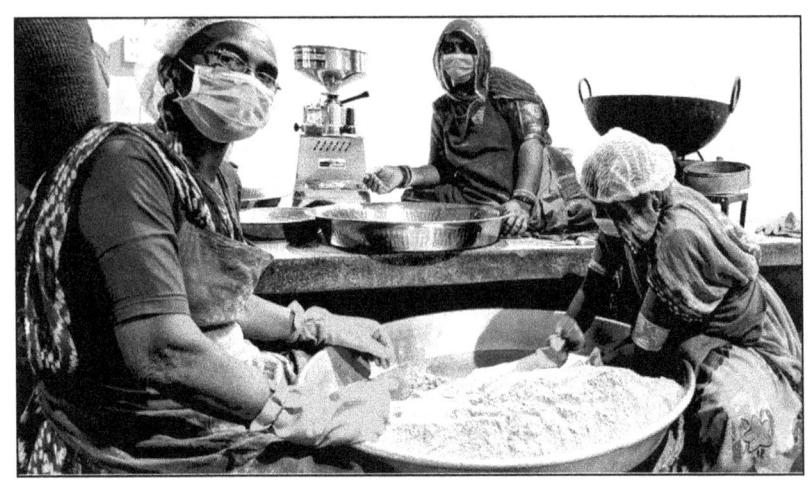

'Superfive' preparation during Covid

Something to celebrate

Appendix I: Glossary and Notes

A

adda – hangout, e.g., a chai shop

anganwadi – village child day care centre worker

Ayurvedic – pertaining to the ancient Indian medical system, based on a natural and holistic approach to physical and mental illness

B

babu – educated man of high standing

bal mandir – school for small children (literally, temple of learning)

Balai – caste found in the states of Madhya Pradesh, Maharashtra, Rajasthan and Uttar Pradesh. Their occupation has traditionally revolved around working with cotton and weaving

balwadi – village child day care centre

bania – trader or merchant

baori – community well

barfi – dense, milk-based sweet

bawadies – step wells

bawdi – open well

bell tota – mobiles consisting of a string of brightly coloured birds. They are traditionally made in northern India from fabric scraps and bells

Bhanu Pratap Singh – Indian politician and Minister of State in Ministry of Micro, Small and Medium Enterprises in Government of India. He stood for the 1996 Lok Sabha elections as BJP candidate and is currently a Member of Parliament from Jalaun

Bharat – ancient and original name for India

Bharat Sevak Samaj – National Development Agency sponsored by the Government of India's Planning Commission to ensure public co-operation for implementing government plans

bigha – a local measurement of land, 1/3rd of an acre

biri (also *beedi*) – a cheap cigarette made of unprocessed tobacco wrapped in leaves

Bua – Aunty (father's sister)

C

Chacha – Uncle (father's brother)

chai – tea

chappals – open sandals, worn in India

chaprasi ka kaam – labourer (peon's work)

chaupal – village community space/stage

Chet sako to chet – Women wake up

chula – a small earthen or brick stove fuelled by twigs, dry cow dung, and which produces toxic smoke

crore – 10,000,000 (ten million)

D

dacoity – banditry, thuggery

dai – midwife, traditional birth attendant (TBA)

dal – lentils

Dalit – an overarching term, coined by Dr. Ambedkar, for India's lowest castes. It is a euphemism meaning 'oppressed' and is often used in literature

dandi – stick

Dandi March – Gandhi's long walk in 1930 from Sabarmati Ashram in Ahmedabad to Dandi on the Arabian Sea coast, in protest against the British Raj's salt tax and prohibition against people making/collecting it themselves

Dastangoi – art form of oral storytelling, in Urdu, dating from the 13th century

degchi – cooking vessel

dhaba – roadside food stall

dhobi – someone who washes clothes by hand for a fee

Didi – Big sister. Used to address any young woman respectfully

dimaag – mind

Dr Kurien – architect of India's 'White Revolution', which helped India to emerge as the largest milk producer in the world. Founder-Chairman of the National Dairy Development Board (NDDB) from 1965 to 1998

dunda – big stick

G

gaon – village

girwa – custom whereby someone lending money takes the right to farm land belonging to the borrower until such time as the loan is repaid

governmentwallahs – important government people

gram panchayat – elected village council

gram sevak – man employed to advise and assist villagers in matters of community welfare and development

Gramdan villages – reference to the practice advocated by Mahatma Gandhi in which village landowners in India transfer the title, and the management of their property, to a village assembly that represents the interests of all the villages

H

hakim – a physician using traditional remedies in India and Muslim countries

Harijan – 'Child of God', a euphemism used by Mahatma Gandhi for the low caste 'Untouchable'. Deemed derogatory by the lower caste themselves

Hathi Committee – set up by the Indian Government in 1974 under the chairmanship of Jaysukhlal Hathi to take a comprehensive look into the pharmaceutical industry. The Committee emphasised the need for self-sufficiency in medicines and the abundant availability of essential medicines at reasonable prices

J

Jal Nigam – the apex body responsible for formulation, execution, promotion, financing, fixing tariffs, etc., for the implementation of water supplies, sewerage, sewage treatment and disposal, river pollution abatement projects, etc., including fixing state standards for water supply and sewerage services

Jat – caste name for a member of an Indo-European people widely dispersed throughout north India

Jaycees – a community of active citizens aged 18-40 who share the belief that in order to create positive change they must take collective action. Engaging in activities ranging from community development to international projects, members demonstrate their social responsibility and improve themselves through participation, leadership and action

jhijhak – apprehensions

K

Kabaad se Jugaad – from Trash to Treasure. It is also the name of the recycling/upcycling division of Barefoot College

kadhai – round cooking pot or Indian style wok

kalakand – sweet milk cake

kankari milai chuna – gravel and limestone

karigars – artisans

karishma – miracle

karo – try

katputli – puppetry

khadi – hand spun and hand woven Indian cotton fabric. Khadi is made by hand in homes in Indian villages, using a cotton yarn spun on a wheel, or charkha

Khadi Board – the All India Khadi Board was set up in 1923 as an integral part of the Indian National Congress organisation to help promote the economic value of khadi as a means of finding work for spinners and weavers

khadi kurta-paijama – handloom made, traditional Indian loose fitting pants and long shirt

Khatik – caste name indicating 'butcher' or 'hunter'

Khol community – a tribe in North India who migrated there from central India around five centuries ago. Mostly landless and dependent on forest produce to make a living, they are Hindus and are designated a Scheduled Caste

khulla – open

kilim – a pile-less piece of hand woven textile, often but not always a rug

kisan – farmer

Kudal Commission – headed by Purushottam Das Kudal, this was set up in February 1982 to probe into the working of three Gandhian institutions (the Gandhi Smarak Nidhi, the Gandhi Peace Foundation, and the Sarva Seva Sangh) and the Association of Voluntary Agencies for Rural Development

kulak – well-to-do peasant farmer [from the Russian]

kulhads – earthenware

kulhad chai – tea served in earthenware cups

kurta – long, loose handloom shirt with deep pockets

L

Ladakh – the highest plateau in India, with most of it being over 9,800 feet. It extends from the Himalayan to the Kunlun Ranges and includes the upper Indus River valley. In the past, it was strategically located at the crossroads of important trade

lakh – 100,000 (one hundred thousand)

lambardar – village headman

Lok Adalat – People's Court: a statutory organisation under the Legal Services Authorities Act 1987. It was created as an alternative dispute resolution mechanism. It is a forum where cases pending on *panchayat* or at a pre-litigation stage in a court of law, are settled

lok geet – folk song

Lok Utsav – a cultural festival

M

Malgudi Days – a collection of short stories by R.K. Narayan, adapted for a long-running TV show, set in the fictional South Indian village of Malgudi, which is a microcosm of a typical Indian village

mate system – system whereby a 'mate', the man responsible for the roster, determines who will work and who will not. He is also responsible for measuring the work that each individual does

mazdoor – an unskilled labourer

mela – fair; a public event organised to celebrate a special occasion, or an event where goods can be bought and sold

mess – dining hall where people eat together as a group (originally a military term)

mistri – mechanic

Mohan Singh Mehta – (1895–1986) was founder of the Vidya Bhavan group of institutions and Seva Mandir in Udaipur in Rajasthan

Morvi – on 11 August 1979, the Machhu-2 earth dam, situated about 6 km upstream of the town of Morvi in the Saurashtra region of India, collapsed under the onrush of an unprecedented volume of water. An 8-10 m high flood wave rolled down Machhu valley, entirely submerging Morvi and nearby villages

Munsif – Court Judge

Munsif magistrate – judge or presiding officer of a district, in charge of its tax inspectors

N

nadi – pond

Naxalite – a member of a left-wing, extremist, armed revolutionary group advocating Maoist communism

Nehru yuvak kendras – networks established in 1972 with the objective of providing young rural people with avenues to take part in the process of nation building, as well providing opportunities for the development of their personality and skills

nirdaliya – independent

Nirmna (nirman) – development

not playing cricket – metaphor for being unfair

P

padha-likha – literate

padyatras – walks from village to village

paise – monetary sub-unit of the rupee

panchayat – elected village council

Panchayat Samiti – a local government body at the block development level

Panchayati Raj – panchayat government

Pani Panchayat – Water Council

Parameshwara Rao – (1933-2017) a senior advocate practising in the Supreme Court of India. An acclaimed social worker and Gandhian and widely considered a doyen of Constitutional Law, he argued a number of landmark cases before the Supreme Court

Parikh – a name found among Hindus of the Bania caste and also Jains. It means 'assayer' in the Gujarati language and has its roots in the Sanskrit word for examiner

Parishad – assembly

patta – type of land deed issued by the Government to an individual or organization. Used for a small piece of land granted by the Government to an approved cultivator with a land revenue exemption

patwari – government official who keeps records regarding the ownership of land

pradhan – prime

Prembhai – (1935-1994). Social activist and Gandhian voluntary worker who was appointed as a socio-legal, investigating Commissioner by the Supreme Court to look into the incidence of child-bonded labour in the carpet industry

Preyatna – 'effort', 'exertion', 'endeavour', 'perseverance', 'activity' or 'action in general'

Professor Raj Krishna – Indian economist who taught at the Delhi School of Economics. He is most famous for the phrase 'Hindu rate of growth' which he coined for India's low rate of GDP growth between the 1950s and 1980s

pucca – genuine

puri (or poori) – puffy, fried wheat cake

Pushkar – a bohemian temple town and tourist hub an hour's drive from Tilonia, famous for its annual Camel Fair

R

rajnaitik samajh – political wisdom

Rajput – caste name (from Sanskrit *raja-putra*, 'son of a king'). Any of about 12 million landowners organised in patrilineal clans and located mainly in central and northern India. They are especially numerous in the historic region of Rajputana/Rajasthan ('Land of the Rajputs')

Ramakrishna (a) – follower of Swami Vivekananda's Ramakrishna movement

Regar – caste living in Rajasthan. 'Regar' comes from their work of dyeing or tanning leather

S

Sahib – Sir

salwar kameez – salwar is a pair of light, loose, pleated trousers typically worn with a *kameez*, which is a long loose shirt

sangharsh – struggle

sari – 'strip of cloth' in Sanskrit. Varying lengths from 4, 6, 9 yards in silk, cotton, synthetic, are wrapped elegantly around Indian women – and a few men

sarpanch – elected Head of the Panchayat (village-level constitutional body of local self–government)

Sarvoday (a) – a follower of the Gandhian Sarvodaya movement, which aims at rural reconstruction and to uplift the people of rural India by peaceful and co-operative means

Scheduled Caste – the legally approved, politically correct and overarching term that covers the entire low caste population of India

Scheduled Tribes – legal term from Article 366 (25) which defined Scheduled Tribes as 'such tribes or tribal communities or parts of or groups within such tribes or tribal communities as are deemed under Article 342 to be Scheduled Tribes for the purposes of this constitution'

sewa – service

Shastra Sahitya – Kerala Sastra Sahitya Parishad is a progressive outfit in the state of Kerala, India. It was conceived as a people's science movement. At the time of its founding in 1962, it was a 40-member group consisting of science writers and teachers with an interest in science from a social perspective

sheeshe ke – glass drinking vessels

shiksha karmi – education assistants

shramdan – a voluntary contribution towards community welfare involving physical effort.

shura – Arabic word for 'consultation'. The Quran encourages Muslims to decide their affairs in consultation with each other *sifarish* – recommendation

T

tamasha – a show

tanka – small dam (small rainwater harvesting tank)

tehsil – local unit of administrative division in some countries of the Indian subcontinent that is usually translated to 'township'

tehsildar – officer in charge of the collection of revenues, etc., in a *tehsil*

thanedar/thanadar – police chief

U

up-sarpanch – deputy head of a Gram Panchayat

V

vaid – doctor/medicine man

vakil – lawyer

Valmiki – community term preferred by the people who used to be known as 'Harijan'

wallah – 'man', used in combination with other words, e.g., *subziwallah* (vegetable man)

Y

yak – long-haired, short-legged ox-like mammal, probably domesticated in Tibet but which has been introduced wherever there are people living at elevations of 4,000-6,000 metres

Appendix II: Abbreviations and Acronyms

ADA – Afghan Development Association

AFPRO – Action for Food Production

aH – battery capacity in Ampère hours

ANM – auxiliary nurse midwife

ARC – Agricultural Refinance Corporation

ASARRD – Asian Survey of Agrarian Reforms and Rural Development

ASVIN – Application of Solar Voltaics in Villages in India and Nepal

B.Ed – Bachelor of Education

B.Sc – Bachelor of Science

BDO – block development officer

BJP – Bharatiya Janata Party

CAG – Comptroller and Auditor General

CAP – Common Action Programme

CBI – Central Bureau of Investigation

CBO – community-based organisation

CCA – Co-operative Centre for Afghanistan

CEO – chief executive officer

CHA – Co-ordination of Humanitarian Assistance

CIA – Commissioner of Indian Affairs (India); also, Central Intelligence Agency (USA)

CIDA – Canadian International Development Agency

CM – Chief Minister (of an Indian state)

DC – district collector

DC/DM – district collector/district magistrate

DG – diesel-generating

DRDA – District Rural Development Agency

ELCI – Environment Liaison Centre International

FAO – Food and Agriculture Organisation

FG – Future Generation

GIC – General Insurance Corporation of India

GRV – goods receiving voucher

GRWHC – Global Rain Water Harvesting Collective

ha – hectare

HPM – hand pump mistri

IAS – Indian Administrative Service

ICAR – Indian Council of Agricultural Research

ICDS – Integrated Child Development Service

ICMR – Indian Council of Medical Research

ICS – Indian Civil Service

IIT – Indian Institute of Technology

IRD – Integrated Rural Development

ISRO – Indian Space Research Organisation

LIC – Life Insurance Company of India

LLB – Bachelor of Law

M.Sc – Master of Science

MBBS – Bachelor of Medicine, Bachelor of Surgery

MDG – Millennium Development Goal

MKSS – Mazdoor (Labour) Kisan (Farmer) Shakti (Strength) Sangathan (Organisation)

MLA – Member of the Legislative Assembly

MP – Member of Parliament

MYRADA – Mysore Resettlement and Development Agency, registered in 1968 under the Mysore Societies Registration Act 1960. Today, the acronym MYRADA has been retained even though it no longer handles any resettlement projects

NCA – Norwegian Church Aid

NDPDC – National Drugs and Pharmaceutical Development Council

NGO – non-governmental organisation

NREP – National Rural Employment Programme

NRSA – Nuclear Safety Regulatory Authority

OXFAM – Oxford Committee for Famine Relief (charitable organisation for poverty alleviation)

PCR – protection of civil rights

Ph.D – Doctor of Philosophy

PHC – Primary/Public Health Centre

PHED – Public Health Engineering Department

PM – Prime Minister (of India)

PR – public relations

pro forma – done as a matter of form; a standard form

PDS – public distribution system

PUCL – People's Union for Civil Liberties

PUDR – People's Union for Democratic Rights

PWD – Public Works Department

RIOD – Réseau International des Organisations Non-Governmental Sur Désertification (International NGO Network on Desertification and Drought)

RWH – rain water harvesting

SAMPDA – Society for Activating, Motivating, and Promoting Development Alternatives. This is the Barefoot College network around India. Each unit is patterned after Tilonia, but is fully autonomous. Currently 19 organisations, including the Barefoot College, are members

SC/ST – Scheduled Caste/Scheduled Tribe

SDO – sub-divisional officer

SEWA – Self-Employed Women's Association

SGP – Small Grants Programme

SHO – station house officer in charge of a police station in India and Pakistan. The SHO holds the rank of inspector or sub-inspector

Smt. – abbreviated form of "Shrimati". It is a widely accepted form of honorific similar to "Mrs"

s/o – son of

SP – superintendent of police

SPV – solar photovoltaic unit

STC – State Trading Corporation

SWRC – Social Work and Research Centre (which became The Barefoot College)

TB – tuberculosis

TBA – traditional birth attendant

TRYSEM – Training of Rural Youth for Self-Employment

UN – United Nations

UNAPEC – United Nations Asia-Pacific Economic Cooperation

UNCTAD – United Nations Conference on Trade and Development

UNDP – United Nations Development Programme

UNEP – United Nations Environment Programme

UNESCO – United Nations Educational, Scientific and Cultural Organisation

UNICEF – United Nations Children's Fund

UNIDO – United Nations Industrial Development Organisation

UP – Uttar Pradesh

VLHW – village-level health worker

W – Watt, unit of electrical power

WAMI – Water and Mountain Initiative

WHO – World Health Organisation

www.ingramcontent.com/pod-product-compliance
Lightning Source LLC
Chambersburg PA
CBHW040252170426
43191CB00019B/2384